Rubén Darío
and the Romantic Search for Unity

The Texas Pan American Series

Rubén Darío
and the Romantic Search for Unity

The Modernist Recourse to Esoteric Tradition

CATHY LOGIN JRADE

 University of Texas Press, Austin

First Edition, 1983

Requests for permission to reproduce material from this work should be sent to
Permissions, University of Texas Press, Box 7819, Austin, Texas 78712.

The Texas Pan American Series is published with the assistance of a revolving
publication fund established by the Pan American Sulphur Company. Publication of
this book was also assisted by a grant from the Andrew W. Mellon Foundation.

LIBRARY OF CONGRESS CATALOGING IN PUBLICATION DATA

Jrade, Cathy Login, 1949–
 Rubén Darío and the romantic search for unity.

 (The Texas Pan American series)
 Bibliography: p.
 Includes index.
  1. Darío, Rubén, 1867–1916—Criticism and interpretation.
 2. Modernism (Literature). I. Title. II. Series.
 PQ7519.D3Z743 1983   861   82-24847
 ISBN 0-292-75075-7

For Ramón

Contents

Preface

This book developed over a number of years, growing in size and vision at every stage. I first began to explore the impact of esoteric symbols and beliefs upon Darío's poetry during my graduate studies at Brown University. These early probes were encouraged by provocative references in Octavio Paz's "El caracol y la sirena" and in Enrique Anderson Imbert's *La originalidad de Rubén Darío* as well as by stimulating discussions with my professors Frank Durand, Juan López-Morillas, and, above all, Alan S. Trueblood, who directed my dissertation with extraordinary care and attention.

While this early research brought into sharp focus Darío's pervasive recourse to occultist elements, it simultaneously raised broader questions about Spanish American Modernism. It underscored the need to investigate the profound philosophic concerns that motivated the Modernist departure from traditional poetic patterns and belief systems. For providing the vantage point from which these concerns began to become clear, I am indebted to three remarkable books: Octavio Paz's *Los hijos del limo* and Meyer Abrams's *Natural Supernaturalism* and *The Mirror and the Lamp*. After examining the widespread resurgence of interest in esoteric beliefs on the part of European writers of the nineteenth century, I sought to shed light on how and why this tendency to envision the world in terms of occultist doctrine was adopted and developed by Darío and other Modernist authors. The resulting analysis alters many of the predominant perceptions regarding Modernist verse.

During the time that this book was taking shape, I had the good fortune to make many dear friends whose advice and support have been crucial to the completion of this project. From the beginning Professor Roberto González Echevarría of Yale University unselfishly took time from his unrelenting schedule to make insightful comments and invaluable suggestions. Professor Andrew P. Debicki of the University of Kansas generously offered detailed advice and enthusiastic encouragement at every stage of the book's development. Professor Enrico Mario Santí of Cornell University reviewed the first chapter with exceptional care. Discussions with and suggestions by professors Miguel Enguídanos, Luis Beltrán, Willis Barnstone, and Maryellen Bieder of Indiana University and Enrique Pupo-Walker of Vanderbilt University helped keep this project moving forward. More recently, advice and suggestions have come from the University of Texas Press. Since 1980, Suzanne Comer, humanities editor, has been a friendly voice on the other end of the phone and has helped me through the publication process. But the one who has been there throughout, steadfastly encouraging me to do my best, has been my husband, Ramón. He has been a stimulating colleague, an entertaining friend, a loving companion, and an unflagging source of strength.

Finally, I wish to express my appreciation to Indiana University for the various travel, research, and publication grants it has awarded me during the past six years.

Rubén Darío
and the Romantic Search for Unity

1. Modernism and the Romantic/Esoteric Tradition

A new awareness of the presence of unorthodox doctrines in Hispanic literature has opened the way for the study of esoteric tradition in the work of Rubén Darío and in the Modernist movement.[1] As early as 1964 Octavio Paz recognized that "the academic critic has generally preferred to close his eyes to the current of occultism that pervades Darío's work." Paz added that, "this silence damages comprehension of his poetry. It is a question of a central current that constitutes a system of thought and also a system of poetic associations."[2] In 1967 Ricardo Gullón examined the eclectic occultism of Modernist writers, while Enrique Anderson Imbert documented Darío's familiarity with the sundry esoteric systems that were popular in Europe at the turn of the century.[3] These studies indicate a connection between occult doctrine and Modernism but do not examine it in detail. Not only does esoteric tradition lie at the heart of Modernist poetics, but it is also the key to understanding Modernism's place in the "modern tradition," that is, with regard to the European literature that preceded it and the contemporary Hispanic literature for which it prepared the way.

For many years critics have been dissatisfied with attempts to define the nature of Modernism. The shortcomings have stemmed from a nearsightedness that limited the examination of Modernism to its Spanish American context—in spite of their awareness of Modernism's "cosmopolitanism." This perspective hindered perception of the movement's true nature, which departed from Hispanic tradition and its cultural emphasis on a Catholic faith in an orderly, meaningful universe. While the impact of Catholicism upon Modernist authors is as pervasive as it is undeniable, a growing sense of doubt about established beliefs defines the movement much more than its Catholic background. Therefore, when more than sixty years ago Unamuno complained, "I don't exactly know what this business of Modernists and Modernism is, such diverse and opposing things are given these names that there is no way to reduce them to a common category," or when Ned Davison, in the introduction to his book on the topic, confesses that "we may have no clearer notion of Modernism today than Unamuno did in 1918. . . ," they both were falling into the same error.[4] They were focusing on the multifarious surface manifestations of a poetic movement that is held at the core by a common vision of the human predicament, one that reflects the modern sense of having been set adrift alone in a world of uncharted realities. The Modernist author deals with feelings of fragmentation and alienation by attempting to rediscover a sense of belonging and "wholeness." In so doing, he or she stands squarely in the mainstream of modern European literary currents, the source of which is English and German Romanticism.

It no longer seems necessary to enter into the debate between the position taken by Pedro Salinas, who believed that Modernism was characterized by its limited scope and its focus on the renovation of poetic language, and that of Juan Ramón Jiménez, who held that Modernism was not a school but an epoch.[5] As Donald L. Shaw suggests, a resolution of this disagreement is to be found in Romanticism. "It is here surely and not in *modernismo* that we find the 'total' phenomenon to which Onís and Juan Ramón Jiménez refer. The former's postulation of a 'crisis universal de las letras y del espíritu que inicia hacia 1885' is unsupported either by facts or arguments." Shaw explains that "no such crisis occurred; and for a very simple reason: it had occurred already. Even the technical renovation of the medium of expression in poetry which is so often insisted on as the primary characteristic of *modernismo* is a continuation of romantic experiments with metre and diction."[6] Shaw postulates a crisis of beliefs and ideals spreading outward from Romanticism into Spanish American literature and argues that Spanish American *modernismo* arose at least as much from a desire to find in art a release from the tension generated by this crisis as from mere desire to regenerate the poetic medium of expression. Central to Modernist innovation was the desire to respond to the collapse of the belief systems dominant at the end of the nineteenth century.[7] Modernist writers established music as their poetic ideal, like the French Symbolists before them, and aspired to evoke with the musical language of their poetry an untarnished vision of the universe. They denounced fossilized language because it interfered with their attempts to rediscover the pristine world that had been lost to them and to their contemporaries. Poetry was not the escapist's path but rather the discoverer's tool.

For the most part Shaw is accurate in his analysis of the situation, but his statement requires clarification. Shaw's "Romanticism" resembles much more closely English, German, and—to a lesser degree—French Romanticism than it does the Spanish version.[8] In Spain the ideological foundation of Romanticism met tenacious opposition from Catholic traditionalists who were already alarmed by the ideas of the Enlightenment. If, as pointed out by Angel del Río, it was impossible for the unorthodox philosophy of Romanticism to take root in the orthodox and Catholic soil of Spain, it was impossible because such new ideas were inappropriate.[9] These ideas had originated as responses to the metaphysical crisis at the end of the eighteenth century, a crisis that had not taken place in Spain, precisely because of its unchallenged orthodox world view.[10] It is profoundly significant, for example, that E. A. Peers finds that an emphasis on Christianity is a dominant characteristic of the Romantic movement in Spain and that the major writers of the period were at peace with the world.[11] As a result, Spanish Romanticism remained, in general, superficial, echoing the tone but not reflecting the substance of the European movement.

In Spanish America, on the other hand, the crisis that arose out of the positivistic criticism of the established religion and metaphysics had become acute toward the end of the nineteenth century. The imperial expansion of the European industrial powers that restructured the countries of Spanish America along the lines of the economic and social order of their own capitalist organization compounded this upheaval.[12] Prosperity and a growing faith in science had transformed widely held assumptions about life. According to the evangelists of the day, the society of the future would be organized upon a more rational basis than ever before, and humanity would find itself living in a world without problems. Messianism was intrinsically present in the attitude of scientists who thought of themselves as the bearers of a demonstrable truth, that is, of the "Truth," and trustees of the future. Yet in time it was recognized that, far from becoming more understandable, the world appeared more enigmatic, and the great inventions did not reduce the mystery.[13] Or, as Darío himself would write: "El progreso moderno es enemigo del ensueño y del misterio en cuanto a que se ha circunscrito a la idea de la utilidad. Mas, no habiéndose todavía dado un solo paso en lo que se refiere al origen de la vida y a nuestra desaparición en la inevitable muerte, el ensueño y el misterio permanecen con su eterna atracción."[14]

Thus a profound crisis of beliefs—virtually unprecedented in the modern Hispanic tradition—arose at the end of the nineteenth century. Yet it is not simply the confrontation of similar crises that unites Romanticism and Modernism, but the similarity of their poetic solutions. Octavio Paz has shown that the concept of analogy is the unifying thread that runs throughout modern poetry and that illuminates the relationship between the two literary movements. It was with this and ancillary esoteric concepts that Romantic writers filled the spiritual void they sensed in the new science of the Enlightenment and Modernist writers responded to the materialism of Spanish American positivism. Paz points out that modern poetry has always represented a reaction against the modern era and its various manifestations, whether they be the Enlightenment, critical reason, liberalism, positivism, or Marxism. He adds: "In their opposition to modern rationalism poets rediscover a tradition, as ancient as man, which was kept alive by Renaissance Neoplatonism and the hermetic and occultist sects and tendencies of the sixteenth and seventeenth centuries. This tradition crosses the eighteenth century, penetrates the nineteenth, and reaches our own. I am referring to analogy, the vision of the universe as a system of correspondences and of language as the universe's double."[15]

Like the English and German Romantics and the French Symbolists, the Spanish American Modernists perceived the anxiety of their age as generated by fragmentation: individuals were out of touch with themselves, with their companions, and with nature. The hope for amelioration resided in integration on all three levels. The design that the Romantics elaborated for possible recovery (and that was later adapted by the Symbolists and the Modernists) had its roots in esoteric and biblical conceptions of the world and centers on the analogical vision of the universe underscored by Paz.[16]

Renaissance vitalism, in which everything is interrelated by a system of correspondences and the living is continuous with the inanimate, is at the heart of the Romantic answer to the Enlightenment, its mechanistic world view, its analytic divisiveness, and its conception of the human mind as totally diverse and alien from its nonmental environment.[17] In broader terms, Abrams has shown that the basis of Romantic thought lies in "highly elaborated and sophisticated variations upon the Neoplatonic paradigm of a primal unity and goodness, an emanation into multiplicity which is *ipso facto* a lapse into evil and suffering, and a return to unity and goodness."[18] Within this framework, absolute unity functions both as the source and supreme mode of all existence and as the criterion of all value.

A powerful pictorial medium that has sustained the doctrine that perfection is identical to simple unity is the myth of primordial man as a cosmic androgyne, who has fallen into evil and multiplicity (the material and bisexual world), yet retains the capacity for recovering his lost integrity and for returning to the One and the Good. In its Western form this myth has its roots in Plato's *Symposium*, in Gnosticism, and in the Orphic and other mysteries. It appears today as a central component of esoteric tradition, two branches of which have remained deeply influential throughout the centuries, namely the Hebrew Kabbala and the Christian version of Hermetic lore. Recent scholarship has demonstrated the prevalence of Hermeticism and Christianized versions of Kabbalist doctrine in the major writings of the European Renaissance.[19] This occult tradition was in turn communicated to later thinkers by various philosophers, including Giordano Bruno and Jacob Boehme. Boehme, for example, elaborated the ancient myth of primal man, who fell into sexual, material, and psychological division, and whose redemption is made possible by Christ, who united the attributes of both sexes in himself. Hegel, Blake, and Coleridge are among the Romantics directly influenced by Boehme and other occult writers.[20] Along more traditional lines, many Romantic writers perceived a significant coincidence between the Neoplatonic/esoteric design for the circular course of the soul and the Christian figure of the prodigal son. As a result, the post-Adamic individual is often seen as a wayfarer in an alien land and the course of life as a pilgrimage in search of the homeland to which he or she belongs.

In short, Romantic writers adapted various versions of the Neoplatonic paradigm in order to explain what they felt to be personal fragmentation, estrangement, or alienation. They sought to help redeem humanity by fostering a reconciliation with nature, from which it had severed itself. In other words, central to Romantic poetry is a nostalgia for a primordial time in which the individual is reconciled with nature. Many of the myths and imagery that supplied the hope for reconciliation are recognizably esoteric in origin. In particular, the attribution of a life and soul to nature allowed for the transformation of a dead and alien milieu into a human and companionable environment in which one could feel at home and with which one could share one's life.

Abrams suggests that English and German Romantics used the myths and images of esoteric tradition as "symbolic conveniences" or "metaphors for poetry," and that the older view of the world helped them to define the malaise of their own time and dramatize their feeling that they did not belong in the intellectual, social, and political milieu of their oppressive and crisis-ridden age.[21] The French heirs of English and German Romanticism looked deeper into their legacy of esoteric thought and developed a new dimension to both the role of the poet and the place of poetry. By making analogy the basis of their poetics, they made the poet a seer who is in touch with the World-Soul, and poetry a means of discovery, a modern religion.[22] Whereas for Wordsworth, Coleridge, and Carlyle the poet was the individual whose vocation is to liberate the vision of readers from the bondage of habitual categories and social customs so that they may see the new world that the poet had come to see, for Baudelaire and Rimbaud the poet is the one who can rearrange the disordered material of perception into a symbolic vision that reflects both the soul of the poet and the essence of the supernatural. This "deciphering" was possible because they believed the soul, by virtue of its divine origin, maintains a means of communication with the spiritual beyond.[23] The special language through which the macrocosm and microcosm reveal themselves to each other is the language of symbols, metaphors, and analogies. The mission of poetry is to rediscover this means of communication and to achieve a renewed unity of spirit. As in Baudelaire's famous "Correspondances," the poet perceives in the "forest of symbols" the "dark and profound unity" and senses that all things correspond with one another.

Baudelaire, in effect, encouraged the free use of words and images, which are to be employed not according to their logical usage but rather in accord with universal analogy. The poet's art was becoming an "evocative magic," a sacred function. Mallarmé, in turn, hoped to increase the magical powers of poetry by separating the crude and immediate from the "essential" condition of words. The "essential" word does not function as an intermediary between two minds, but as an instrument of power capable of awakening the soul to its original innocence. Implicit in this conception is the belief that, when restored to its full efficacy, language will evoke, like music, a pure, untarnished vision of the universe, a vision that recalls the first day of creation. Music, because it is indefinite and innocent of reference to the external world, thus became the ideal of poetic creation. For the Symbolists, the purposeful use of the musical resources of language, the internal adjustment of ideas, words, and sounds to the impressions that evoke them, became a means of transcending the here and now and of achieving unity with the universe. Poetry thus becomes a magic double of the cosmos.

Finally, Rimbaud took the Romantic and Symbolist concept of the visionary poet one step further. He openly assigned to the poet the task of "making himself a seer." He was determined to go beyond accepted human limitations, which he saw as the product of habit and laziness. It was necessary to break with "culture" and to "cultivate his soul" by "disordering his senses." Rimbaud was, in part, following the lead of Baudelaire, who engaged in unconventional behavior for the purpose of extending the range of his sensations and of expanding his experience.

Even the most radical stance adopted by the Symbolist writers reveals the traditional basis of their position. Like the Romantics before them, they were concerned with the paradise that had been lost. The fundamental thrust of nineteenth-century poetry is an unquenched hope for innocence, a key principle of which is the reconciliation or synthesis of whatever is divided, opposed, and conflicting. Their search led them to discover the analogical vision of esoteric doctrine. Modernism is heir to these movements, and it is in terms of Modernism's unique adaptation of the trends that they embody that the Spanish American movement can be defined and its place in modern poetry can be determined.[24]

The centrality to Modernism of this search for unity comes to the fore in Darío's poetry. Not only is Rubén Darío the movement's most widely read and admired poet; he was also, shortly after 1896, its undisputed head, spokesman, and intellectual center of gravity. He found in the Romantic and Symbolist writers models that took him and the movement beyond the confines of traditional religions into the area of alternative belief systems. Aspects of these unorthodox world views have routinely been identified as Pythagorean.[25] But what most students of Modernism have failed to recognize is that the Pythagoreanism that influenced Darío was reinterpreted through esoteric doctrine and freely combines elements not only from historical Pythagoreanism but also from Neo-Pythagoreanism, Platonism, and Neoplatonism.[26]

Actually "Pythagoreanism" even when used in the strictest sense is a term of uncertain dimension. Although a fully historical figure, Pythagoras underwent a kind of canonization, and his life was quickly obscured by legend. Therefore, in discussing the theories of the Pythagoreans, it cannot be determined how much was due to Pythagoras himself and how much was due to later members of the school. For the literary critic, however, the problem is less complicated in that the concern is not so much with the equivocal body of doctrine called Pythagoreanism as with the prevailing idea of the philosophy at the time. In Darío's case it is well-accepted that his idea of Pythagoreanism was molded by Edouard Schuré's esoteric classic, *The Great Initiates: A Study of the Secret History of Religions*, one of just a few books that Arturo Marasso, in his study of the sources of Darío's poetry, holds to have had a lasting influence on Darío's imagination and poetic thought.[27] In Schuré's work, Pythagoras is ranked among the great religious leaders of the world: Rama, Krishna, Hermes, Moses, Orpheus, Plato, and Jesus, all of whom are described as initiates of occultism. This syncretic approach is a fundamental characteristic of esoteric tradition and, it may be assumed, one that proved particularly attractive to Darío.

In general, the various manifestations of esoteric tradition hold that the ancient wisdom of the sages did not disappear when Christianity became the world's most powerful religion; this knowledge simply assumed the symbolism of the new faith, perpetuating through its emblems and allegories the same truths that have been the property of the wise since the beginning of time.[28] This faith in the fundamental unity of all religions provided Darío with a framework in which he could reconcile Catholic dogma, which left an irrefutable, permanent stamp on his view of the world, with the appealing alternative belief systems that would become intimately linked with his poetic creation. Moreover, Darío, like Schuré previously, endeavored to convince his reading public of the validity of occult creeds by reconciling them with the positivistic approach popular at the time.[29] In an article published in *La Nación* in 1895, he wrote:

> La ciencia de lo oculto, que era antes perteneciente a los iniciados, a los adeptos, renace hoy con nuevas investigaciones de sabios y sociedades especiales. La ciencia oficial de los occidentales no ha podido aún aceptar ciertas manifestaciones extraordinarias—pero no fuera de lo natural en su sentido absoluto—como las demonstradas por Crookes y Mme. Blavatsky. Mas esperan los fervorosos que con el perfeccionamiento sucesivo de la Humanidad llegará un tiempo en que no será ya arcana la antigua *Scientia occulta, Scientia occultati, Scientia occultans*. Llegará un día en que la Ciencia y la Religión, confundidas, hagan ascender al hombre al conocimiento de la Ciencia de la Vida.[30]

In the same article Darío demonstrates an intimate acquaintance with the key names and philosophies associated with the occult revival of the nineteenth century. He divides the occultists into three groups: (1) the Theosophical Society founded by Madame Blavatsky and Colonel Olcott, (2) the Rosicrucians headed by Sâr Péladan, and (3) the Independent Group of Esoteric Studies directed by Gérard Encausse, "Papus." In addition, he concludes that the last group is the most important, because it is the widest in scope, encompassing under its broad title "Kabbalism," astrology, magnetism, hypnotism, Gnosticism, freemasonry, and alchemy. Though in this article Darío does not confide a personal commitment to any of these occultist sects, his participation in the major literary circles of Europe, which were saturated with believers and proselytizers, and his intense interest in the current vogues and intellectual trends would indicate a serious predisposition to a wide range of esoteric beliefs. His broad knowledge of Romantic and Symbolist literature would have shown him the relevance of these unorthodox beliefs to his conceptualization of the world and the role of poetry.

Actually Darío became aware of the possibility of alternative belief systems as early as 1881, when he came into contact with José Leonard y Bertholet, who was brought to León, Nicaragua, as director of the Instituto de Occidente, where Darío studied for two months. Charles Watland explains Leonard's importance: "Like many others in the nineteenth century, Leonard believed in the perfectibility of mankind and that science would soon solve all major problems. He was impatient with established religion and violently opposed to the Jesuits. He was an active freemason and is regarded as the founder of the Managua Lodge."[31] The receptive and restless youth followed the model set for him. In his poems, Darío denounced the mystery of the trinity, the dogma of papal infallibility, and the sacraments. Moreover, he became active in the masonic temple. He recounts the process: "Cayó en mis manos un libro de masonería, y me dió por ser masón, y llegaron a serme familiares Hiram, el Templo, los caballeros Kadosch, el mandil, la escuadra, el compás, las baterías y toda la endiablada y simbólica liturgia de esos terribles ingenios."[32] Despite Darío's return to the Church shortly thereafter, he never ceased to be attracted to alternative beliefs. Around 1890, after reading Madame Blavatsky and falling under the influence of his Guatemalan friend Jorge Castro, he began to consider himself a Theosophist.[33]

Throughout his career Darío continued to explore large numbers of nontraditional doctrines. While most share a common core of beliefs, it was esoteric Pythagoreanism—with its emphasis on order, harmony, and music—that captured his poetic imagination and became the philosophic and metaphoric center of his poetry. Though Darío's cosmic vision and his poetics are merely two sides of the same coin, the conceptual framework requires detailed explanation first.

As was the case with the Romantics and the Symbolists, harmony, as a philosophic ideal associated with divine perfection, forms the basis of the Pythagorean cosmology to which Darío turned in order to find unity where others saw discord and dissonance. Darío learned that Pythagoreans hold that the entire universe is one harmonious extension of God, whose soul permeates all and is identical with the great soul of the world. Since both the individual and the universe are made in the image of God, each being is a microcosm that should strive to implant in his or her soul the harmony seen in the macrocosm. Schuré's description, which Darío knew well, highlights these points.

> Pythagoras called this [the Great Monad, the essence of the Uncreated Being] the first One, composed of harmony, the Male Fire which passes through everything, the Spirit which moves by itself, the Indivisible, great non-manifest, whose creative thought the ephemeral worlds make manifest, the Unique, the Eternal, the Unchangeable hidden under the many things which pass away and change. . . . [Philolaus, the Pythagorean,] added that the work of initiation was to get closer to the great Being by resembling Him, by making oneself as perfect as possible, by mastering things through intelligence, by thus becoming active like Him, and not passive like them. "Your being is yours; is your soul not a microcosm, a little universe?—But it is filled with storms and discords. Therefore, it is a question of effecting unity in harmony. Then,—only then—will God descend into your consciousness; then you will share His power. . . ."[34]

The Neoplatonic paradigm of a primal unity and goodness, a lapse into evil and suffering, and a return to unity and goodness that Darío was reading in Romantic and Symbolist literature is clearly evident in this rendition of Pythagoreanism. Schuré also explains that this view that the universe is harmonious, well-ordered, and the paragon for the soul came to Pythagoras largely from his discoveries in mathematics. "Pythagoras called his disciples mathematicians because his higher teaching began with the study of number. But his sacred mathematics or science of principles was both transcendent and more alive than the secular mathematics known to our modern scientists and philosophers. Number was not considered an abstract quantity but an intrinsic and living nature of the supreme *One*, of God, the Source of universal harmony" (p. 311).

Historically the germ of Pythagoras's mathematical philosophy was a discovery in the field of music. He found out that the perfect consonances of the musical scale can be exactly expressed as ratios between the numbers 1, 2, 3, and 4, which, added together, make the perfect number, 10. Pythagoras saw in his discovery a principle that could illuminate the whole economy of nature. If the chaotic welter of sounds that besiege our hearing can be reduced, by the simple principle of limiting measure, to the harmonious order of art and finally to proportions of number, he believed that the whole order of nature, with its acknowledged beauty, could also be framed on the principle of form and measure, proportion and harmony.[35] An outgrowth of the view that universal harmony is demonstrated both in the beauty of music and in the regularity of the heavenly bodies is the image of celestial music, to which Darío often referred. The seven planets were comparable to the seven strings of the heptachord; the various distances to lengths of chord; and the supposed sounds produced by the spheres revolving around the center to the tones of the lute. This close relationship among universal harmony, number, and music is incorporated into Schuré's history of Pythagoreanism. He writes (pp. 307–308):

> He [the novice] was allowed to see this truth only in part through what was called the power of Magic and Number. For numbers, the master taught, contain the secret of things, and God is universal harmony. The seven sacred modes built on the seven notes of the heptachord correspond to the seven colors of light, to the seven planets, and to the seven forms of existence, which are reproduced in all the spheres of material and spiritual life, from the least to the greatest. The melodies of these modes, wisely instilled, should bring the soul into harmony, making it capable of vibrating exactly with the breath of truth.

These highly suggestive passages served to reinforce the principal Romantic and Symbolist tenets under the influence of which Darío was writing, and he came to formulate a poetic cosmology predicated on the Pythagorean concept of universal harmony.[36] The entire universe is one harmonious, living, rhythmically pulsating extension of God, and all elements of nature are signs that indicate the unity of the universe in and through God. A corollary holds that the poet is a magus who can read and interpret the signs of nature, conveying their message of unity and harmony to the rest of humanity. It is, of course, the goal of all initiates of Pythagoreanism to comprehend the order of the macrocosm, to imitate it, and to implant a similar order in the microcosm, thus becoming orderly of soul. Yet it is recognized that there are certain superior individuals who are more conscious than others of the divine element within them and, consequently, more able to recognize the transcendent order of the world around them. Romantic literary theory encouraged the identification of these special individuals with poets. Combining Platonic and Neoplatonic vocabulary, the prominent Romantics commented upon the newly elevated role of poets. Shelley held that the objects imitated by great poets are eternal Forms perceived through the veil of fact and particularity and that poetry "strips the veil of familiarity from the world, and lays bare the naked and sleeping beauty, which is the spirit of its forms." A poet, therefore, "participates in the eternal, the infinite, and the one." Coleridge also believed that the artist must copy not the external world but the essence "which is within the thing." Carlyle's hero-poet is transformed into a man-god, a prophet, a priest, or a king who lives "in the True, Divine, and Eternal, which exists always unseen to most, under the Temporary, Trivial."[37]

As noted previously, this tendency to raise the poet to the status of high priest, who is credited with the power to express in poetry, through the magic of language, a transcendent vision of the universe, was continued and strengthened among the Symbolists and, later, adopted by the Modernists. Darío found further support for this view in the writings of nineteenth-century occultists. Annie Besant, for example, wrote that the poet is the most perceptive of people and the best qualified to share with humanity findings regarding the harmonious universe, for the poet has attained the ideal held by occultists, namely, to rise to the plane of unity, to be one with one's brothers and sisters through the unity of a common life.[38]

In esoteric Pythagoreanism, the elevation to the plane of unity is seen as a dynamic process through which the human soul, which is part of the great Soul of the world, that is, a spark of the divine spirit, passes through all the kingdoms of nature, gradually becoming developed through a series of innumerable existences. In other words, an individual reaches a higher plane of existence through the transmigration of souls. Darío discovered in this third tenet a means of describing the conflicts within his being between his physical desires and his sense of poetic responsibility. The final goal of humanity is "attained when the soul will have decisively conquered matter; when, developing all its spiritual faculties, the soul will have found within itself the principle and goal of all. Then, since incarnation will no longer be necessary, the soul will enter the divine state through a complete union with divine intelligence" (p. 344). Within this framework, Darío presumed that the enlightened poet had achieved highly developed intellectual and expressive talents through successive lives, finally mastering, in his or her last incarnation, perfect harmony and unity with God and the universe. As two nineteenth-century occultists wrote: "The poet hath no Self apart from his larger Self. . . . He is supreme and ubiquitous in consciousness: his heart beats in every Element. The Pulse of all infinite Deep of Heaven vi-

brates in his own and responding to their strength and their plenitude, he feels more intensely than other men."[39] This point of view
lies at the heart of Darío's regard for all poets and is the basis of his
judgment of his own life and accomplishments.

The thrust toward integration and harmony that underpins the
first three tenets is particularly important in the fourth, through
which Darío reconciles his sexual drive with universal accord by affirming the sexual nature of the godhead and by appropriating the
esoteric myth of the primordial man as a cosmic androgyne.[40] Darío
read the following explanation of the twofold nature of God in *The
Great Initiates*: "Pythagoras said that the Great Monad acts as a *creative Dyad*. From the moment God is manifest, He is double; indivisible Essence, divisible Substance, masculine, active, animating
and passive feminine principle. Therefore the Dyad represented the
union of the Eternal Masculine and Eternal Feminine in God, the
two basic, corresponding divine faculties. . . . This eternal Nature,
this great Wife of God, is not only earthly nature but heavenly nature, invisible to our eyes of flesh, the Soul of the world. . . ." (p.
315).

In this conception of the cosmos, woman plays an integral role,
and the attraction between man and woman is placed within the
context of universal harmony, becoming a path to perfection. Sexual
love becomes a means of approximating the androgynous state of
the primal man, and, since his fall into evil is identified with his entrance into the material and bisexual world, a return to the union of
male and female becomes a means of perceiving the prelapsarian,
primordial bliss of unity as well as of intuiting the divine state.

Students of Darío will recognize in this view of sexuality not
only a satisfying alternative to the Catholic concept, which proved
particularly troublesome to him, but also the basis of a large segment of his artistic creation. A modified but similar design had been
prevalent in the major German and English literature of the beginning of the nineteenth century. For the Romantics, the quest for self-
knowledge and wisdom begins with a fall from primal unity into
self-division, which is an indispensable first step along the journey
toward higher unity. The end of the journey is the return to man's
ancestral home, which is often linked with a female contrary from
whom he has, upon setting out, been separated. The achievement
of the goal is often signaled by a loving union with the feminine
other.[41] In France, Hugo, in *Les contemplations*, Balzac, in *Séraphita*,
and Fourier, to mention just a few, drew directly upon the myth of the
androgyne.

The fifth and final tenet of the world view that Darío formulated under the influence of the dual esoteric/Romantic tradition re-affirms the occultist belief in the unity of all religions. This syn-cretic perspective made it possible for Darío to "harmonize" esoteric doctrine with the Catholic heritage that he could not disown. The persistence of this strongly Catholic outlook in the works of Darío and other Modernist authors forms the basis of their unique position in modern poetry.

The importance of Catholicism to Darío's poetry is not limited to religious vocabulary or references to the divine liturgy. Its impact is far more pervasive and subtle. As uncertain as the poet was of Catholic dogma, throughout Darío's poetry runs a persistent under-current of hope that behind the symbolic universe, which he has come to see as beautiful and harmonious, stands God, a personal God who will answer his anguished cries. It is very likely that this Catholic perspective has persisted longer in Hispanic letters than in any other Western literature. Curtius notes that it was only in Spain that "Biblical poetics" was able to develop into a theological poetics, and it did so during the Spanish revival of theology in the sixteenth century. In contrast, French Classicism confined to separate com-partments poetry and faith, Christianity and culture. In Spain all the arts—from the poetry of Luis de León, the novels of Miguel de Cer-vantes, the plays of Lope and Calderón, to the painting of Zurbarán and El Greco—have their origin in God and, therefore, are able to reconcile terrestrial images with the supraterrestrial.[42]

The opposite perspective is adopted by most modern poets, for whom the heart of analogy is, in the words of Octavio Paz, an "empty space." Paz's point of comparison is Dante, for whom the center is a "knot":

> . . . it is the Trinity which reconciles the One and the Many, substance and accident. Therefore, he knows—or thinks he knows—the secret of analogy, the key with which to read the book of the universe; this key is another book: the Holy Scrip-tures. The modern poet knows—or thinks he knows—pre-cisely the contrary: the world is illegible, there is no book. Negation, criticism, irony, these also constitute knowledge, though of the opposite kind to Dante's. A knowledge which is not the contemplation of otherness from the vantage point of unity, but the vision of the breaking away from unity. An abys-mal knowledge, an ironic knowledge.[43]

For Darío the heart of analogy is neither completely deciphered nor completely indecipherable. Though often overtaken by doubts and despair, Darío appears unable to reject out of hand the basis of hope provided by Catholicism. In this attitude, also, he resembles many Romantic poets who "deliberately elected their stance, not of optimism, but of qualified hope. . . . in the Romantic view dejection breeds sterility, and to persist in a state of apathy and hopelessness is to live what Coleridge called a 'death-in-life'; while to commit oneself to hope . . . is an essential obligation, without which we are indeed doomed. For while hope, by holding open a possibility, releases man's powers of imagination and action, despair is self-fulfilling, because it guarantees the condition to which it surrenders."[44] It is this qualified hope that makes Darío's poetry seem at times naive, anachronistic, *cursi*, and out of touch with contemporary cynicism and irony. Modern readers, therefore, tend to prefer his poems of anguish and doubt.

The dominant Catholic culture of Latin America left Darío with another heritage, that of guilt, which he also attempts to resolve with the help of esoteric doctrine. The strongly instilled sense of sin modified, for example, Darío's view of the role of the poet. Like other Modernist authors, he could not forgive himself the unrestrained behavior of a Baudelaire or a Rimbaud—even for the sake of achieving a clearer vision of the supreme order of things. The price was simply too high to pay. The only time the Modernist writer assumed the martyrdom of one predestined to the damnation of the poet's sacred calling was when one was able to claim, as Rimbaud did on occasion, the holiness of sin.[45]

The five tenets outlined above underscore Darío's debt to the dual esoteric/Romantic tradition. Under the influence of occultist beliefs—as presented by Schuré and others—and of Romantic and Symbolist writings, Darío created a poetic cosmology based on the Pythagorean concept of world harmony, in which the elements of nature are seen as signs that indicate the harmonious order of the universe. It is the poet/magus who can interpret and translate into human language nature's message of unity and harmony. Faith in this unity, which is dynamic, forms the basis of Darío's third tenet, the doctrine of transmigration of souls. Through the belief in the sexual nature of God, Darío found in human love a microcosmic parallel to the macrocosmic order and developed a mystical concept of love. Finally, Darío's appeal to syncretism allowed him to extend his concern for reconciliation to religious doctrine and symbolism. But this listing of tenets that are the germ of several key poems merely emphasizes the most obvious aspect of Darío's interaction with the dual esoteric/Romantic tradition. To appreciate the centrality of this influence, Darío's poetry must be examined in detail. Poems must be analyzed in order to try to resolve the enigmatic and explicate the seemingly inexplicable as well as to reveal uncharted levels of intensity in Darío's poetry, which has, in great part, been admired like fine filigree—fanciful, ornate, and well-crafted but superficial, lacking philosophic and emotional depth. A comprehensive awareness of his reliance on the dual esoteric/Romantic tradition highlights his unrelenting attempts to come to terms with the modern predicament.

These detailed readings will also demonstrate that the impact of the dual legacy was not limited to the formulation of the Modernist *Weltanschauung*. Darío's personally modified esoteric Pythagoreanism forms the basis of Modernist aesthetics as well. If the universe is one harmonious extension of God and both individuals and the universe are made in God's image, all the elements of creation are analogous and correspond to each other; they are signs to be "read" and deciphered. This view makes the world comprehensible and defines a special role for poetry. As Paz explains, "Poetry is one of the manifestations of analogy: rhymes and alliterations, metaphors and metonymies are modes of operation in analogical thought. If analogy turns the universe into a poem, a text made up of oppositions which become resolved in correspondences, it also makes a poem a universe." [46] Darío, using a more traditional image, affirms this special relationship between language and creation.

> En el principio está la palabra como única representación. No simplemente como signo, puesto que no hay antes nada que representar. En el principio está la palabra como manifestación de la unidad infinita, pero ya conteniéndola. *Et verbum erat Deus.*
>
> La palabra no es en sí más que un signo, o una combinación de signos; mas lo contiene todo por la virtud demiúrgica. Los que la usan mal, serán los culpables, si no saben manejar esos peligrosos y delicados medios. Y el arte de la ordenación de las palabras no deberá estar sujeto a imposición de yugos, puesto que acaba de nacer la verdad que dice: el arte no es un conjunto de reglas, sino una armonía de caprichos. [47]

Darío's poetic goal is therefore a perfect "translation" of the "unidad infinita," or, in other words, a "re-creation" of the pristine order of the world undistorted by established patterns of perception or speech. He aspires to have his poetry emulate the pre-Babelic language with which God speaks in nature, and he denounces the fossilized poetic language of his time because it interferes with the poetic vision through which author and reader rediscover the paradise that has been lost to them. Darío, therefore, like the Symbolists before him, established music as the ideal of poetic creation. He aspires to evoke with the musical language of his poetry a pure, untarnished vision of the universe. He writes: "No gusto de *moldes* nuevos ni viejos. . . . Mi verso ha nacido siempre con su cuerpo y su alma, y no le he aplicado ninguna clase de ortopedia. He, sí, cantado aires antiguos; y he querido ir hacia el porvenir, siempre bajo el divino imperio de la música—música de ideas, música del verbo" (p. 697).

Melody implies harmony and a well-ordered universe. It was in the linking of harmony and melody with rhythm that the impact of esoteric Pythagoreanism upon Modernist aesthetics is most evident. Perhaps the first to recognize the importance of this connection was Paz, who saw that the search for a modern and cosmopolitan tongue led the Spanish American poet to rediscover the Hispanic tradition of rhythmic versification. Paz also recognized that this tendency was universal; it was the same principle that ruled the work of the great Romantics and Symbolists. Rhythm was the source of poetic creation and the key to the universe.[48] In this way, the fundamental harmony of creation was associated with a cosmic pulse—perhaps an outgrowth of the basic Plotinist image of emanation that enjoyed popularity among Romantic writers and that was picked up later by Darío, in which the One and the Good are habitually analogized to such objects as an overflowing fountain or a radiating sun—a cosmic pulse with which the poet had to synchronize soul and poetry in order to perceive and "transmit" the hidden truths of the universe.

Darío often perceived in the poetic language of others—especially the French—in their rhythms and rhymes, in their vocabulary and images, means of coming into contact with the hidden truths of the universe. Severo Sarduy explains: "En la percepción que Darío tiene del mundo como un código significante hay un intermediario. Ese intermediario es *siempre* de orden cultural, es decir, que Darío introduce en la literatura esta dimensión fundamental. . . : el poema se sitúa en una esfera absolutamente cultural, en lo que los estructuralistas llaman 'el código de papel.' Este intermediario, siempre plástico en él, es con frecuencia también de orden literario, y cuando digo literario, digo Verlaine."[49] But Darío does not allow this "intermediary" to become a fixed pattern or mold. He writes, "El clisé verbal es dañoso porque encierra en sí el clisé mental, y, juntos, perpetúan la anquilosis, la inmovilidad" (p. 695). His poetics is based on the freedom to aspire to the level of music, that is, to the language before all languages that contains the "unidad infinita."

Darío recognized that this need for freedom was common to all poets and, therefore, refused to write a manifesto establishing his work as a model for others. In "Palabras liminares" of *Prosas profanas* he commented: "Yo no tengo literatura 'mía'—como lo ha manifestado una magistral autoridad—, para marcar el rumbo de los demás: mi literatura es *mía* en mí; quien siga servilmente mis huellas perderá su tesoro personal. . . ." (p. 545). The origin of this strong individualism is to be found in the Romantic, Symbolist, and esoteric view that the enlightened poet, whose soul is a spark of divine intelligence, creates in accord with the harmony of the universe. To dictate the form that poetry must take would be to inhibit what the poet most hopes to achieve, namely, the direct contact between language and universe. Darío turns to a Neoplatonic figure common in Romantic poetry, the spring, to make this point.[50]

> Joven, te ofrezco el don de esta copa de plata
> para que un día puedas calmar la sed ardiente,
> la sed que con su fuego más que la muerte mata.
> Mas debes abrevarte tan sólo en una fuente.
>
> Otra agua que la suya tendrá que serte ingrata;
> busca su oculto origen en la gruta viviente
> donde la interna música de su cristal desata,
> junto al árbol que llora y la roca que siente.
>
> Guíete el misterioso eco de su murmullo;
> asciende por los riscos ásperos del orgullo;
> baja por la constancia y desciende al abismo
>
> cuya entrada sombría guardan siete panteras:
> son los Siete Pecados las siete bestias fieras.
> Llena la copa y bebe: la fuente está en ti mismo.[51]

Poetry is the silver goblet that the young man will use some day to calm his burning thirst for beauty and knowledge. But his longing will be satisfied only when the goblet is filled with water from the spring that flows harmoniously in tune with the responsive and feeling nature that surrounds it. This spring is within the poet; it is that part of him that "speaks" with the primordial language of music and understands the primal order of the world before the fall. It may be hidden by habit and custom, but he must search it out. To drink from some other source will leave him parched and disillusioned.

Implicit in this identification of the free-flowing spring with the essence of poetry are the restrictions that "form" must impose. Inevitably the music of the spring must be muted in the goblet. This is

the complaint that Darío voices in "Yo persigo una forma . . ." also
from "Las ánforas de Epicuro" of *Prosas profanas* (p. 622).

> Yo persigo una forma que no encuentra mi estilo,
> botón de pensamiento que busca ser la rosa;
> se anuncia con un beso que en mis labios se posa
> al abrazo imposible de la Venus de Milo.
>
> Adornan verdes palmas el blanco peristilo;
> los astros me han predicho la visión de la Diosa;
> y en mi alma reposa la luz, como reposa
> el ave de la luna sobre un lago tranquilo.
>
> Y no hallo sino la palabra que huye,
> la iniciación melódica que de la flauta fluye
> y la barca del sueño que en el espacio boga;
>
> y bajo la ventana de mi Bella-Durmiente,
> el sollozo continuo del chorro de la fuente
> y el cuello del gran cisne blanco que me interroga.

Darío only finds "the word that escapes" because as he attempts to
capture the ideas that float in his head—like the ship of dreams in
space—they elude his verbal constraints. What is left instead is the
melodic introduction or, to use Darío's words, the soul of the word.
(What is lost is its body.) In "Palabras liminares" of *Prosas profanas*,
he wrote, "Como cada palabra tiene un alma, hay en cada verso, además de la harmonía verbal, una melodía ideal. La música es sólo de
la idea muchas veces" (p. 574). The melody that remains is the ideas
that are in their essence music. Through the fusion of verbal harmony and ideal music, language becomes poetry and "recovers its
original being, becomes music again."[52]

Despite the acknowledged difficulty in achieving this perfect
combination, Darío, as is evident in "Yo persigo una forma. . . ,"
continues to search for the ideal form that has only begun to develop
in his mind. This form, which is heralded by the kiss placed on his
lips in the impossible embrace of the Venus de Milo, is clearly identified with woman, the goddess that the stars have predicted that he
will see.[53] Woman, the womb of existence, the primordial matrix, is
the "flesh" of poetry as well. She is language and to become poetry
must be inseminated with ideas, that is, the "ideal music." This conceptualization of poetry parallels the mythic view of the creation of
the world. "In the beginning the Spirit conceived, the waters [i.e., the
maternal womb of the universe] gave birth, and the world which was

born from their conjunction was the first material image of the World, of God the Son, the Logos who was the ideal pattern after which the creation was modeled."[54] Among Romantic writers it was common to identify the poem as a "second nature" created by the poet in an act analogous to God's creation of the world, but Darío appeals to the more blatantly sexual conceptualization of creation of esoteric tradition.[55] Thus, in union with the poet, woman holds the key to deciphering the universe by making possible the creation of a microcosmic "translation" of the pristine cosmos. "Eva y Cipris concentran el misterio / del corazón del mundo" (p. 668).

Darío's search for the ideal woman, whose purity of form will permit the "re-creation" of the time before the loss of innocence, leads him to the ultimate female, to "Ella," to Death. At the end of "Coloquio de los centauros," she is described as "la victoria de la progenie humana" (p. 578):

> La virgen de las vírgenes es inviolable y pura.
> Nadie su casto cuerpo tendrá en la alcoba obscura,
> ni beberá en sus labios el grito de victoria,
> ni arrancará a su frente las rosas de su gloria.

The very materiality of language prevents poetry from attaining the spirituality of music. Paz, commenting on similar attempts by Mallarmé, concludes that "he has left reflections, confidences, doubts, fragments, odds and ends—but the book does not exist; it was never written. Analogy ends in silence."[56] Darío himself was aware that the Symbolist aesthetics would lead him, like the French writers before, to silence. As early as 1888, in "Catulo Méndez [sic]. Parnasianos y decadentes," he writes:

> Es dar toda la soberanía que merece el pensamiento escrito, . . .
> es utilizar todas las claridades del espíritu que concibe. . . .
> Juntar la grandeza o los esplendores de una idea en el cerco
> burilado de una buena combinación de letras; lograr no escribir
> como los papagayos hablan, *sino hablar como las águilas
> callan*; tener luz y color en un engarce, aprisionar el secreto de
> la música en la trampa de plata de la retórica, hacer rosas ar-
> tificiales que huelen a primavera, he aquí el misterio. Y para
> eso, nada de burgueses literarios, ni de frases de cartón.[57]

Darío's success, despite the unattainability of his ultimate goal, lies in the creation of artificial roses that evoke spring or, as suggested by

Merrim, in his "utilization of the Iconic potential of poetry to renew the direct contact between language and the universe."[58]

It is in this poetics and the cosmology formulated by Darío under the influence of the dual esoteric/Romantic tradition—and not in the many surface features of the movement—that the true nature of Modernism can be perceived. Modernism is a movement born of crisis; it is Spanish America's response to the fragmentation and alienation generated in modern society; its final goal is to recover, through art, a sense of belonging and integration.[59] The paradigms for possible recovery were supplied by the esoteric doctrine that was first rediscovered by Romantic writers.

Whereas Davison places "attitude of cultural reform" (i.e., the widespread crisis of beliefs) on the same level as the five other characteristics of the movement—along with "renewal of form and techniques," "voluntad de estilo," "cosmopolitanism," "aestheticism and sensation," and "spiritual quest and mysticism"—it is, in reality, the origin of the movement. Both Alberto Zum Felde and Octavio Paz recognize that Modernism is a genuine literary movement, rather than a shallow reflection of literary trends, because its members respond with true revolutionary vision to the personal and spiritual crises of their age. While Zum Felde holds that Modernism is a period of profound spiritual crisis and uneasiness of mind, Paz emphasizes the profound nature of the Modernist response. "Our critics and historians have been insensitive to the contradictory dialectic uniting positivism and modernismo. Consequently, they insist upon seeing the latter only as a literary trend and, above all, as a cosmopolitan and rather superficial style. No, modernismo answered spiritual needs. Or, more precisely, it was the answer of imagination and sensitivity to the positivist drought."[60]

"The spiritual quest and mysticism" of Modernism, which Davison acknowledges to have received less attention than other characteristics, is the ideological answer to the spirit of crisis outlined by both critics above. Since the standard answers no longer appeared viable, Modernist writers sought solutions in unorthodox beliefs and belief systems. Their rejection of established answers included literary commonplaces; they turned away from linguistic clichés and stylish trends and carried out a "renewal of form and techniques." They aspired to achieve a more flexible and subtle linguistic vehicle that would enable them to maximize the musical attributes of their poetry. Through the magical powers of language they hoped to break the set patterns of perception, to see beyond disordered appearances, and to capture the perfect harmony of creation.

With the rejection of the dominant ideologies of the day, the Modernists turned inward, to their souls, in order to achieve the desired, unencumbered vision of the world. They recognized that they had to intuit their responses directly from the world that had been cut off by rationalism and positivism. They willed unique manners of expression—"voluntad de estilo"—because they believed, not unlike other later literary movements, that any attempts to arrive at truth were predicated on the acceptance of individual truths. Zum Felde explains this position in broad terms: "The common principle is *individualism*, the most genuine and characteristic intellectual product of the last third of the nineteenth century. Individualism— in its diverse ethical and aesthetical manifestations—is a child of the philosophical pessimism that, considering as *illusions* what man had held until then to be immutable *principles* of his reason and as fundamental ideals of his existence, left in its place, as the only truth, the individual, the *I*, the irreducible limit of all reality. . . ."[61] In short, enlightened poets must trust themselves to find the truth they seek.

The ideal recognized and singled out by all Modernists is beauty, but this aestheticism is far from frivolous. They aspired to emulate in their poetry the perfection of the universe that is hidden from most. Their models were found both in nature and in art. For as much as Modernists may have turned away from the molds and braces of their own culture, they found in the art of other cultures the freedom and beauty that they sought. As Sarduy indicates, the Modernist author often viewed the world filtered through an aesthetic landscape which provided a harmonious and well-ordered vision of the universe. Along similar lines, the Modernist author attempted to cultivate materials and devices for defining and evoking sensation in order to put people in touch once again with the beauty of the world around them.

These characteristics of Modernism are widely recognized. What has been overlooked is their basis in the cosmology developed under the influence of esoteric tradition that was adopted by the Romantic and Symbolist writers of the nineteenth century. The foundation of this cosmology is the Pythagorean concept of world harmony, and, as is shown in the next chapter, it is in esoteric Pythagoreanism that Darío found a philosophic framework to structure his poetic world, his hopes, and his fears.

2. Esoteric Pythagoreanism in Darío's Vision of the Universe

Though the centrality of esoteric Pythagoreanism to Darío's poetic creation has generally been overlooked, the importance of his search for unity and harmony has not. Pedro Salinas, in the conclusion to his *La poesía de Rubén Darío*, finds the common ground that unites the three diverse themes of love, art, and society in Darío's frustration with the inadequacies of the human condition—especially in the face of time—in his struggle with fate, and, finally, in his increasing longing for peace.[1] Miguel Enguídanos, taking Salinas as a point of departure, sees the tension generated by this constant dissatisfaction with human destiny as the source of Darío's artistry.[2] In his own terms, Enguídanos emphasizes Darío's refusal to accept the imperfect world that he was given to live in. Both critics therefore indirectly highlight Darío's continuation of the Romantic and Symbolist longing for the paradise from which the modern individual has been exiled. The poet struggles to discover the hidden order of the cosmos—an order that he trusts to be, in its essence, ideal music and beauty—and to incorporate that order into his life and works. Tension results from the possibility of failure: the possibility that he will fail either to recognize the pulse of creation or to control the human frailties that disrupt it. Darío eventually finds a philosophic framework for his hopes and fears in esoteric Pythagoreanism.

Like the Romantics and Symbolists before him, the youthful Darío rejects the dominant ideologies of the day, for they offered few solutions to his sense of alienation and fragmentation. He turns instead to an older conception of the universe. His sensitivity to the lush tropical environment that surrounded him from his birth and his religious and even superstitious character combined to produce a propensity to see God in nature.[3] As early as 1879 Darío links nature and God by describing the roar of the sea as "el eco tremendo / de la voz del Señor." He also perceives the entire world as a living organism, for in the sea's "seno profundo / fuerte palpita el corazón del mundo."[4] In 1880, in "Desengaño" he wrote (p. 7; first ellipsis in original):

> Era en fin, todo armonía;
> era todo allí grandeza;
> sonreía Naturaleza
> al contemplar aquel día . . .
>
> Pero del Sol asomó
> la faz pura y soberana
> y entre celajes de grana
> la aurora se disipó,
>
> y derramó los fulgores
> de su lámpara esplendente,
> dando vida a la simiente
> y fecundando las flores. . . .

Here Darío adapts Genesis 1:31, "And God saw every thing that he had made, and, behold, it was very good," to his pantheistic notion of the fusion of God and nature. The harmony described derives from the unity of life manifested in the well-working union of sun and earth. In "El año lírico" of *Azul* (1888), Darío transforms the Pythagorean universal monochord into a "lira universal" and envisions the song of birds in sympathetic resonance with one of its chords (p. 517). In this brief but telling passage, he reaffirms his faith in the musical order of the universe that may be hidden but that can be recovered and reestablished as the basis of poetry and life.

Darío found support for this intuitive response to and poetic interpretation of the universe in the intellectual currents coming to him from Europe. His youthful tendency to a pantheistic view of the world was given impetus by his early familiarity with the writings of Victor Hugo and, shortly thereafter, by his extensive readings of Romantic and Symbolist poets.[5] These readings were soon complemented by his own zealous immersion in occult doctrine, particularly as summarized by Edouard Schuré in *The Great Initiates*. As a result of the confluence of literary and esoteric traditions, Darío's early attitudes began to jell into a coherent conception of the universe as a single living being animated by a single divine soul. This belief that God is the One that is everything is the foundation of esoteric Pythagoreanism and the key to Darío's vision of unity. Through it he discovers not only the unity of all the elements of creation but also the unity of male and female and the unity of life and death.

Esoteric Pythagoreanism holds that the whole universe is God, and since the Great Monad is composed of harmony, the entire universe is considered one harmonious unfolding of his divine being. Though God is one, he acts as a creative Dyad, the union of the Eternal Masculine and the Eternal Feminine. Because both individuals and the universe are thought to have been made in the image of God, primordial man is conceived as a cosmic androgyne who has fallen into the material and bisexual world. It is necessary to understand the harmony of the macrocosm in order to imitate it and establish a similar divine order in the microcosm, thereby becoming "orderly of soul" and approximating the undivided primordial ancestor.

Although Pythagoreans maintain that God is omnipresent, they imagine that all the elements of creation are set up in a hierarchy based on their degree of spirituality and resemblance to God. In order for the human soul to have attained its present position, it had to traverse all the kingdoms of nature, gradually becoming developed through a series of innumerable existences. Furthermore, it is believed that the soul becomes aware that the link between it and its external companion, Spirit, is insoluble even though death breaks the soul's attachment to the body. Accordingly, death is viewed as a "new sleep" or a "delightful swoon" during which the soul receives the hierarchical teaching of the circle of divine love. The alternation between life and death is, therefore, necessary for the development and purification of the soul.[6]

All these tenets are based on and are inextricably linked to the belief in the unity of life. This belief forms the philosophic backdrop to Darío's entire poetic production and underlies his faith in an ordered, intelligent, decipherable universe. While it seldom appears in isolation, it stands solidly at the core of seven major poems written between 1895 and 1908. In these poems Darío explores, through the concepts derived from esoteric Pythagoreanism, the possibilities of human perception and attainment of perfect harmony. Darío recognizes that people aspire to be reintegrated into the order of the cosmos, but he is also aware that their disruptive nature makes failure likely. The resulting tension, alluded to earlier, is at times blatantly expressed in admonitions, but, more generally, it is subtly contained within wishes and self-directed commands. In "Coloquio de los centauros," Darío's first sophisticated recourse to occultist mythology and doctrine, the figure of the centaur, a composite creature that embodies the polar elements of intelligence and bestiality, underscores the poet's awareness of the uncertainty of human destiny. Though some centaurs speak on behalf of immoderate behavior, anger, and discord, Darío optimistically joins ranks with Quirón, the voice of harmony, order, and wisdom. In some later poems, Darío's view of his own fate is less confident.

As Arturo Marasso notes, with the writing of this complex poem in 1895, Darío manifests a change that was taking place during his years in Buenos Aires. "Por su espíritu, Rubén que está escribiendo el *Coloquio de los centauros* pasa a ser un nuevo poeta que encuentra un espacio infrecuentado en la ascensión de sus investigaciones interiores. Se ha iniciado . . . en el saber que anima el estilo. . . . Volverá a transfundir en la lengua lírica la esencia metafísica. . . . Se impregnó de Plotino. . . . Se inicia también en el simbolismo hermético."[7] Though the change in the young poet is probably less radical than Marasso suspects, for the first time Darío focuses on and explores at length the question of the unity of life and all its ramifications, or, as he himself wrote several years later, he examines "las fuerzas naturales, el misterio de la vida universal, la ascensión perpetua de Psique."[8] For this examination, Darío astutely turns to the centaur, for few figures are more suited to discuss the kinship of life than this creature that is half human and half horse.

Like the Egyptian sphinx and the Assyrian man-bull, the centaur signifies for occultists spiritual evolution, for in it the human form rises from the body of the beast. As the sign of Sagittarius, the centaur, generally shown with a bow and arrow in hand, is a symbol of aspiration and ambition. Just as it aims its arrow toward the stars, every human being aims at a mark that is beyond his or her reach. In the poem, the composite nature of the centaur is emphasized by Folo (p. 574):

> El biforme ixionida comprende de la altura,
> por la materna gracia, la lumbre que fulgura,
> la nube que se anima de luz y que decora
> el pavimento en donde rige su carro Aurora,
> y la banda de Iris que tiene siete rayos
> cual la lira en sus brazos siete cuerdas; los mayos
> en la fragante tierra llenos de ramos bellos,
> y el Polo coronado de cándidos cabellos.
> El ixionida pasa veloz por la montaña,
> rompiendo con el pecho de la maleza huraña
> los erizados brazos, las cárceles hostiles;
> escuchan sus orejas los ecos más sutiles;
> sus ojos atraviesan las intricadas hojas,
> mientras sus manos toman para sus bocas rojas
> las frescas bayas altas que el sátiro codicia;

junto a la oculta fuente su mirada acaricia
las curvas de las ninfas del séquito de Diana;
pues en su cuerpo corre también la esencia humana,
unida a la corriente de la savia divina
y a la salvaje sangre que hay en la bestia equina.
Tal el hijo robusto de Ixión y de la Nube.

Since the centaurs are said to have been the offspring of Ixion and a cloud, the more spiritual aspects of their character are supposedly inherited from their mother. Their baser emotions are from their father, whose incorrigible behavior was severely punished by Zeus. The split in the centaurs' personality emphasizes the fusion of contraries. It also parallels human nature and the tension within Darío's poetry.[9]

Like Darío, the centaurs aspire to comprehend the heavenly phenomena of lights, clouds, rainbows, and seasonal changes at the same time that they respond with unrestrained sensual delight to their physical surroundings. Though Darío has them perceive the harmonious order of the universe in the seven bands of the rainbow, which recall the seven strings of the lyre and the music of the spheres, he also captures, in the second half of the section quoted, the centaurs' potential for destructiveness. They assert their freedom by crushing the "intractable thicket" that holds them like "hostile jails" as they surge across the landscape. This unbridled energy is coupled with unlimited sensuality. They hear, see, touch, and taste with the greatest acumen and pleasure, and their desirous looks "caress" the nymphs of Diana's retinue. But it is the unity of their being that is emphasized in the concluding lines: "pues en su cuerpo corre también la esencia humana, / unida a la corriente de la savia divina / y a la salvaje sangre que hay en la bestia equina" (p. 574).

In his usual, summary manner, Quirón, the pivotal figure of the poem, confirms Folo's emphasis on the unity of opposites: "Sus cuatro patas, bajan; su testa erguida, sube." The verbs "bajar" and "subir" highlight the poles of the centaur's behavior. He aspires toward the divine but may fall toward the bestial. In effect, the poem grows out of the search both for the reconciliation of the tension within the centaurs and for their reintegration into a harmonious and well-working universe. They discover on the magical "Isla de Oro" the hidden order of the cosmos, which, in turn, illuminates the proper role of sexuality and death. As a result, "Coloquio" represents a paradisiacal interlude in the harried, modern world, or, in other words, a poetic utopia. The resolution of strife and discord is directed by Quirón, the wisest of all centaurs, who, according to Reto, is the source of the truth sought by the human race.

The conspicuous placement of the word "harmonía" as well as the carefully constructed description of the poem's setting underscore from the very beginning the underlying harmony of nature to which the centaurs will strive to attune themselves. The entire colloquy takes place "En la isla en que detiene su esquife el argonauta / del inmortal Ensueño, donde la eterna pauta / de las eternas liras se escucha" (p. 572). The argonaut who sails the seas alone in search of the immortal Dream and who stops only at the island where the fundamental accord of existence is felt is the poet. This association of the poet with an argonaut continues throughout Darío's poetry and may have its roots in the Romantic connection linking the visionary with the prodigal son, who wanders in search of "home." Certainly the word "esquife" carries with it overtones of Rimbaud's "Le bateau ivre." As María Teresa Maiorana notes, "Un 'argonauta.' Se habla de ellos, por lo general, en plural. El singular destaca fuertemente una soledad acentuada aún más por la palabra 'esquife.' La soledad que desafía al mar en su cáscara de nuez no puede ser sino la del poeta."[10]

The pulse of celestial music sensed by the poet is echoed in the rhythmic gallop of the centaurs and in the throbbing movement of the ocean, to which the centaurs are instinctively attracted. The sea is more than an ornament in the verbal picture of the poem's location, and Darío's own statement about "Coloquio" underscores its importance: "Y bajo un principio pánico, exalto la unidad del Universo en la ilusoria Isla de Oro, ante la vasta mar."[11] As Alan S. Trueblood, in his article "Rubén Darío: The Sea and the Jungle," observes, the sea holds a unique place in Darío's poetic imagination, for from the beginning of his career, he senses in it the beating of a giant heart.[12] Trueblood's conclusions regarding the symbolism of the cicada apply equally to the image of the sea.

> [It] leads us to the genetic core of Darío's art, a zone where nature, man's sentient life, and his creative impulse become coordinated in a kind of symbiosis from which the poem takes its life. The beat and echo of human hearts, the stresses and sonorities of the poet's lines, the pulsating call of the insect, and the lappings on the ocean's shore are rhythms and sounds belonging ultimately to a single harmony and it is this music which the poet seeks to apprehend. We detect here a predisposition on Darío's part to the Pythagoreanism which will become marked later on in his view of art, life and spirit and of

their essential concordance, and we see an early intimation of the "harmony of the spheres" to which he will seek to attune his art.[13]

In "Coloquio" the sea recalls the single pulsating heart of the world which echoes throughout the universe and within Darío's poetry. Darío relays the message of this universal pulse in the staccato rhythm of the second, third, and fourth strophes. The beat of these lines and the description of the thundering sounds of the approaching centaurs serve as a drum-roll introduction to the colloquy and emphasize its basic theme: all life is one harmonious extension of God.

This sense of harmony is reinforced by the sound patterns established throughout the poem. The rather rigid *alejandrino pareado* is given new life and flexibility in "Coloquio" through various forms of enjambment as well as through the free alteration among various alexandrines. Trochaic uniformity disappears, and Darío relies upon the *alejandrino mixto* to express movement and speed and upon the *alejandrino dactílico* in more musical passages.[14] In addition, the rhythmic recurrence of the sounds of the paired consonantal rhymes evokes the ordered pulse of the cosmos.

The fundamental accord among the elements of the universe that is alluded to and suggested acoustically in the first twenty-two lines is demonstrated immediately. Quirón's attempt to open the colloquy is assisted by nature; the Tritons and the Sirens grow silent and the winds die down. He proposes to discuss: "la gloria inmarcesible de la Musas hermosas / y el triunfo del terrible misterio de las cosas" (p. 573). His injunction reflects certain basic assumptions. The glory of the Muses is unfading, for the arts that they represent, like the attractive goddesses themselves, embody the eternal harmony of the universe. As a result, the female form serves as one more example of the universal order that the poet must strive to emulate in his creations. This association of the female body with poetry is particularly strong for Darío. As indicated in the first chapter, creation—poetic or otherwise—is conceived of in sexual terms. He, therefore, links language, the "flesh" of poetry, with woman. To become poetry language must be inseminated with "ideal music." Therefore, the glory about which Quirón wishes to speak is present only in those cases where the artist has succeeded in inseminating the materials of artistic creation with ideas that sustain the perfection of the cosmos. This perfection is the "mystery of all things"; it is rooted in the unity of all life in and through God.

Quirón's suggestion is taken up after Reto's speech praising him with allusions to the stories that surround his death. Chiron was known everywhere for his goodness and wisdom, so much so that the distinguished heroes of Grecian mythology, like Jason, Achilles, and Aesculapius, the great physician, were entrusted to him. Hercules, too, was his friend; but while fighting with the other centaurs he inadvertently injured Chiron, who, although immortal, chose to die. He gave his immortality to Prometheus, who, in one story, was being punished for arranging that human beings get not only fire but also the best part of the animals sacrificed. Prometheus had been warned that there would be no end to his suffering until a god would freely die for him. Although it seemed unreasonable to expect such a sacrifice from another, Chiron offered himself, and Zeus accepted him as a substitute. After his death, Chiron was placed among the stars as Sagittarius.

These introductory remarks about Quirón are picked up toward the end of "Coloquio." The later references to Quirón's death bring the poem full circle and shed light on the role of mortality within the Pythagorean vision of life. Discussion of this perspective, which continues throughout the poem, is initiated by Abantes, who, following Quirón's command, begins by praising Nature, the womb of existence, and the seed of life (p. 573):

> Himnos a la sagrada Naturaleza; al vientre
> de la tierra y al germen que entre las rocas y entre
> las carnes de los árboles, y dentro humana forma,
> es un mismo secreto y es una misma norma:
> potente y sutilísimo, universal resumen
> de la suprema fuerza, de la virtud del Numen.

Genesis is again imagined in sexual terms with all matter as the womb of creation. With the implantation of spirit, the divine seed of life, the inanimate becomes animate, the trees come alive and have flesh like their kin of the human race. The germ that lies at the heart of all mineral, vegetable, and animal life is one, "un mismo secreto." It is the extract, the essence of the supreme deity that permeates all.

Quirón supports and elaborates upon Abantes's statement (pp. 573–574):

> ¡Himnos! Las cosas tienen un ser vital: las cosas
> tienen raros aspectos, miradas misteriosas;
> toda forma es un gesto, una cifra, un enigma;

en cada átomo existe un incógnito estigma;
cada hoja de cada árbol canta un propio cantar
y hay un alma en cada una de las gotas del mar;
el vate, el sacerdote, suele oír el acento
desconocido; a veces enuncia el vago viento
un misterio, y revela una inicial la espuma
o la flor; y se escuchan palabras de la bruma.
Y el hombre favorito del numen, en la linfa
o la ráfaga, encuentra mentor:—demonio o ninfa.

Quirón emphasizes the presence of life everywhere, even in what is normally regarded as inert matter. The kinship that exists between "inanimate" objects and people is further reflected in Darío's choice of a humanizing vocabulary. They have appearances, looks, and gestures; the leaves sing, the wind enunciates, and the foam reveals. These human qualities not only point out nature's sympathetic relationship with people—which makes it possible for it to communicate its message to them. They also suggest that "humanity" is rooted in the lower forms of life and is perfected through the transmigration of souls.

It is, of course, the poet/magus who is most sensitive to the signs of life and harmony present in all things. It is the *vates* who can "read" the gesture, the sign, or the puzzle of external forms as indications of the order of the universe and the immanence of God, both of which are generally hidden from human experience. The difficulty of this apprehension is highlighted by the adjectives used in this section. The signs of nature are odd, mysterious, unknown, and unfamiliar. Yet the poet understands them like his own language. He sees in them a text to be interpreted and translated.[15]

The final two lines summarize the points made in this twelve-line section. The poet is God's favorite, for wherever he looks, whether in water or in the air, he finds a guiding spirit that will teach him the secrets of the cosmos. The "linfa" and "ráfaga" are correlated in reverse order with the previously mentioned "viento" and "espuma." Darío capitalizes on the images connected with these two elements. The wind is often linked with life by virtue of its association with creative breath or exhalation. The foam of the sea recalls the ebb and flow of the ocean and the throbbing of a giant heart. Together they evoke the natural pulse and movement of the universe and convincingly assert the presence and unity of life.

In the next two sections, the unity of life is discussed from the perspective of apparent discord. First Folo, in the section already examined, deals with the split in the centaur's personality. Then Orneo outlines the problem of good and evil in the traditional Western manner (p. 574):

> Yo comprendo el secreto de la bestia. Malignos
> seres hay y benignos. Entre ellos se hacen signos
> de bien y mal, de odio o de amor, o de pena
> o gozo; el cuervo es malo y la torcaz es buena.

Orneo segregates all creatures into absolute, dualistic categories: goodness and evil, love and hate, pleasure and pain. Quirón disagrees and insists upon the basic oneness of life. He holds that all creatures are manifestations of a single life force. "Ni es la torcaz benigna ni es el cuervo protervo: / son formas del Enigma la paloma y el cuervo" (p. 575).

As in an actual conversation, where a single word occasions a series of responses, the word "enigma" calls forth remarks by both Astilo and Neso. As used by Quirón, the "enigma" was the apparent paradox of Pythagoreanism: what is in essence one is in appearance many. Astilo reminds the assembled centaurs that the underlying unity is found in mathematics and music. His comment is: "El Enigma es el soplo que hace cantar la lira" (p. 575). The impersonal "viento" mentioned previously becomes a "soplo," a "puff" exhaled by some invisible anthropomorphic force that activates the universal lyre and causes celestial music. Similarly, this "breath" infiltrates the soul of the artist, driving him to translate universal harmony into music or poetry. The connection between artistic creation and the harmonious order of the universe is clear. Neso's response to Astilo draws attention to their link with woman. "¡El Enigma es el rostro fatal de Deyanira!" Skyrme's conclusion is thus supported: "Whatever physical stimulus the man may have found in woman, the poet certainly saw in the female body the incarnation of the enigma of the universe, and in the act of love a sacrament of communion with its motive spirit, music and mystery in one. . . . Love is a means to knowledge, and in this sense Darío's erotic images are metaphors for mystical cognition."[16]

But as much as love is a means to knowledge, passion is a means to destruction. This dichotomy in the nature of love and in the relationship between man and woman is explored in the sections spoken by Neso, Eurito, Hipea, Odites, and Quirón. These sections draw heavily upon the account of the battle between the centaurs and the Lapithae described by Ovid in *The Metamorphoses*, book

12.[17] Neso begins with recollections of his encounter with Deianira.

According to the myth, Nessus met Deianira when she was on her way home after her marriage to Hercules. The newlyweds came upon the river where the centaur acted as ferryman, carrying travelers over the water. He took her on his back and in midstream insulted her. She shrieked, and Hercules shot Nessus as he reached the other bank. Before Nessus died, he told Deianira to take some of his blood and use it as a charm if Hercules ever loved another woman more than her. When she heard about Iole, she anointed a robe with the blood and sent it to Hercules. As he put it on, he was seized with excruciating pain, but he did not die. To relieve the suffering, he ordered the construction of his own funeral pyre.

It is only in the context of this original story that the meaning of the adjective "fatal" can be understood. Deianira's beauty aroused a passion that led to the death of her suitor. Neso actualizes the memory of this meeting with Deianira and makes her a presence that is just barely removed by stating: "Mi espalda aún guarda el dulce perfume de la bella; / aún mis pupilas llama su claridad de estrella." He continues: "¡Oh aroma de su sexo!, ¡oh rosas y alabastros!, / ¡oh envidia de las flores y celos de los astros!" His uncontrolled emotions are reflected in the final two lines, in the breakdown of sentence structure and in the projection of envy and jealousy onto the flowers and stars.

On the other hand, Quirón directs the discussion away from the baser emotions aroused by women by turning to the figure of Venus, who represents the feminine attributes of the godhead. He does not reject Neso's claims on behalf of feminine beauty. He simply highlights its integration into the harmony of creation. Quirón takes Neso's sensual phrase "¡oh rosas y alabastros!" and develops a unified vision of woman's role in the cosmos. The erogenous pink and white of the female body are related to the genesis of Venus, who sprang from the white foam of the sea impregnated by Uranus's red blood (p. 575).[18]

> Cuando del sacro abuelo la sangre luminosa
> con la marina espuma formara nieve y rosa,
> hecha de rosa y nieve nació la Anadiomena.

Her marine birth places her within a context that is for Darío laden with rhythmic and harmonious associations: the curves of the seahorses are echoed conceptually in the curling green waves and Venus's well-rounded hips; these "ondas" are echoed aurally in the "redondas" describing the goddess's feminine shape (p. 575):

Al cielo alzó los brazos la lírica sirena;
los curvos hipocampos sobre las verdes ondas
levaron los hocicos; y caderas redondas,
tritónicas melenas y dorsos de delfines
junto a la Reina nueva se vieron. . . .

The rhythmic undulations of the verbal picture, which, as Marasso indicates, has many possible sources, spotlights Darío's novel conclusions regarding Venus's impact upon the world.[19]

For the poet, Venus's creation is identified with the birth of her concept or with her being named; both acts fill the void with a deep, resonant harmony of meaningful existence and communication, a dual phenomenon that can only be compared with poetic creation (p. 575):

. . . . Los confines
del mar llenó el grandioso clamor; el universo
sintió que un nombre harmónico, sonoro como un verso,
llenaba el hondo hueco de la altura: ese nombre
hizo gemir la tierra de amor: fué para el hombre
más alto que el de Jove, y los númenes mismos
lo oyeron asombrados; los lóbregos abismos
tuvieron una gracia de luz. ¡VENUS impera!

The mention of her name sends a sympathetic moan of love throughout the earth, and the gloomy abysses are filled with light. Venus, indeed all women, illuminates the path to consonance. She is the Eternal Feminine in God, the divine substance of creation, and the embodiment of harmony. She is "the living earth and all earths, along with the bodies they enclose, into which souls are incarnated. . . . [She is] the great Soul of the World who gives birth, preserves, and renews. . . ." (p. 575):[20]

Ella es entre las reinas celestes la primera,
pues es quien tiene el fuerte poder de la Hermosura.
¡Vaso de miel y mirra brotó de la amargura!
Ella es la más gallarda de las emperatrices,
princesa de los gérmenes, reina de las matrices,
señora de las savias y de las atracciones,
señora de los besos y de los corazones.

Beauty, as epitomized by Venus, is the manifestation of divine perfection and universal accord. She is "la lírica sirena" because the harmonious proportions among her parts and her consonance with the cosmic order reveal her essence to be music. She is, for this reason, Darío's standard for artistic achievement, and, like poetry, she is able to convert all bitterness into honey and myrrh.[21] She leads man away from discord toward the goal of the assimilation of the music of the spheres. In addition, as the feminine aspect of the godhead, Venus is also the universal source of the vital fluid of existence ("las savias") that flows throughout all the elements of nature. This image reinforces the underlying associations of the first few lines of this section. If Darío senses in the ocean the beating of a giant heart that attests to the perpetuation of life, he establishes in love and its resulting quickened heartbeats a microcosmic parallel. Venus, born of the ocean, contains within herself the lifeblood of creation that continues to flow because of her human counterparts, women, and the emotions that they arouse.

These emotions mean but one thing for Eurito, for his thoughts about women revolve exclusively around his abduction of Hippodamia, whom he carried off at her wedding to Pirithous, starting the battle between the Lapithae and the centaurs. The Lapithae, mythical people inhabiting the mountains of Thessaly, were governed by Pirithous, who, being a son of Ixion, was a half brother of the centaurs. When Pirithous married Hippodamia and invited the centaurs to the marriage feast, the latter attempted to carry off the bride and other women. The bloody conflict evoked led to the defeat of the centaurs. For this reason, Hipea angrily denounces women as cunning, traitorous, and deadly (p. 576):

> Yo sé de la hembra humana la original infamia.
> Venus anima artera sus máquinas fatales;
> tras los radiantes ojos ríen traidores males;
> de su floral perfume se exhala sutil daño;
> su cráneo obscuro alberga bestialidad y engaño.

It is, according to Hipea, woman's external grace and apparent accord with creation that hide her true bestial and deceitful nature. Her amphoral shape and her laughter, which recalls a rippling, iridescent brook, belie her poisonous temperament. Therefore, in Hipea's judgment, she is worse than the female of any other species (p. 576):

> Tiene las formas puras del ánfora, y la risa
> del agua que la brisa riza y el sol irisa;

> mas la ponzoña ingénita su máscara pregona:
> mejores son el águila, la yegua y la leona.
> De su húmeda impureza brota el calor que enerva
> los mismos sacros dones de la imperial Minerva;
> y entre sus duros pechos, lirios del Aqueronte,
> hay un olor que llena la barca de Caronte.

As physical heat saps physical strength, the heat of passion that emanates from woman's "humid impurity" weakens man's powers of
reason. The consequent irrational behavior manifests a complete
disregard for life. As a result, Hipea describes female breasts as lilies
from the river Acheron, the river of woe that flows toward the outer
limits of the underworld. They have the same odor as the boat that
Charon uses to ferry the souls of the dead across the water to the
adamantine gates of Hades: they smell of death.

The contrast between Hipea's speech and Quirón's underlines
the fundamental split in the centaurs' perception of woman. Whereas Hipea asserts that woman is the cause of discord, destruction, and
death, Quirón upholds that she is the origin of harmony, art, and life.
The resolution of this conflict is not found, as suggested by Odites,
in earthly woman's enchantingly attractive features. Rather it is discovered in the oneness of the universe. Quirón is the first to return
to this primary theme. He does so by introducing the esoteric belief
in the androgynous nature of human beings.

According to esoteric doctrine, though God is one, he acts as a
creative Dyad and contains within himself the Eternal Masculine
and the Eternal Feminine. Adam is similarly imagined as androgynous since he was made in God's image. His fall into evil is identified with his entrance into the material and bisexual world. A return
to the union of male and female becomes a means of perceiving the
prelapsarian bliss of unity and of intuiting the divine state. In general, marriage is the way humans reattain the original androgynous
state or, as Quirón expresses it, the way Cinis [sic] can become Ceneo.
This image, like many others of the poem, is derived from the tale of
the battle between the centaurs and the Lapithae. Caeneus was originally a maiden named Caenis who was beloved by Poseidon and who
was, upon her request, changed into a man by this god (p. 576):[22]

> Por suma ley, un día llegará el himeneo
> que el soñador aguarda: Cinis será Ceneo;
> claro será el origen del femenino arcano:
> la Esfinge tal secreto dirá a su soberano.

According to Quirón's statement, the marriage that the visionary awaits and that is ordained by the highest law of the universe will place sexual love within the context of universal accord. It will restore human beings to their original androgynous state and allow them to comprehend the order of the cosmos. One who comprehends the order of the cosmos will understand the role of woman and be master of the Sphinx's secret—traditionally an ultimate meaning which remains forever beyond human comprehension. This individual will have achieved a degree of spiritual perfection that approximates his or her original, noncorporeal existence in union with God and will be prepared for immortality, which is a theme of central importance to the concluding sections of the poem.

The question of the unity of the sexes brings the colloquy back to the discussion of the oneness of creation. Clito holds that humans are the highest form of life on earth and the goal of all earthly evolution. Of all individuals, visionaries are the most elevated because they perceive the hidden meaning of existence. But Caumantes rejects this emphasis on humanity. Instead he holds that all creatures, though externally divergent, are forms of a single life force. He therefore turns to the figure of the monster, which represents the unity of creation despite apparent diversity. His only concession to Clito comes in the final three lines of his speech (p. 577):

> Naturaleza sabia, formas diversas junta,
> y cuando tiende al hombre la gran Naturaleza,
> el monstruo, siendo el símbolo, se viste de belleza.

Monsters—or composite beings—are created by an intelligent nature that willfully chooses to join divergent forms. Though nature tends toward human status through a series of incarnations, the monster is the symbol of the spectrum of life, a symbol that is beautiful in its eloquence or, as Darío states, "El monstruo expresa un ansia del corazón del Orbe" (p. 577).

The composite beings to which Caumantes refers are, in addition to the centaur, the satyr, Pan, the siren, and the Minotaur. In Greek mythology, satyrs are woodland deities represented as men with the characteristics of a goat and associated with the luxuriant vital powers of nature. Pan, a merry, musical god, resembles the satyr in that he also has goat's horns and goat's hooves instead of feet and lives in the wild thickets, forests, and mountains. Sirens are sea nymphs who lured sailors to their destruction by their sweet singing; they have come to be identified with mermaids, legendary marine creatures with the head and upper body of a woman and the tail of a fish. The Minotaur, the fruit of the union of Minos's wife Pasiphae with a bull, is half man and half bull. Caumantes sees in all these creatures the fusion of opposites: animal and human life are united in the centaur, sexual passion and harmonious fury in the satyr, the harmony of rustic life and the rhythm of the cosmos in Pan, bewitching incantations and idyllic music in the voice of the siren, Pasiphae and the bull in the Minotaur (p. 577):

> en el Centauro el bruto la vida humana absorbe;
> el sátiro es la selva sagrada y la lujuria:
> une sexuales ímpetus a la harmoniosa furia;
> Pan junta la soberbia de la montaña agreste
> al ritmo de la inmensa mecánica celeste;
> la boca melodiosa que atrae en Sirenusa,
> es la fiera alada y es de la suave musa;
> con la bicorne bestia Pasifae se ayunta.

The contrasting elements that form the center of Caumantes's argument are carefully selected to exemplify the apparent, though fallacious, diversity of life. "La selva sagrada" is contrasted with "la lujuria," "sexuales ímpetus" with "la harmoniosa furia," and "la soberbia de la montaña agreste" with "el ritmo de la inmensa mecánica celeste." As Darío makes clear in "Yo soy aquel que ayer no más decía," the introductory poem of *Cantos de vida y esperanza,* the sacred forest is where the initiate can sense the palpitation of the divine heart and learn from it the art of harmony and rhythm (p. 629):

> Mi intelecto libré de pensar bajo,
> bañó el agua castalia el alma mía,
> peregrinó mi corazón y trajo
> de la sagrada selva la armonía.
>
> ¡Oh, la selva sagrada! ¡Oh, la profunda
> emanación del corazón divino
> de la sagrada selva! ¡Oh, la fecunda
> fuente cuya virtud vence al destino!

The "sagrada selva" is a forest in which the wild movements of life have been disciplined and made to beat in rhythm with the divine heart (which also appears in the first line of Caumantes's speech). It is united with the concept of "lujuria" in that it is an enlightened, rhythmic development of the lower form. The same is true for "la harmoniosa furia" and "sexuales ímpetus," which parallel the former pair. A similar correspondence is found between "la soberbia de la montaña agreste" and "el ritmo de la inmensa mecánica celeste." The perfect order that is the rhythm of the celestial mechanism is, in a rougher, less refined state, the pride of the rustic mountain. The same life pulse is present both on the distant mountaintop and in the magnificent structure of the heavens.

These paired comparisons also underscore again the underlying tension that is central to Darío's work and to "Coloquio." They highlight Darío's awareness that human beings have within themselves the power—indeed the responsibility—to ascend, to become more spiritual, divine, and orderly of soul or the capacity to descend toward the bestial and uncontrolled.

Whereas Caumantes's speech focuses on the resolution of contraries in composite beings, Grineo directs his attention further down on the scale of existence. He speaks of inanimate objects, which he claims to love as much as Hesiod, the great poet of the simple life. Quirón supports Grineo's unusual affection by reaffirming the most fundamental belief of esoteric Pythagoreanism: the entire universe is permeated by a single, divine soul. Grineo's response to Quirón explains his attachment to stones and rocks (p. 577):

> He visto, entonces, raros ojos fijos en mí:
> los vivos ojos rojos del alma de rubí;
> los ojos luminosos del alma del topacio,
> y los de la esmeralda que del azul espacio
> la maravilla imitan; los ojos de las gemas
> de brillos peregrinos y mágicos emblemas.
> Amo el granito duro que el arquitecto labra
> y el mármol en que duerme la línea y la palabra.

Grineo does not perceive the stones and rocks as inanimate; rather he sees locked within them inchoate beings that peer out, attempting to communicate with higher forms of life. They are "pilgrims" about to begin their journey through the evolutionary process made possible by the transmigration of souls. He sees the fiery gems as sparkling eyes through which—like human eyes—their souls make contact with others. Moreover, as the gránite is worked by the architect and the marble by the sculptor, a special relationship arises between the artist's soul and that of the stone. The hidden figure and word through which nature speaks are released from their stony confines by art. The artist who understands the order of creation awakens the sleeping "línea" and "palabra."

The discussion regarding the presence of the universal soul in stones and rocks is continued in Quirón's reference to the Greek myth of the destruction of the world. When Zeus resolved to destroy the degenerate race of human beings, the pious Deucalion and his wife Pyrrha were the only mortals saved. Deucalion built a ship in which he and his wife floated in safety during the flood of nine days that killed all other inhabitants. At last the ship rested. Deucalion and Pyrrha consulted the sanctuary of Themis as to how the population might be restored. The goddess directed them to cover their heads and throw the bones of their mother behind them. Interpreting the cryptic message to refer to the Great Mother of all creatures, Mother Earth, Deucalion and Pyrrha picked up loose rocks and cast them behind them. From those thrown by Deucalion there sprang up men, from those thrown by Pyrrha, women.

The occultist reading of this allegory strengthens the connection between Grineo's comments and Quirón's brief remark. It holds that the story of Deucalion and Pyrrha epitomizes the mystery of human evolution. Spirit, by ensouling matter, becomes the indwelling power that propels the mineral to the status of the plant, the plant to the plane of the animal, the animal to the dignity of humanity, and humanity to the glory of the gods. This interpretation of the myth also sheds light on the speech by Abantes that opened the discussion regarding the unity of life. The "vientre" is the womb of the Great Mother where the "germen," spirit, is implanted. The seed develops until it is liberated from matter and returns to the godhead.

These beliefs regarding the origin and destiny of the human soul bring the poem to its final theme, namely, the proper role and function of death. The esoteric view of death, alluded to throughout the poem, ties together all the ideas already examined. It is introduced by Lícidas with a reference to lemurs, the name given by Romans to disembodied spirits associated with ghosts and apparitions (pp. 577–578):[23]

> Yo he visto los lemures flotar, en los nocturnos
> instantes, cuando escuchan los bosques taciturnos
> el loco grito de Atis que su dolor revela
> o la maravillosa canción de Filomela.
> El galope apresuro, si en el boscaje miro
> manes que pasan, y oigo su fúnebre suspiro.
> Pues de la Muerte el hondo, desconocido Imperio,
> guarda el pavor sagrado de su fatal misterio.

Darío once again brings inanimate elements to life, this time by mixing Greek mythology with his own view of nature. Atys is remembered as a youth who was driven into a frenzy by a jealous Agdistis and who, in that moment of wild abandon, castrated himself. Zeus thereupon turned him into a fir-tree. A similar story of metamorphosis is the background to Darío's reference to Philomela. Philomela was a princess of Athens who was raped by her sister Procne's husband, Tereus, who also cut out her tongue. In revenge Procne killed her son, Itys, and fed him to her husband. When Tereus was about to kill both of them, they were turned into birds, Philomela into a swallow and Procne into a nightingale, whose song is the sweetest of all birds because it is the saddest. Roman writers, however, got the sisters confused and identified Philomela with the nightingale.[24] Darío, like the Greeks, sees nature populated by human forms struggling to express human emotions. The forest is, therefore, taciturn as it listens to Atys's wild shouts of pain heard in the whining of the fir-trees or to Philomela's marvelous song. In spite of this sympathetic relationship with nature described by Lícidas, the centaur quickens his pace whenever he sees the manes, the spirits of the dead, pass by. Death remains frightful to him. The concluding speeches respond to Lícidas's fear.

The myth that underlies all the responses recounts Chiron's willful surrender of his immortality so that Prometheus might be freed from his unending punishment. Though any number of literary works with their individual interpretations of the myth may have brought the tale of Chiron's generosity to Darío's attention, his rendering of the myth departs from the traditional and follows instead esoteric doctrine.[25] Quirón finds that "La Muerte es la victoria de la progenie humana" (p. 578), because it is through death—or the deaths that precede and make possible each new, more advanced reincarnation—that one is able to attain union with God. Schuré may have influenced Darío's thinking on this subject, for a passage from *The Great Initiates* elucidates the entire concluding section of "Coloquio."

The law of incarnation and excarnation emphasizes the real meaning of life and death. It constitutes the main link in the evolution of the soul, allowing us to follow the latter backward and forward to the depths of nature and of divinity. For this law reveals to us the rhythm and measure, the reason and purpose of immortality. . . . Earthly birth is a death from the spiritual point of view, and death is a heavenly birth. The alternation between the two lives is necessary for the development of the soul, and each of the two is both the result and the explanation of the other. . . .

It is therefore in a very deep sense that the ancient initiate poets called sleep the brother of death. For a veil of forgetfulness separates sleep from waking as it does birth from death.[26]

This statement clarifies what is meant by Arneo's statement: "La Muerte es de la Vida la inseparable hermana" (p. 578). It also explains Medón's description of death: "No es demacrada y mustia, / ni ase corva guadaña, ni tiene faz de angustia" (p. 578). Death is not horrible or fearsome as in traditional Christian iconography; rather "es semejante a Diana, casta y virgen como ella," because it is unsullied by the flesh, by matter. The "palmas triunfales" represent death's victory over life and the "agua del olvido" the forgetfulness which separates birth from death.

In this context, it is reasonable for Quirón to conclude, "La pena de los dioses es no alcanzar la Muerte" (p. 578), and for him to give up his immortality to Prometheus, who is mentioned in this last section by Eureto [sic] in relation to the creation of human beings. Legend states that Prometheus created man out of earth and water and gave him a portion of all the qualities possessed by the other animals. Eureto, therefore, suggests that if human beings, through Prometheus, could steal life, they should be able to understand the key to death that is presented, in conclusion, by Quirón (p. 578):

> La virgen de las vírgenes es inviolable y pura.
> Nadie su casto cuerpo tendrá en la alcoba obscura,
> ni beberá en sus labios el grito de la victoria,
> ni arrancará a su frente las rosas de su gloria.

By supernatural communication or intuitive accord with nature, the centaurs conclude the colloquy as Apollo, the sun god, rises to the highest point in his journey through the sky. At the same time, the thundering sounds that are produced by his passage through the heavens (an adaptation of the image of the universal monochord) are echoed by the ocean.[27] The winds that died down begin to blow, and the various sounds of nature replace the sounds of voices. The light rustle of the west wind is pierced by the strident song of the Greek cicada, the voice of inextinguishable life (pp. 578–579):[28]

> Mas he aquí que Apolo se acerca al meridiano.
> Sus truenos prolongados repite el Oceano.
> Bajo el dorado carro del reluciente Apolo

vuelve a inflar sus carrillos y sus odres Eolo.
A lo lejos, un templo de mármol se devisa
entre laureles-rosa que hace cantar la brisa.
Con sus vibrantes notas, de Céfiro desgarra
la veste transparente la helénica cigarra,
y por el llano extenso van en tropel sonoro
los Centauros, y al paso, tiembla la Isla de Oro.

The conclusion of the poem is, thus, a perfect echo of and balance to the introduction. In both sections Darío underscores the rhythms and sounds that ultimately belong to the single harmony of the universe, to the rhythmic pulse of the life to which the poet aspires to attune his life and art.

Shortly after composing "Coloquio de los centauros," Darío wrote a series of thirteen poems entitled "Las ánforas de Epicuro," which he added to the 1901 edition of *Prosas profanas.* Four of the thirteen deal with occultist themes; two ("La espiga" and "Ama tu ritmo . . . ") center on the Pythagorean concept of the unity of life. In the first of the series, "La espiga" (p. 615), the peaceful tone of the harmonious accord is the same as in "Coloquio." The setting, however, is different. The Greek temple and mythological figures disappear. What is left is a scene of timeless, natural beauty undefined as to period or style. Indeed, time stands still, and, unlike "Coloquio," which provides a harmonious interlude limited to the confines of the poem, "La espiga" takes place in an eternal setting of idyllic and unchanging peace. Moreover, with the disappearance of artistic intermediaries, Darío declares his confidence in his ability to perceive the order of creation directly from nature.

Though "La espiga" will be considered in greater detail in the chapter on syncretism, a few additional points that are particularly relevant to the present discussion require comment. In the first three lines of the sonnet, Darío establishes the scene in which the underlying concepts of the poem germinate. A sign is seen in the movement of a plant which is being stirred by "los dedos del viento." The sign is subtle, noticed only by the enlightened poet, who now directs the reader's attention to it. He sees the swaying plant as a golden brush with which the fingers of the wind paint upon the blue canvas of the sky. They sketch "el misterio inmortal de la tierra divina / y el alma de las cosas." In other words, it is in all the elements of nature working together in universal harmony that the poet perceives the mystery of the divine and the soul of all things.

The pantheistic belief that God is present throughout creation is reinforced by the transitional ninth line, "Pues en la paz del campo la faz de Dios asoma." Darío concludes the poem on a syncretic note by introducing standard Christian symbols, which clarify his previous allusions to the Eucharist. He is thus able to reconcile Catholic doctrine with his pantheistic vision.

As "La espiga" unfolds, Darío builds upon the elements present in the initial scene, preparing the way for the final, syncretic image. The elements gradually become more and more invested with supernatural and religious significance. In contrast to this deepening religious experience of "La espiga," in the fifth sonnet of "Las ánforas de Epicuro," "Ama tu ritmo . . ." (p. 617), Pythagorean pantheism is seen through a cool, calculating, mathematical eye. Not that religion and mathematics represented to Pythagoras opposing points of view. Rather they were two inseparable factors in a single world view.[29] The central notions which held these two elements together were those of contemplation, orderliness, and purification. By contemplating the order revealed in the universe, especially in mathematics, music, and the regular movement of the heavenly bodies, and by assimilating themselves to that orderliness, individuals are progressively purified until they eventually escape from the cycle of birth and attain immortality.[30]

As has been pointed out, Pythagoras derived the fundamental doctrines of his philosophy from observing the mathematical ratio that exists between the lengths of string required to produce different notes at a particular tension. Indeed, the key Pythagorean view that the real and comprehensible nature of things was to be found in proportion and number came to him largely from these observations, which formed the basis of both the belief in universal harmony and the image of celestial music. Many times these various ideas became fused into a simplified conception of Pythagoreanism as holding that the universe is regulated by rhythm.[31]

In "Ama tu ritmo. . . ," one senses, through the poet's use of self-directed commands and the shorter, eleven-syllable lines, the imperative quality both of his desire to attune himself to the all-pervading pulse of the universe and of the universal beat itself. No longer, as in "La espiga," is the setting idyllic or the unity of life immediately evident; rather the poet must strive to perceive and to achieve harmony. Thus the lyricism of the previous poem gives way to a crisp, assertive tone; its long, flowing lines to short, abrupt phrases; and its pastoral scene to arithmetic and geometric signs and symbols. The poet tells himself: "Ama tu ritmo y ritma tus acciones / bajo su ley, así como tus versos." He feels an obligation to obey the rhythm of the universe—seen here as divine law—because he has singled himself out as the most capable of integrating himself into this rhythm, thereby achieving harmony in his life and in his poetry.

Since Pythagoreans hold that from the moment that God is manifest he is simultaneously indivisible essence and divisible substance and that the physical manifestations of God, both human beings and the universe, are made in his image, Darío's conception of himself and his works is enhanced. This traditional solution to the problem of the One and the Many and its implications are elaborated and reworked in lines 3 through 8 of "Ama tu ritmo. . . ."

> eres un universo de universos,
> y tu alma una fuente de canciones.
>
> La celeste unidad que presupones,
> hará brotar en ti mundos diversos;
> y al resonar tus números dispersos
> pitagoriza en tus constelaciones.

The poet is told that he is a universe of universes, for he is a microcosm which ideally should be a perfect reproduction of that harmonious macrocosm.[32] His soul is a source of songs, for the enlightened poet distills and transforms into poetry the music of the spheres that reverberates within him. Yet clearly the poet's accord with the universe does not stop there. As Darío contemplates the divine unity, he assimilates its productive qualities and becomes the origin of new life and diverse worlds. Since these diverse worlds of art and beauty are patterned on universal harmony, their fundamental nature is proportion and number. Hence, at the same time that the celestial unity is harmoniously reflected within the constellations of Darío's poetic worlds, the reading of Darío's poetry causes his "números dispersos" to reecho within the universe. In this way, Darío establishes within the quatrains a series of parallel mirrors in which the harmonious universe is reflected in the artist and his or her works while the artist's image and views of the universe are reflected back. Acoustically Darío communicates the sensation of echo through the purposeful use of repetition throughout the poem. The word "versos" reappears in "uni*verso* de uni*versos*" and in "di*versos*," "divina" reappears in "a*divina*," and "urna" in "noct*urna*" and "tacit*urna*." In addition, "dispersos" echoes "diversos" in the second quatrain.

After the normal pause, the sonnet "resumes" with a series of commands that continue the injunctions of the first line and maintain the imperative tone of the poem.

> Escucha la retórica divina
> del pájaro del aire y la nocturna
> irradiación geométrica adivina;
>
> mata la indiferencia taciturna,
> y engarza perla y perla cristalina
> en donde la verdad vuelca su urna.

Once again the poet is told to attune himself to universal harmony: to listen to the enlightened song of the bird and to solve the riddle of the geometric movement of the stars.[33] The chiasmus of the first tercet and the greater fluidity of these lines suggest that Darío senses that he is approximating his goal. The commands remain as a warning that he always be vigilant. For this reason the poem concludes with an appeal that the poet eliminate silent indifference and neglect and that he string together "perla y perla cristalina / en donde la verdad vuelca su urna." The final imagery is more fully understood in light of another of Darío's poems, "Lírica," written in 1902 (p. 765):

> Todavía está Apolo triunfante, todavía
> gira bajo su lumbre la rueda del destino
> y viértense del carro en el diurno camino
> las ánforas de fuego, las urnas de armonía.

As the later poem clearly indicates, Darío envisions the sun as a giant urn of truth and harmony. In "Ama tu ritmo . . . ," the poet is told to string together his crystalline creations, which, like the pearls of a necklace, catch and reflect the light of the sun.[34] The ultimate mission of the enlightened poet is, as implied in the quatrains, to produce works that mirror the truth and harmony that he perceives around him.

Approximately seven years later, in April, 1908, Darío wrote another sonnet, "En las constelaciones" (p. 1035), which bears a strong resemblance to "Ama tu ritmo . . . " but which reflects a fundamental change in attitude. The undefined "nocturna irradiación geométrica" reappears as "constelaciones pitagóricas," and the repetition, with minor variations, of the words "constelaciones," "Pitágoras," and "leía" recalls the repetition within the first line of "Ama tu ritmo. . . ." More importantly, the poet's concern with following the rhythm of the universe is the same in both sonnets. But the differences are crucial. In the earlier of the two, one senses the poet's recently awakened awareness of the universal law of harmony and his faith—perhaps at times a bit shaky—in his ability to follow his own commands. In the later poem, he seeks to explain—or to justify—his often unsuccessful attempts to do so. He no longer tells himself what to do; the "tú" of the earlier poems is now a "yo," and the imperatives are now indicatives. The poet states:

> En las constelaciones Pitágoras leía,
> yo en las constelaciones pitagóricas leo;
> pero se han confundido dentro del alma mía
> el alma de Pitágoras con el alma de Orfeo.

The "but" of line 3 marks the introduction of the poet's explanation of his loss of harmony—both with nature and within himself. The use of the adjective "pitagóricas" to describe the constellations emphasizes this loss. When Darío tries to read harmony in the stars, he loses touch with them; they become Pythagorean and alien. "En las constelaciones" relates the poet's internal struggle and his attempt to overcome the chaos within his soul by reestablishing contact with the order inherent in nature, an order that he seeks to re-create in his poetry.

As Erika Lorenz points out, it certainly is not surprising that Pythagoras and Orpheus should become confused in Darío's syncretic imagination, for both serve a dual, musical-religious function. Pythagoras, who is, of course, closely associated with the "music of the spheres," also symbolizes the "rhythm of all that exists." Thus, the Pythagorean law which demonstrates the unity of all life in number and proportion is linked with Orpheus's magic song, which fuses all that exists in a unity of feeling.[35]

Darío does not deny that great beauty can be created under the aegis of feeling. He does find, however, that in his life feelings often turn into wild impulses which interfere with the pursuit of harmony. To illustrate this point, the two facets of Darío's soul that are alluded to in the first quatrain are delineated in the second as opposing forces of dissonance and consonance and as the result of two antithetical incarnations (ellipsis in original):

> Sé que soy, desde el tiempo del Paraíso, reo;
> sé que he robado el fuego y robé la armonía;
> que es abismo mi alma y huracán mi deseo;
> que sorbo el infinito y quiero todavía . . .

On the one hand, Darío feels that his permanent, reincarnating soul has been sinful since the beginning of time and, as a result, that he has been an outcast. On the other, he believes that he is aspiring and benevolent and deserving of paradise—a fact signaled by his appropriation of both fire and harmony.[36] This split recalls the split in the personality of the centaurs and the other composite beings of "Coloquio." It is emphasized by the repetition of the initial "sé" of lines 5 and 6 and by the parallels established in lines 7 and 8. The "abismo" that is his soul is contrasted with the "infinito" that he is able to absorb, thereby attaining communion with the soul of the world, and his wildly uncontrollable and destructive desire is contrasted with his open-ended aspiration.[37]

The anguish caused by the struggle within his soul is clear in the choppy, almost disjointed, structure of the first tercet, and his confusion is apparent in the use of the extended rhetorical question that begins with: "¿qué voy a hacer . . . ?" The fundamental problem, as Darío sees it, is that he cannot satisfy both aspects of his being simultaneously, and he therefore always wishes to be different from what he is. The path toward reconciliation and harmony is indicated in the second tercet by the "tortuga de oro," which shows the poet God's will.

> En la arena me enseña la tortuga de oro
> hacia dónde conduce de las musas el coro
> y en dónde triunfa, augusta, la voluntad de Dios.

As previously indicated, Darío learned from esoteric Pythagoreanism that because the entire universe is the visible unfolding of God in space and time, there is life everywhere, even in what is generally regarded as dead and inert matter. It is most often the enlightened poet who can interpret the external signs that indicate deeper meanings and internal life. Consequently, it is not unusual that the tortoise should lead Darío to the choir of the Muses or show him where God's will triumphs.[38] Similarly, in an earlier sonnet, "La tortuga de oro . . ." (p. 1004), written in 1900, it is the tortoise—through the signs that it traces on the carpet, the enigma that is engraved on its carapace, and the circle that is drawn in its shadow—that identifies the God that usually remains unnamed and unrecognized. In both poems, Darío concludes with a reference to the underlying music of reality and, by extension, to the universal harmony to which he seeks to attune himself in spite of his "pecho süave" and his "pensamiento parco."[39] "La tortuga de oro . . ." also shows the close linking of God's will with the concept of the eternal return, an association which is only alluded to in "En las constelaciones" in the reference to reincarnation.[40]

God's will is seen not in the ploddings of a tortoise across the sand but in the sweep of the birds across the sky in "Pájaros de las islas" (p. 1016), written on the island of Mallorca during the winter of 1906.

> Pájaros de las islas: en vuestra concurrencia
> hay una voluntad,
> hay un arte secreto y una divina ciencia,
> gracia de eternidad.

Here again the elements of nature reveal "la única Verdad," that is, the oneness of the universe in and through God, and once again Darío aspires to learn the divine wisdom captured in their flight in order to establish in his poetry and his soul the idyllic harmony unseen by most people.

Darío finds in the graceful movement of the birds a sign or "cifra" of a perfectly ordered and proportionate universe. He also responds to their flight aesthetically, by proclaiming it a work of art. Although ordinarily these two points of view are considered incompatible—one based on a mathematical or scientific grasp of the universe, the other on an intuitive reaction to it—Darío, following in the tradition of the Romantics and Symbolists, is able to reconcile these two approaches to nature. Harmony, which within esoteric Pythagoreanism is based on number and proportion, is for Darío an artistic standard associated with divine perfection, the Good, and the Beautiful. Nature is the supreme work of art, in which the divinely gifted and inspired poet recognizes the perfect proportions of universal harmony.[41] By drawing upon the harmony behind the disorganized appearance of external realities, the poet is able to capture the essence of the supernatural in his art. In this way, the complementary pairs established in stanzas 1, 2, and 5—"arte"/"ciencia," "academia"/"signos," "dicha de mis ojos"/"problemas de mi meditación"—deal with a single truth about the birds.

Darío's desire to imitate their flight and thereby capture in his poetry the secret art and divine wisdom that they embody becomes clear in the final stanza. Artistically he has achieved this objective throughout the poem. The alternating glide and flapping of the birds' wings is captured by the alternation between fourteen- and seven-syllable lines, and the oxytone rhyme in the shorter lines, all but one of which are end-stopped, contributes to a feeling of calm and order.

At the same time it is evident that the attainment of harmony is more than an artistic goal. It is a means of achieving inner peace, accord with all life, and, in turn, immortality through reunion with the single soul of the universe. For this reason, in addition to "una voluntad," "un arte secreto," and "una divina ciencia," Darío sees "gracia de eternidad" in their sweep across the heavens. He more closely joins the image of the birds with the concept of immortality by drawing upon traditional symbolism which links the soul with winged creatures. In the last stanza, Darío represents his soul as a bird that aspires to fly in unison with the others that had previously been described as "almas dulces y herméticas." As his soul is metaphorically converted into a bird, the birds are metaphorically changed into souls that have, for ages, flown in harmony with nature: "a vuestras alas líricas son las brisas de Ulises, / los vientos de Jasón." It is in this way that Darío underscores the evolutionary aspect of "la única Verdad," namely, the doctrine of transmigration of souls, at the same time that he relates his sense of elation as his soul takes flight "con las alas puras de mi deseo abiertas / hacia la inmensidad."

The fusion of the diachronic and synchronic aspects of the oneness of the universe is evident in "Filosofía" (p. 664), published in *Cantos de vida y esperanza* (1905) not long before the composition of "Pájaros de las islas." The first of the two four-line stanzas is directed to the lower creatures of the world who are informed that, because of the kinship of all life and the resulting laws of reincarnation, they can expect to advance on the scale of existence and even, perhaps, attain reunion with God. For this reason, they should be grateful that they are alive. The tone of optimism and exaltation is established by the initial phrases of lines 1 and 2: "Saluda al sol, araña, no seas rencorosa. / Da tus gracias a Dios, oh sapo, pues que eres." The spider and the toad are to turn skyward and to speak to the sun and to God, respectively. Yet, because the harmonious unity of life has a punitive aspect, Darío reminds these creatures that they can descend as easily as ascend on the scale of existence. The prickly crab is linked to the rose by its thorns, and mollusks have reminiscences of women. The graphic connection between women and mollusks appears to indicate that it is the sexual facet of women that has caused their return to a lower form of life.

In the second stanza, Darío once again turns to the discussion of the signs of nature and introduces the concept of "norms," which are probably demiurgic emanations of divine thought (ellipsis in original):[42]

> Sabed ser lo que sois, enigmas, siendo formas;
> dejad la responsabilidad a las Normas,

que a su vez la enviarán al Todopoderoso . . .
(Toca, grillo, a la luz de la luna, y dance el oso.)

The demiurge acts on behalf of the supreme being by putting into "formas" God's concept of the world, "el enigma." Neither the forms nor the norms, which are merely divine agents, have responsibility, for all is passed on to the all-powerful. The final, fantastical commands underscore the poet's belief that it is by becoming attuned to the rhythm of life and to the music of the spheres that universal harmony can be achieved.

Most of the "signs" of the oneness of life examined so far come from the land. But in "Marina" (p. 670), "Caracol" (p. 679), and "Revelación" (p. 712) the universal life force is seen in the rhythmic movement of the sea and the beating of its great heart, both of which serve as models for the poet's art and soul. Detailed studies of these three poems are presented in the article by Trueblood cited earlier. In tracing the development of the symbol of the sea from "Sinfonía en gris mayor" (probably from 1889) and "Tarde del trópico" (1892) to "Marina" and "Caracol" (both from 1903) and "Revelación" (1907), he discovers that "behind the various marine rhythms which Darío carried into the beat of his lines, behind the sea-sounds he transposed into verbal music, lay in addition all the sense of a single limitless life which the sea more than any other force in nature arouses."[43] Thus it is in all the elements of nature—on land, on sea, and in the sky—that Darío perceives the single soul of the universe.

In the seven poems analyzed, Darío aspires not only to affirm the unity of life and the harmony of existence but also to integrate himself and his poetry into the hidden order of creation, thereby translating the perfection of the cosmos into a language more generally understood by humanity. He relies upon the creative use of images, acoustical patterns, verbal effects, and figures of speech in his struggle to illuminate the harmonious and living nature that—perhaps through no fault of his own—he fears he might not be able to emulate. This fear haunts him and affects his perception of his ultimate fate. As a poet and interpreter of the orderly universe, he trusts that he is among a chosen few. Yet the possibility of failure—because of the intractability of language or because of his own spiritual weaknesses—is forever present. The next chapter explores Darío's recourse to the doctrine of transmigration of souls as a philosophic and metaphoric framework with which he attempts to resolve this tension generated by his desire to fulfill his poetic responsibility.

3. "Under the Sign of a Supreme Destiny": Reincarnation and Poetic Responsibility

In the Pythagorean belief in universal harmony, prevalent in the literature of the nineteenth century, Darío finds the philosophic context out of which grows his aspiration to capture in his art the musical perfection of the macrocosm. This conception of harmony illuminates the core of his poetics. It is also the underlying principle of the doctrine of reincarnation, a doctrine that addresses the personal dimensions of the poet's search for harmony. If Darío relies upon esoteric Pythagoreanism to clarify his positions regarding the purpose of art and the community of life, he turns to the transmigration of souls to refine his views regarding the nature of his soul and the possibility of immortality.

Darío's fascination with the doctrine of reincarnation—demonstrated by its early and continued appearance in his poetry—may stem from his well-recognized preoccupation with death. In *Historia de mis libros*, as an extension of his comment on "Lo fatal," he writes:

> Ciertamente, en mí existe, desde los comienzos de mi vida, la profunda preocupación del fin de la existencia, el terror a lo ignorado, el pavor de la tumba, o más bien, del instante en que cesa el corazón su ininterrumpida tarea y la vida desaparece de nuestro cuerpo. . . . Me he llenado de congoja cuando he examinado el fondo de mis creencias y no he encontrado suficientemente maciza y fundamentada mi fe cuando el conflicto de las ideas me ha hecho vacilar, y me he sentido sin un constante y seguro apoyo.[1]

This profound fear of death is intimately related to Darío's fear of eternal damnation, and his lack of constant and certain religious support refers to his inability to find an absolute and unqualified promise of salvation—either in the Catholic beliefs of his childhood or in the esoteric belief in the transmigration of souls. He therefore vacillates between the two conceptions of immortality. But resolution cannot be found in either of them, for the anxiety stems from his sense of wrongdoing. As indicated in the last chapters, Darío sees himself pulled toward the spiritual on the one hand and toward the bestial on the other. It is for this reason that Darío turns to the doctrine of transmigration of souls. In it he finds not only a philosophic and metaphoric framework that is integrated into his larger vision of the universe but also one that helps him to imagine and discuss poetically the conflict within his being, for within this framework all the elements of creation are torn between their aspiration toward a harmonious union with God and the temptations of the flesh. Darío's earlier poems reflect a youthful optimism, but, with a mature appreciation of the unrelenting passage of time, the carefree tone gives way to a melancholy reflectiveness. Under the influence of esoteric Pythagoreanism, the anxiety of growing old develops a metaphysical dimension which Darío lives as intensely as the purely physical. As Anderson Imbert points out with regard to his use of autumnal imagery, "Además de esta experiencia del tiempo biológico y psicológico—envejecer, cambiar—Darío se imaginaba un tiempo metafísico. Sus lecturas teosóficas, esotéricas, ocultistas lo habían iniciado en la idea de preexistencias y reencarnaciones, de tiempos cíclicos y eternos retornos."[2]

According to esoteric tradition, there is a unity of existence; all things form a community animated by a single life force that can pass from one to another. As Kingsford and Maitland wrote: "The doctrine of a universal soul is the doctrine of love, in that it implies the recognition of the larger self. It represents, moreover, Humanity as the one universal creation of which all living things are but different steps either of development or of degradation, progression or retrogression, ascent or descent. . . ."[3] For the human soul to have become what it is, it had to traverse all the kingdoms of nature, gradually becoming developed through a series of innumerable existences. In the series of lives, the soul can regress or advance depending upon whether it surrenders itself to its lower or to its divine nature. As a result, the very nature of its new existence is determined by the good or evil use it made of its freedom. In general, however, human beings are born again with the instincts and faculties that they developed in preceding incarnations. They can come to recognize these previous existences by putting themselves in contact with the permanent ego, the *anima divina*, for something of each personality survives, as it leaves its eternal impress on the incarnating permanent self. It is held that the final goal has been achieved when the soul has decisively conquered matter, reached the threshold of divinity, and escaped the cycle of incarnation. This end is possible because the life within each creature is a spark of divine fire.

Many of these tenets are shared by Buddhists. Both Buddhism and Pythagoreanism posit a single, universal life force (in Buddhism called Brahman), and they both hold that, according to the law of retribution or "karma," each being has a kind of specific gravity at death; the next form to be assumed is determined by its weight. Although references to Buddhism are virtually nonexistent in Darío's poetry—despite his tendency toward syncretism—the Oriental religion and Pythagoreanism often become fused in derivative esoteric sects as well as in the poetic imagination of other writers of the period.[4] Gullón suggests that their longing for immortality, if not their belief in it, led to this association of disparate doctrine.[5] It is equally reasonable to assume that the poets—including Darío—rediscovered in either the Buddhist or the Pythagorean cosmology an aesthetically satisfying conception of time, one which offers the promise of the rhythmic repetition of the perfect, timeless past.[6]

The two earliest references to reincarnation that appear in Darío's poetry more closely resemble experiments with esoteric doctrine than expressions of conviction. The rather naive tone of the poems and the prefatory nature of their titles, "Reencarnaciones" (p. 939) and "Metempsícosis" (pp. 702–703)—which in the latter case is really the only indication that the poem is to be read from the perspective of the reincarnated Rufo Galo—reveal the hand of a neophyte. The earlier of the two, "Reencarnaciones," was written in Guatemala in 1890 and draws upon esoteric tenets to recount the history of the poet's soul, a history which seems to be offered as proof of a deeply ingrained artistic temperament.

> Yo fuí coral primero,
> después hermosa piedra,
> después fuí de los bosques verde y colgante hiedra;
> después yo fuí manzana,
> lirio de la campiña,
> labio de niña,
> una alondra cantando en la mañana;
> y ahora soy un alma
> que canta como canta una palma
> de luz de Dios al viento.

In the soul's passage through the kingdoms of creation, it maintains a harmonious accord with nature and finally, as it becomes increasingly more perfected, achieves synchronization with the musical pulse of the universe.

In the second poem, "Metempsícosis," which is generally believed to have been written in 1893, Darío alludes to the esoteric notion of retribution, which holds that, because people are free, they are responsible for the good or evil use they make of their existence on earth. Failure to live in harmony with the world is punished by descent on the scale of existence. Though upon approaching middle age Darío appropriates these concepts to express the profound anxiety he feels regarding his own fate, in this poem he evokes a past life of Rufo Galo, who, as an emancipated slave, represents humanity. Rufo appreciated the value of freedom, struggled to attain it, but later forfeited it by succumbing to the disordering temptations of the flesh.

> Yo fuí un soldado que durmió en el lecho
> de Cleopatra la reina. Su blancura
> y su mirada astral y omnipotente.
> Eso fué todo.
>
> ¡Oh mirada! ¡oh blancura! y ¡oh aquel lecho
> en que estaba radiante la blancura!
> ¡Oh la rosa marmórea omnipotente!
> Eso fué todo.
>
> Y crujió su espinazo por mi brazo;
> y yo, liberto, hice olvidar a Antonio
> (¡oh el lecho y la mirada y la blancura!)
> Eso fué todo.
>
> Yo, Rufo Galo, fuí soldado, y sangre
> tuve de Galia, y la imperial becerra
> me dió un minuto audaz de su capricho.
> Eso fué todo.
>
> ¿Por qué en aquel espasmo las tenazas
> de mis dedos de bronce no apretaron
> el cuello de la blanca reina en broma?
> Eso fué todo.
>
> Yo fuí llevado a Egipto. La cadena
> tuve al pescuezo. Fuí comido un día
> por los perros. Mi nombre, Rufo Galo.
> Eso fué todo.

Darío relies upon the expressive possibilities of the various types of eleven-syllable lines to convey, in each half of the poem, a different perspective on the event that is described in the first one and one-half lines, namely, Rufo's love affair with Cleopatra. In stanzas 1 through 3, the initial, unidentified "yo" is completely subordinated to the memory of the captivating Egyptian queen, emerging only in a moment of extreme pride ("y yo, liberto, hice olvidar a Antonio"). The lack of predication that runs from the second half of the first stanza through the second communicates a sense of stupefaction or trancelike calm, which is heightened by the even flow of the melodic hendecasyllables. The series of exclamations, the repetition of the words "lecho," "blancura," "mirada," "omnipotente," and the refrain, "Eso fué todo," highlight Rufo's total surrender to the seductive monarch and to the pleasures of the flesh.

A more cogent account of his story begins in the fourth stanza, as the poem "resumes" with an echo of the first line. This time the unidentified "yo" gives his name and explains his dignified past. This change reflects Rufo's reawakening to his own worth and his growing resentment of his voluntary subjugation to the will of another. Rufo's anger is sensed in the predominance of emphatic hendecasyllables and in the biting vocabulary of the fifteenth line, in which he voices his indignation at having been the queen's momentary whim. Rufo wonders why he did not—if only in jest—demonstrate to Cleopatra the ease with which he could destroy her, thus showing her the disdain that she showed so many. His outrage carries into the refrain, altering its meaning though the words remain the same. It now proclaims: "That was all it was, nothing more, and now it is all over."

The short phrases of the last stanza heighten the already emphatic tone of the second half of the poem. The quickened pace parallels Rufo Galo's rapid fall, and, while the reader does not know what form his soul has taken, the degradation that was inflicted upon him in life seems intended to foreshadow his descent, after death, on the scale of existence. He lost his freedom, was chained like an animal, and, finally, was fed to the dogs. Although the refrain still proclaims "That was all it was, nothing more, and now it is all over," the "eso" here refers to Rufo Galo's life and, perhaps, future lives.

During the eight years between the writing of "Metempsícosis" and the publication of "Alma mía" (pp. 621–622) in "Las ánforas de Epicuro" of the 1901 edition of *Prosas profanas*, both Darío and his poetry matured, but maturing had not yet become aging and death had not yet become an imminent possibility. On the contrary, Darío's creative energies and sense of self-worth were at their zenith, he enjoyed fame and respect, and, under the dual influence of Romantic and esoteric traditions, he considered himself among the noblest men on earth, at the threshold of divinity. Understandably, "Alma mía" presents an optimistic view of reincarnation, one in which reunion with God appears attainable. At the same time, however, Darío's confidence is not blind. All the barriers to success are not yet behind him. For this reason optimism is combined with caution.

This ambivalence is reflected in the acoustical features of the poem: the optimism in the even, balanced rhythm, the caution in the end-stopped alexandrine lines that spotlight the series of short injunctions to be followed by the poet's soul. The exception to this rhythmic pattern is the enjambment between lines 11 and 12, which stresses the simultaneity of the three adverbial clauses. The rhyme scheme of the quatrains follows that of the classical sonnet— ABBA : ABBA—but that of the tercets does not—CCD : EED. This departure heightens the suspensive quality of the last directive, which ends with the word "dios" linked in rhyme with the unstressed "los" of the previous tercet (ellipses in original):

> Alma mía, perdura en tu idea divina;
> todo está bajo el signo de un destino supremo;
> sigue en tu rumbo, sigue hasta el ocaso extremo
> por el camino que hacia la Esfinge te encamina.
>
> Corta la flor al paso, deja la dura espina;
> en el río de oro lleva a compás el remo;
> saluda al rudo arado del rudo Triptolemo,
> y sigue como un dios que sus sueños destina . . .
>
> Y sigue como un dios que la dicha estimula;
> y mientra la retórica del pájaro te adula
> y los astros del cielo te acompañan, y los
>
> ramos de la Esperanza surgen primaverales,
> atraviesa impertérrita por el bosque de males
> sin temer las serpientes; y sigue, como un dios . . .

The conviction that the poet is the highest form of humanity is based on the premise that he shares a consciousness with all the elements of nature and that he can articulate in human language the cadence of universal life and the divine wisdom manifest therein. In accordance with this view, Darío interprets his calling to be a "sign" that he has a "supreme destiny," which he trusts that his soul will achieve if it maintains its present condition and continues its present course. The religious significance of Darío's statement unfolds through the astrological and theological reverberations of the word "signo." Similarly his command that his soul continue "hasta el ocaso extremo," along the road that leads toward the Sphinx, brings to the fore the theme of immortality. Inasmuch as the idea of the restoration of life from death was drawn from the sun's daily reappearance in the east after its nightly disappearance in the west, Darío's desire that his soul reach the final sunset symbolizes his wish that it break the cycle of reincarnation by achieving reunion with God. The road that leads to the last sunset also leads toward the Sphinx, who, as the embodiment of the doctrine of the universal soul and the mystery of nature, represents the final lesson of esoteric doctrine. All who cannot solve her riddle perish; those who know the answer proceed to attain immortality.

The road imagery continues into the second quatrain, and the next three injunctions concern elements from the symbolic landscape through which the poet's soul must pass. While the proverbial flower and thorn recall pseudo-Epicurean doctrine and Darío's unending search for beauty, Triptolemus's plough brings to mind the early stages of human progress toward the artistic and the divine. The image of the golden river takes its meaning from the fusion of two metaphors: the occultist identification of the soul as a spark of God's own being and Darío's representation of the human soul as a *fuente.*[7] As the spark is to the fire, so the spring is to the river and the human soul is to the soul of God. Thus the second command of the second quatrain is not only a vibrant elaboration of the travel symbolism, an elaboration that underscores the poet's struggle to remain on course and in harmony with nature; it is also a poetic restatement of the Pythagorean principle that the soul must assimilate the musical pulse of the divine soul that flows throughout the cosmos in order to achieve perfection.

Darío reaffirms his confidence in his soul's ability to emulate divine perfection by comparing it to a god who controls his dreams and who is inspired by good fortune. Like all poets, he can read the signs of nature—in the song of the birds, in the patterns of the stars, and in the springtime branches of hope. Since the signs are clearly propitious, he urges his soul to pass intrepidly through the forest of evils without fearing the serpents. The branches of hope that are in blossom are Darío's renewed hopes for eternal life. He therefore concludes optimistically with the directive "y sigue, como un dios. . . ," with which the poem returns to the point of departure. The circularity of form achieved through the restatement of the first thought, "perdura en tu idea divina," subtly supports the doctrine of trans-migration of souls at the same time that the suspensive quality of the last injunction reinforces Darío's desire for an end to the cycle of reincarnation.

A similarly confident view of the poet's soul is expressed in "Palabras de la Satiresa" (p. 616), another sonnet from "Las ánforas de Epicuro." But whereas the cautious tone of "Alma mía" merely implies that there are pitfalls on the road to immortality that should be avoided, "Palabras de la Satiresa" deals directly with the greatest danger to Darío's aspiring soul. He acknowledges his tendency to fall to the temptations of the flesh and to behave in a manner un-becoming the elevated status of his soul. The resulting tension be-tween the flesh and the spirit is embodied in the Satiresa, who, like the composite creatures of "Coloquio," is a figure of opposites. The sexually arousing, pleasure-seeking aspects of the Satiresa dominate the poet's attention in the quatrains; her understanding of the har-monious integration of apparently divergent elements speaks in the tercets.

> Un día oí una risa bajo la fronda espesa;
> vi brotar de lo verde dos manzanas lozanas;
> erectos senos eran las lozanas manzanas
> del busto que bruñía de sol la Satiresa.
>
> Era una Satiresa de mis fiestas paganas,
> que parece clavel o rosa cuando besa
> y furiosa y ríente y que abrasa y que mesa,
> con los labios manchados por las moras tempranas.
>
> "Tú que fuiste—me dijo—un antiguo argonauta,
> alma que el sol sonrosa y que la mar zafira,
> sabe que está el secreto de todo ritmo y pauta
>
> en unir carne y alma a la esfera que gira,
> y amando a Pan y Apolo en la lira y la flauta,
> ser en la flauta Pan, como Apolo en la lira."

The laughter and the lush landscape establish the initial tone. The junglelike surroundings from which the Satiresa emerges evoke a region of rich, uncontrolled vegetation. This forest symbolism, which links the setting of the poem with the poet's unconscious, is enhanced by the identification of the Satiresa's breasts with lux-uriant apples free of prohibition.[8] More than a brilliant visual image, this description contrasts this locale with the Garden of Eden. Darío finds himself in a region of unlimited pleasures, unchecked by conscience or reason. The Satiresa, who is painted in bold, red brushstrokes, emerges from his pagan dreams rather than from his Catholic nightmares.

In the tercets, however, the Satiresa cautions against excesses and indulgences. Echoing Darío's own advice to himself in "Alma mía," she reminds him that he has an advanced soul that exists in accord with the universe and that reflects the majesty of the natural world. Like the poet/observer of "Coloquio" who travels in search of harmony, Darío has the soul of an argonaut. For these reasons, he should know that the key to attaining synchronization with the cadence of universal life lies in the reconciliation of opposites. Under the divine illumination of the sun, the poet must reconcile the flesh and the spirit, the Panic and the Apollonian. With music as a model, he will harmonize the natural and the artistic, the pagan and the Christian, and the transient and the eternal.[9]

The exuberance of "Palabras de la Satiresa," despite its appeal for moderation, stands in marked contrast with the subdued tone of "Divina Psiquis" (pp. 665–666), published in *Cantos de vida y esperanza* just four years later. The inevitable approach of death combined with Darío's confessed weakness for "el vino del Diablo," "los senos," and "los vientres" to alter his view of the fate of his soul. In his attempts to express his changing attitudes toward the desires for his soul, he summons up images from the Pythagorean account of the incarnation of Psyche and from traditional Christian doctrine. The fusion of images conveys more than the poet's search for a way out of the situation in which he feels imprisoned. It reflects his touching aspiration to find the magical language that will enable him to decipher the enigmas of the core of his being.

According to the Pythagorean myth, after a series of existences, Psyche reached the level of humanity, acquired intelligence, and remembered her celestial origins. She then wished to return to heaven, but she was also drawn to the pleasures of her body. As a result, she constantly struggled between her desire for spiritual happiness and her enjoyment of physical delights. Death constituted only a temporary liberation, since her failure to conquer the material world condemned her to wander across the earth in successive incarnations. Only souls that have totally mastered matter and have become perfect enter the divine state.

In keeping with the broad outlines of the myth, Darío begins "Divina Psiquis" by underscoring the divine nature of the soul, which converts inanimate matter into the living substance of existence. In the same way that he imagines the ensouling of matter as turning rock and wood into flesh in "Coloquio" (p. 573), Darío sees his body, despite its complex system of nerves and muscles, as little more than a "statue of mud" without the heavenly spark of life.

> ¡Divina Psiquis, dulce mariposa invisible
> que desde los abismos has venido a ser todo
> lo que en mi ser nervioso y en mi cuerpo sensible
> forma la chispa sacra de la estatua de lodo!

The steady, even flow of the alexandrine lines and the gentle repetition of sibilants reinforce the sense of tenderness established by the poet's description of his soul as "dulce mariposa invisible." The traditional butterfly imagery becomes a term of endearment spoken by the poet to his beleaguered and fragile soul at the same time that it enlivens—with the butterfly's imagined fluttering—the references to Darío's "ser nervioso" and the flickering of the holy spark.

This representation of the soul as a winged creature presupposes its earthly confinement within the body. But whereas esoteric mythology emphasizes Psyche's struggle to overcome temptation in order to regain the freedom she enjoys in the state of pure spirit, Darío sees her as defeated, a prisoner of war locked within the cage of his body. This sense of spiritual weakness is expressed through a poetic synthesis of the cage metaphor with the common association linking the body with the house of the soul and the eyes with its windows.

> Te asomas por mis ojos a la luz de la tierra
> y prisionera vives en mí de extraño dueño:
> te reducen a esclava mis sentidos en guerra
> y apenas vagas libre por el jardín del sueño.

The soul is imprisoned within the thick, impregnable walls of the body, but Darío is not the captor. He subtly joins ranks with his soul as he describes it as locked within a body of which he is no longer in charge. Psyche does not even find a temporary reprieve from the restrictions of the flesh in the "garden of dreams." Unlike the dreamed conclusion of the earlier "El reino interior" (pp. 603–605), in which Darío's soul is freed to embrace both sin and virtue, in "Divina Psiquis" Psyche is unable to reconcile her physical and spiritual wants.

Despite Darío's portrayal of his soul as unable to counter the forces of the flesh, he maintains a faith in its hidden strengths. This admiration, which is implicit in the respectful language of the first two quatrains, becomes the focus of the third.

> Sabia de la Lujuria que sabe antiguas ciencias,
> te sacudes a veces entre imposibles muros,
> y más allá de todas las vulgares conciencias
> exploras los recodos más terribles y obscuros.

Psyche is wise; she understands the ancient sciences, for she has learned them in death, during those periods when she escapes the walls of flesh that have held her in life. Once free from the body she suffers a period of frightening disorientation in which she is overtaken by darkness. Schuré explains: "Darkness encloses him; around him, in him, everything is chaos. He sees but one thing, and that thing attracts and horrifies him. . . . It is the sinister phosphorescence of his own cast-off skin; and the nightmare begins again. . . . This state can last for months or years. Its length depends upon the strength of the material instincts of the soul" (p. 333). Darío's hope for his soul is that it will have a natural dislike for earthly attractions and that it will ascend to the higher levels of existence.

> Y encuentras sombra y duelo. Que sombra y duelo encuentres
> bajo la viña en donde nace el vino del Diablo.
> Te posas en los senos, te posas en los vientres
> que hicieron a Juan loco e hicieron cuerdo a Pablo.

This hope for salvation is supported in more traditional terms with reference to Saint Paul in the final stanza of the first part.

> A Juan virgen, y a Pablo militar y violento;
> a Juan que nunca supo del supremo contacto;
> a Pablo el tempestuoso que halló a Cristo en el viento,
> y a Juan ante quien Hugo se queda estupefacto.

The final six lines of the first part of "Divina Psiquis" turn the focus of attention away from the fate of the poet's soul toward the underlying question of language. Darío gives the example of John and Paul: the same "sign" in nature drives one crazy and restores the sanity of the other. Darío is compelled to wonder if spiritual peace does not rest as much on the "reading" of nature as on anything else, and, as a result, his search for immortality brings him back to the search for a magical language with which his soul can communicate with the universal life force. He sees in the conversion of Saint Paul two questions: What was the sign that he saw on the road to Damascus that convinced him of the existence of God? What were the words that he spoke to affirm the sincerity of his new faith?

Although the second part of "Divina Psiquis" was probably written as an independent poem, it underscores Darío's dilemma. If the attainment of immortality is at least in part a linguistic problem, he must find the language with which he will set his soul in tune with the divine order. As the rapid pace of the shorter lines suggests, Darío's soul flies swiftly between the rose of the pagan ruins and the cross of the cathedral, resting only momentarily at each. In some poems, Darío's solution is a syncretic blending, finding a satisfactory reading of the universe in symbols that have survived the passage from one religion to the next. In others, like "Divina Psiquis," he vacillates between two appealing symbolic systems.

Despite his cautious hesitation to define the nature of his soul, Darío is certain about his sensuality, which he finds impossible to curb. The words of the Satiresa have gone unheeded, and he fears the consequences for his soul. This awareness of his failure to meet his spiritual responsibilities becomes a terrible burden. In comparison, the apparent ignorance or insensitivity of the creatures on the lower levels of existence seem blissful. Nevertheless, though he envies their immunity from the pangs of conscience, Darío dreads—even more than the possibility that his soul may remain imprisoned in the flesh for many incarnations to come—the thought that his soul may descend from the human to the animal in retribution for having sullied his elevated status. These anxieties form the background to Anderson Imbert's extensive analysis of "Lo fatal" (p. 688), the last poem of *Cantos de vida y esperanza*.[10] Aware of the influence of occultist doctrine upon Darío's formulation of the poem, Anderson Imbert sees in the line "y el temor de haber sido y un futuro terror" Darío's obsession with both past and future incarnations. The horror of the future stems from Darío's concept of "lo fatal," which, according to Anderson Imbert, includes two dimensions: inevitability and misfortune. It is inevitable that people think and, because they think, they are burdened with regret, which is actually the fundamental issue of the poem.

> . . . es evidente que no se quejaba del pensamiento sino más bien de los escarabajos de la conciencia. La conciencia, aguafiestas de la vida, derramasolaces de la alegría, que avinagra el vino y amarga el beso, adusta, desabrida y acusadora.

> El mineral, el vegetal y el animal no son culpables de nada
> porque son lo que son; el hombre siente culpas porque es de un
> modo y quiere ser de otro.[11]

As already demonstrated in chapter 2, this tension is central to
Darío's entire poetic production. In "En las constelaciones" his anguish explodes in a bitingly rhetorical question "Pero ¿qué voy a
hacer, si estoy atado al potro / en que, ganado el premio, siempre
quiero ser otro, / y en que, dos en mí mismo triunfa uno de los dos?"
(p. 1035). In other poems written after 1906 he sadly confronts the
misspent years that he should have used fulfilling his "supreme destiny." Mallorca proved a propitious place for such introspection.[12] In
"Eheu!" (pp. 737–738) Darío draws not only emotional impetus but
also images and symbols from the Mallorcan setting.

The presence of the sea, whose rhythm is felt in the ebb and
flow of the six- and eight-syllable lines, brings back memories of
a time long past, of a time of primordial bliss and union with the
universe. The poet recognizes, as if from a previous existence, the
rock, the oil, and the wine, all of which are closely associated with
the timeless Mediterranean and its civilization. Bathed by a wave
of nostalgia for an innocence long lost, Darío feels the weight of
the years—his physical age as well as the age of his soul. As he
looks back upon a life that held great promise, a life that could have
been the culmination of many lives and the final step to perfection,
he is overcome by unspeakable remorse. A few years before, in
"Nocturno" (pp. 680– 681), he was able to verbalize the regret he
experienced.

> Y el pesar de no ser lo que yo hubiera sido,
> la pérdida del reino que estaba para mí,
> el pensar que un instante pude no haber nacido,
> ¡y el sueño que es mi vida desde que yo nací!

In "Eheu!," however, it can only be conveyed by his anguished cry of
the second stanza (ellipsis in original):

> Aquí, junto al mar latino,
> digo la verdad:
> Siento en roca, aceite y vino,
> yo mi antigüedad.
>
> ¡Oh, qué anciano soy, Dios santo;
> oh, qué anciano soy! . . .

> ¿De dónde viene mi canto?
> Y yo, ¿adónde voy?

Darío is doubly old—old of body and old of soul. He knows that he has lived before and that his talents have been perfected in other lives. But his grief prevents him from mentioning "the loss of the kingdom that should have been his." He can only allude to it by juxtaposing the question "¿De dónde viene mi canto?" with the uncertainty of his future in this life and those to come.

In spite of the despair that it causes him, Darío does not retreat from his self-examination. Yet, drawing an analogy from the brilliant Mallorcan sun that illuminates no more than the entrances to the island's many caves, he recalls the Kantian precept that the real nature of self (transcendental ego) cannot be known any more than the intrinsic nature of the things it perceives. He therefore wonders, as did the German idealists, whether intellectual clarity is sufficient to distinguish between self and non-self (ellipsis in original):

> El conocerme a mí mismo,
> ya me va costando
> muchos momentos de abismo
> y el cómo y el cuándo . . .
>
> Y esta claridad latina,
> ¿de qué me sirvió
> a la entrada de la mina
> del yo y el no yo . . . ?

Even with the possibility that he was judging himself too harshly, he proceeds to criticize himself for blindly trusting his intuitions as a poet and for assuming that he could read in the signs of nature the wisdom of God. Specifically, he accuses himself of complacently studying the clouds and of believing that he could interpret the wind, the land, the sea, and the vague, fragmentary echoes of previous incarnations (ellipsis in original):

> Nefelibata contento
> creo interpretar
> las confidencias del viento,
> la tierra y el mar . . .
>
> Unas vagas confidencias
> del ser y el no ser,

> y fragmentos de conciencias
> de ahora y ayer.

Reaching the nadir of despair, Darío concludes the poem on a prophetic note or, as Pedro Salinas describes it, "Acentos de Biblia, metales de Jeremías, *vox clamantis in deserto.*"[13] Darío no longer feels the presence of the "mar latino." The shift is significant. Not only is a comparison established between the life and movement of the sea and the aridity and stagnation of the wilderness, but, at the end of the poem, the rhythmic throbbing of the great heart of the world that Darío so often senses in the ocean is absent. He looks up at the sun, the symbol of divine illumination, like a dead man, without hope of salvation. In the end Darío mourns his own spiritual death.

This nostalgia for the ancient Mediterranean appears throughout his poetry in the repeated allusions to Darío's having been, if not specifically an argonaut, one of their contemporaries. As in "Coloquio de los centauros" and "Palabras de la Satiresa," he affirms his special relationship with ancient Greece in "Retorno" (pp. 782–784), the poem that he wrote on his triumphant return to Nicaragua in 1907. Though he expresses great nationalistic pride in his homeland, he cannot escape the memory of his earlier life on the Mediterranean. He explains his extended absence in terms of his spiritual inheritance from Jason.

> Por atavismo griego o por fenicia influencia,
> siempre he sentido en mí ansia de navegar,
> y Jasón me ha legado su sublime experiencia
> y el sentir en mi vida los misterios del mar.
>
> ¡Oh, cuántas veces, cuántas veces oí los sones
> de las sirenas líricas en los clásicos mares!
> ¡Y cuántas he mirado tropeles de tritones
> y cortejos de ninfas ceñidas de azahares!

The transmission of nautical experience is not literature but life for Darío, part of a previous life that still lives within him. This point is emphasized by the construction of the second stanza quoted. The exclamatory "oh" which starts the first line along with the repetition of "cuántas veces" communicates a sense of urgency and a need to convince. The effect of anaphora, the repeated "y," heightens the tone. Darío states without qualification that he has *heard* the sounds of the sirens and *seen* the tritons and nymphs, all of which are not mere mythological ornaments.

In "Caracol" (p. 679), written in 1903, the allusion to Darío's previous existence is more subtle. The conch shell that the poet finds on the beach becomes a means by which he puts himself in touch with Jason, perhaps his own permanent ego, perhaps an old friend. Moreover, when the poet hears in the shell "un profundo oleaje y un misterioso viento," he realizes that "el caracol la forma tiene de un corazón." It thus becomes identified not only with the doctrine of transmigration of souls but also with the great heart of the world, whose pulsation is felt in the rhythm of the ocean. Or, as Octavio Paz points out, "It is a symbol of universal correspondence. It is also a symbol of reminiscence: when he presses it to his ear he hears the surf of past lives."[14] This dual function of the shell reappears in the long letter in verse which Darío wrote for the wife of Leopoldo Lugones (pp. 746–753) during his travels from July to November, 1906. From Mallorca, at the end of his journey, he wrote:

> ¿Por qué mi vida errante no me trajo a estas sanas
> costas antes de que las prematuras canas
> de alma y cabeza hicieran de mí la mezcolanza
> formada de tristeza, de vida y esperanza?
> ¡Oh, qué buen mallorquín me sentiría ahora!
> ¡Oh, cómo gustaría sal de mar, miel de aurora,
> al sentir como en un caracol en mi cráneo
> el divino y eterno rumor mediterráneo!

Both the impact of the Mallorcan setting and the tone of wistful regret are striking. Darío believes that, had he come to this mystical land of spiritual conversion sooner, his life would have taken a different course. While the possibility of reform offers some hope, he recognizes that it is probably already too late. The extravagances of youth have brought on a premature old age of body and soul, cutting short his life on earth and his aspirations for reunion with God. In the first four lines quoted, Darío shares his guilt with fate for not having set him on the right path; in the last four lines he seems angry at the fact that things could have been different. He still hears a constant call to harmony in the roar of the Mediterranean. By imagining these sounds as echoes of a seashell within his skull, Darío underscores their significance. They are divine and eternal: they are the beat of the universal heart and the reverberations of past lives. He is confident that had he always lived with these reminders of the oneness of life, he would be able to enjoy "sal de mar, miel de aurora." But now, without peace of mind, he finds small comfort in the salty sea air that envelops his tired body or in the golden glow of dawn that lights the Mallorcan horizon. By the same token, he finds little solace in his perception of universal unity in the beat of the great heart of the world or in his recognition of the possibility of a new tomorrow symbolically sweetened by honey, which in Orphic tradition is associated with spiritual betterment and rebirth.[15]

Turning from the bittersweetness of the present, Darío becomes exhilarated by the recollection of his life as an argonaut. He therefore describes in long, sweeping phrases what he knows from the past (ellipsis in original):

> Hay en mí un griego antiguo que aquí descansó un día
> despúes que le dejaron loco de melodía
> las sirenas rosadas que atrajeron su barca.
> Cuanto mi ser respira, cuanto mi vista abarca,
> es recordado por mis íntimos sentidos:
> los aromas, las luces, los ecos, los rüidos,
> como en ondas atávicas me traen añoranzas
> que forman mis ensueños, mis vidas y esperanzas.
> Mas ¿dónde está aquel templo de mármol, y la gruta
> donde mordí aquel seno dulce como una fruta?
> ¿Dónde los hombres ágiles que las piedras redondas
> recogían para los cueros de sus hondas? . . .

Convinced that he had landed on Mallorca centuries ago, Darío describes all that he encounters as remembered by his innermost senses, which were imprinted with these images long before his birth. The vividness of his recollection is emphasized in the fourth line by the exclamatory connotation of "cuanto" and by the emphatic balance, in the sixth line by the breathless enumeration of the phenomena that he faces. The aromas, the lights, the echoes, and the noise bombard him like waves from the past, and the remnants of his previous existences surface in his hopes, dreams, and poetry. Thus when he inquires where are the marble temple, the grotto where he bit "aquel seno dulce como una fruta," and the agile men who use slingshots, he is asking for things that he vaguely remembers from the past and that have emerged in other poems, in "Coloquio de los centauros" (p. 579), "Palabras de la Satiresa" (p. 616), and "Hondas" (pp. 739–740), respectively.

The surging movement of the poem ceases at this point. In the next stanza, which begins with "Calma, calma. Esto es mucha poesía, señora," the tone is totally different. For some reason the poet feels compelled to restrain his lyric impulse.

A similar surfacing of reminiscences from an earlier life appears in "Hondas," which, like "Eheu!" and "Epístola," was written during Darío's November, 1906–March, 1907, stay in Mallorca. Since the inhabitants of Mallorca were renowned for their use of slingshots, Darío "dreams" that he was a slinger. "Hondas," while less philosophic than the other poems analyzed, shows Darío's recourse to the doctrine of reincarnation to address the issue of poetic responsibility.

According to his dream, one afternoon during his existence as a brave Mallorcan slinger, he saw an enormous gerfalcon chasing a strange, radiant bird which resembled a ruby streaking across the heavens. While the stone of pure gold that he had hurled into the skies did not return to earth, the angel/bird that had been pursued and that was actually David's luminous soul came directly to him. It explained that Darío's shot had wounded the soul of Goliath, which was imprisoned in the gerfalcon. By some supernatural accord and attraction of souls, Darío saved David's soul in the same way that David had originally saved himself. Here the doctrine of transmigration of souls takes on an interesting prismatic effect: Darío, the poet, is influenced by his previous life as a slinger, which, in turn, had been influenced by the soul of an earlier poet/slinger. In this, Darío appears to imply that, just as David was forced to take arms against Goliath, all poets are called upon—perhaps by intuition, perhaps by the souls of other poets—to speak out against injustice and oppression.

From "Reencarnaciones" through "Hondas," the doctrine of the transmigration of souls is closely related in Darío's mind with the role of the poet and of poetry. The poet aspires to achieve a degree of spirituality that will permit him to share a consciousness with all the elements of nature. Yet, like all creatures, he is simultaneously pulled toward the bestial. This tension to fulfill his responsibility as a poet and to translate into human language the signs of the universe is reflected in his concerns for his soul. During the height of his career, the doctrine of reincarnation offers Darío a symbolic system through which he can express his optimism about the world, poetry, and the fate of his soul. But, as he matures, he demonstrates a loss of certainty in the poetic vision supplied by esoteric Pythagoreanism. He hesitates between the esoteric symbolic system and the traditional Christian system that, as seen in "Divina Psiquis," permits a mystical conversion at any point. Darío's hesitancy highlights his continued faith in the "right words" that will put him in touch with the timeless paradise he strives to envision. It also highlights his recognition that these "right words" may come from any of a number of symbolic systems—or from none at all. His uneasiness in the later poems, therefore, not only reflects his doubts about himself and the degree to which he has fulfilled his "supreme destiny." It also underscores his sensitivity to his inability to "speak with the voice of the spring." That drinking bouts and sexual excesses contributed to his sense of failure is really not the point. Darío believed that he was extraordinarily attuned to the pulse of the universe and to the echo of past lives. Yet he is forced to confront the fundamental limitations of human beliefs and symbols—even those invested with a special aura by the Romantics and Symbolists. Even though esoteric tradition did not provide the ultimate language with which he could articulate a sense of universal accord, it inspired a religious dimension to the role of the poet.

4. The Poet as Magus: Deciphering the Universe

Though ostensibly Darío relies most frequently on the concept of reincarnation to express his judgment of his own ability to achieve spirituality—which he measures against his poetic goal to articulate in human language the divine rhythm of universal life—his concern is often broader in scope, reaching beyond the question of his personal destiny. This concern reflects a convergence of literary and religious trends that elevated the poet to the status of magus. In his discussion of the poet's responsibilities, privileges, and burdens, Darío adopts the attitudes that originated in English Romanticism and developed among the French Romantics and Symbolists. These attitudes were formulated under the influence of esoteric doctrine, to which the writers of the nineteenth century turned in order to fill the void left by their loss of faith in traditional belief systems.

The Romantics, who inherited a world in which the rational view of life had separated individuals from their nonrational powers, hoped to reintegrate people and foster a reconciliation with nature, from which they felt estranged. Many of the myths which supplied the hope for reconciliation were derived from ancient esoteric beliefs. The attribution of a life and soul to nature, for example, allowed for the conversion of a dead and alien milieu into a human and companionable environment in which people could feel comfortable. Combining Platonic and Neoplatonic vocabulary, the prominent Romantics underscored the poet's special relationship with this living, knowledgeable nature. Shelley, Coleridge, and Carlyle held that the poet does not imitate the familiar external world but rather exposes the essential and eternal realities of existence that are often hidden behind the trivial. This first generation of Romantics nevertheless kept poetry separate from religion, assigning to the poet the task of liberating the vision of readers from the bondage of habitual categories and social customs.[1] The second generation of Romantics and the Symbolists, however, saw in this penetration of the veil of appearances and in this discovery of the verities of life a "compensatory function" in their society.[2] They turned poetry into a religion and made the poet the magus of the day.

No single artist strove to live out this poetic ideal as did Victor Hugo, who identified himself as "the *voyant*, the *entendant*—the crystal soul that vibrates sympathetically to the forces of the world."[3] Under the influence of esoteric doctrine, Hugo formulated his goals in mythic terms.[4] "He displayed," as Shroder points out, "the sense of Orphic mission, with all its necessary attributes: the conviction that he was the recipient of divine inspiration, that his task was to be performed with divine sanction, and that the task was an obligatory one." Perhaps the most important aspect of his poetic mission was to reveal to people the mysteries of life by "reading" the symbols of nature and by attending to the supernatural forces of the universe. He thus aspired to make possible the perception of God himself.[5]

The Symbolists followed in Hugo's footsteps. Their quest for an understanding of life went beyond the superficial and variable and was linked with the ideal of beauty. They developed a religion of "le Beau," and their aspiration to superior beauty took on a mystical quality. They sought to utilize the disordered material of the visible universe to create an order that would capture the expression of the poet's soul and the essence of the supernatural. In short, they credited the poet with the power to express in poetry, through the magic of language, a transcendent vision of the universe. This view of the unique relationship between the poet and nature was further supported by the esoteric sects popular throughout the nineteenth century.

As indicated in Chapter 1, occultists hold that the soul of God permeates all things and that the universe is one harmonious extension of God. As a result, they perceive nature to be the revelation of God and the great teacher of people. The poet, as the most perceptive of individuals, is nature's best student and the best qualified to share with humanity findings regarding the harmonious universe. By rising to the plane of unity, the poet has attained the ideal held by occultists and has become able to share wisdom with others through the oneness of life.[6] The following detailed elaboration of the mission of the poet presented by Kingsford and Maitland not only typifies these esoteric beliefs but brings into focus the image of the poet that emerged from the widely read and discussed esoteric literature of the day.

> Thou mayest the more easily gather somewhat of the character of the heavenly Personality by considering the quality of that of the highest type of mankind on Earth,—the Poet.

The Poet hath no Self apart from his larger Self. Other men pass indifferent through Life and the World, because the Self-hood of Earth and Heaven is a thing apart from them, and toucheth them not.

The Wealth of Beauty in Earth and Sky and Sea lieth outside their being, and speaketh not to their heart.

Their interests are individual and limited: their Home is by one Hearth: four walls are the boundary of their kingdom—so small it is!

But the Personality of the Poet is Divine: and being Divine it hath no limits.

He is supreme and ubiquitous in consciousness: his heart beats in every Element.

The Pulses of all the infinite Deep of Heaven vibrate in his own: and responding to their strength and their plenitude, he feels more intensely than other men.

Not merely he sees and examines these Rocks and Trees: these variable Waters, and these glittering Peaks.

Not merely he hears this plaintive Wind, these rolling Peals:

But he *is* all these: and with them—nay, *in* them—he rejoices and weeps, he shines and aspires, he sighs and thunders.

And when he sings, it is not he—the Man—whose Voice is heard: it is the Voice of all the Manifold Nature herself.

In his Verse the Sunshine laughs; the Mountains give forth their sonorous Echoes; the swift Lightnings flash.

The great continual cadence of universal Life moves and becomes articulate in human language.

O Joy profound! O boundless Self! O god-like Personality![7]

Beginning with his earliest works, Darío describes the poet as a divinely inspired, illuminating force. Consequently, the poet's art appears not only as a translation of the divine perfection of the universe but also as a magical influence on all surrounding elements. In return, however, humanity, true to the Romantic tradition, fails to perceive the wisdom of the poet's words and mocks the sensitive artist. The poet must, nevertheless, tolerate human ingratitude to fulfill a superior destiny.[8]

Later, as Darío became more directly involved with the occultist foundations of these beliefs, he refined his perception of the poet's mission, accepting for himself and others the challenge of poetic responsibility. As he grew older, however, the goals that had seemed challenging began to appear unattainable. His frustrations—with the intractability of language and with his lifestyle, which exacerbated his feelings of artistic impotence—led him to reassess his goals. A struggle developed between the ideal that was established for him by both his literary predecessors and esoteric tradition and what Darío came to believe was the reality of his poetic nature. Despite this growing tension, Darío never renounced the image of the poet as magus. It functions throughout his poetry as his ultimate artistic yardstick.

Several of the poems already examined in the chapter on the Pythagorean concept of universal harmony convey Darío's faith in the poet's talent for interpreting and translating the signs of nature. In "Coloquio de los centauros," for example, this optimism is expressed by Quirón, who praises the poet/magus for his ability to "read" external forms and gestures (pp. 573–574). In "La espiga" (p. 615) it is in the elements of nature working together in cosmic harmony that the poet sees the mystery of the divine and the soul of all things. In "Ama tu ritmo . . . " (p. 617) the poet cautiously orders himself to follow in his poetry the patterns that he recognizes in the cosmos. Significantly, however, by the time that Darío writes "En las constelaciones" (p. 1035), in 1908, the rhythm of the universe and the order of the stars that the poet readily perceived in "Ama tu ritmo . . . " are no longer clear to him. The later poem underscores the heightened tension between Darío's spiritual aspirations and his baser urges. As discussed in chapters 2 and 3, Darío finds these diametrical desires, common to all living beings, to be particularly burdensome, for he is a poet who feels an obligation to fulfill his divine destiny.

In "La página blanca" (pp. 588–589) published in 1896 in *Prosas profanas* Darío looks at the blank page for insight and inspiration.

> Mis ojos miraban en hora de ensueños
>   la página blanca.
>
> Y vino el desfile de ensueños y sombras.
> Y fueron mujeres de rostros de estatua,
> mujeres de rostro de estatuas de mármol,
> ¡tan tristes, tan dulces, tan suaves, tan pálidas!
>
> Y fueron visiones de extraños poemas,
> de extraños poemas de besos y lágrimas,
> ¡de historias que dejan en crueles instantes
> las testas viriles cubiertas de canas!
>
> ¡Qué cascos de nieve que pone la suerte!
> ¡Qué arrugas precoces cincela en la cara!

> ¡Y cómo se quiere que vayan ligeros
> los tardos camellos de la caravana!

The first thing that comes into view is a parade of dreams and shadows, which is then more clearly identified as "mujeres de rostros de estatua, / mujeres de rostro de estatuas de mármol." The rigid echo of the phrase and the uninspired repetition of the "tan" in the following line ("¡tan tristes, tan dulces, tan suaves, tan pálidas!") reinforce the lifeless quality of these first images. The poet rejects the stale, outmoded artistic models that spring into his imagination. He opts instead to grapple with the profound issues of life, even at the expense of his personal happiness. He rejects the poems and stories of the second quatrain in favor of the artistic order in nature which "chisels" precocious wrinkles on his face.

At this point, the white page appears to him like a frozen desert across which the camels of inspiration plod, all too slowly, carrying the images of life into focus. This description of the blank page establishes an aura of messianic religiosity. It is the poet who will guide the reader across the blank page of existence by filling it with symbols that lead to salvation through a total comprehension of life. This image is developed with a reference to "the Christs."

> Los tardos camellos
> —como las figuras en un panorama—,
> cual si fuese un desierto de hielo,
> atraviesan la página blanca.
>
> Este lleva
> una carga
> de dolores y angustias antiguas,
> angustias de pueblos, dolores de razas;
> ¡dolores y angustias que sufren los Cristos
> que vienen al mundo de víctimas trágicas!

More than a powerful turn of phrase that metaphorically transforms the poet into a savior, this reference emphasizes the poet's assumption of a profoundly religious role. The Christs are, according to Annie Besant, the holiest of men who come into this world to suffer, to be "tragic victims," because by suffering each gains the strength to be a savior and one of the peace-centers of the world.[9]

This view of poetry does not eliminate its impulse toward beauty. The first camel is accompanied by a second that carries into view the beautiful queen of poetic inspiration, who brings with her a coffer of dreams, pearls, and gold with which she is to be adorned.

> Otro lleva
> en la espalda
> el cofre de ensueños, de perlas y oro,
> que conduce la reina de Saba.

> Otro lleva
> una caja
> en que va, dolorosa difunta,
> como un muerto lirio, la pobre Esperanza.

> Y camina sobre un dromedario
> la Pálida,
> la vestida de ropas obscuras,
> la Reina invencible, la bella inviolada:
> la Muerte.

Yet, because of the difficulty involved in attaining this twofold aesthetic/religious goal, the poet is haunted by the loss of hope; this loss of hope is the touching third image to cross the white page. The final image is of death, who appears as she did at the end of "Coloquio de los centauros" not as something fearsome but rather as the ultimate female, "la Reina invencible, la bella inviolada." The reason that death can be accepted as the consummate human consort is that the poet, who penetrates the apparent discord of the universe and perceives the harmonious order of the cosmos, captures that order—and its promise of salvation—on the white page.

> ¡Y el hombre,
> a quien duras visiones asaltan,
> el que encuentra en los astros del cielo
> prodigios que abruman y signos que espantan,

> mira al dromedario
> de la caravana
> como el mensajero que la luz conduce,
> en el vago desierto que forma
> la página blanca!

This extraordinary confidence in the visionary power of the poet is the basis of the sonnet "A Juan Ramón Jiménez" (p. 1003) that was written in Paris in 1900 and that first appeared as the

"Atrio" to *Ninfeas*, Juan Ramón's first book of poetry. The even rhythm of the alexandrine lines is echoed by its balanced form of fourteen fourteen-syllable lines. The resulting pervasive sense of calm reflects the questioner's trust that his "young friend" will respond affirmatively to all the inquiries and that he will meet the challenges that await him (ellipsis in original):

> ¿Tienes, joven amigo, ceñida la coraza
> para empezar, valiente, la divina pelea?
> ¿Has visto si resiste el metal de tu idea
> la furia del mandoble y el peso de la maza?
>
> ¿Te sientes con la sangre de la celeste raza
> que vida con los números pitagóricos crea?
> ¿Y, como el fuerte Herakles al león de Nemea,
> a los sangrientos tigres del mal darías caza?
>
> ¿Te enternece el azul de una noche tranquila?
> ¿Escuchas pensativo el sonar de la esquila
> cuando el Ángelus dice el alma de la tarde? . . .
>
> ¿Tu corazón las voces ocultas interpreta?
> Sigue, entonces, tu rumbo de amor. Eres poeta.
> La belleza te cubra de luz, y Dios te guarde.

The younger poet is asked if he is ready to begin the divine struggle against his attackers. While they are brutally physical, his only defense is the strength of his ideas. With this description, the poet is raised above his enemies as a superman of extraordinary courage and perception. This exaltation of poetic prowess is continued in the next two lines: "¿Te sientes con la sangre de la celeste raza / que vida con los números pitagóricos crea?" Implied in this question is that the young man, in order to be a poet, must be a member of the celestial race that creates life by perfectly reproducing in art the "Pythagorean" order of the universe. The poet who assents approaches divinity by creating a new microcosm in which the harmony of the macrocosm has been translated into human language.[10]

As the interpreter of the cosmos, the poet must be aware of the living soul of the universe, which is hidden from most people but can be perceived by the enlightened in all the elements of nature. He, therefore, must be sensitive to the heavenly order of a tranquil night and must hear what the Angelus bell says when it speaks the soul of the afternoon. In short, he must feel in the depth of his being the occult voices of the living universe. Since the interrogator is silently assured of the young poet's abilities, the young man is sent on his way with his title, "Eres poeta," and the older man's best wishes.

The ideas first formulated in "A Juan Ramón Jiménez" and in "La página blanca" are developed shortly thereafter in a group of three poems from *Cantos de vida y esperanza* (1905). In "Pegaso" (p. 639), the seventh poem of the collection, Darío's optimistic view of poetic potential is emphatically personal, that is, almost defiant in its assertion of the first person singular. This somewhat defensive posture, which was also the point of departure in "A Juan Ramón Jiménez," becomes the dominant focus of "¡Torres de Dios! ¡Poetas!" (p. 641), the ninth poem of the collection. In the eleventh poem, "Mientras tenéis, oh negros corazones" (p. 643), Darío reasserts his faith in the messianic potential of poetry in the face of the forces of ignorance and hate.

Because of the strength of spirit and purpose demonstrated by the poet as he strives to fulfill his destiny, to overcome psychological and material obstacles, and to fend off attacks by the critical masses, the poet is portrayed as a hero of mythic proportions. In "Pegaso" the task before Darío is the same as Bellerophon's, namely, to catch and tame the winged horse of the Muses and with it to meet the many challenges placed before him.

> Cuando iba yo a montar ese caballo rudo
> y tembloroso, dije: "La vida es pura y bella."
> Entre sus cejas vivas vi brillar una estrella.
> El cielo estaba azul, y yo estaba desnudo.
>
> Sobre mi frente Apolo hizo brillar su escudo
> y de Belerofonte logré seguir la huella.
> Toda cima es ilustre si Pegaso la sella,
> y yo, fuerte, he subido donde Pegaso pudo.
>
> Y soy el caballero de la humana energía,
> yo soy el que presenta su cabeza triunfante
> coronada con el laurel del Rey del día;
>
> domador del corcel de cascos de diamante,
> voy en un gran volar, con la aurora por guía,
> adelante en el vasto azur, ¡siempre adelante!

To achieve all his goals, the poet must first calm the rebellious, unsteady animal, who represents the heightened power of natural forces, the innate capacity for spiritualization, and, more specifically, the inspiration of the poet.[11] These special qualities, associated with the horse's ability to ascend into the heavens, are underscored in the poem by a star that shines in its forehead. In the final line of the first quatrain, Darío lifts the entire scene by focusing on the blue of the sky, which is thus subtly transformed into the proper place for both horse and rider. At the same time, the clarity of the sky is linked with the poet's nakedness. As a result, Darío reiterates his faith in the poet's ability to control—unassisted by artificial trappings—the animal energy of his steed. In other words, the poet has no need to turn to established structures to bridle his imagination; a sincere expression of his soul will capture his unclouded view of the heavens and will allow him to reach the highest poetic peaks.[12]

This image of the naked poet is also central to the concluding section of "Yo soy aquel que ayer no más decía" (pp. 627–630), the first poem of *Cantos de vida y esperanza*. Darío insists that it is necessary for the soul that enters the sacred forest, where the pulse of creation is sensed, to be naked, that is, in touch with nature and unencumbered by social constructs (pp. 629–630). He prefers (p. 628; ellipsis in original):

> todo ansia, todo ardor, sensación pura
> y vigor natural; y sin falsía,
> y sin comedia y sin literatura . . . :
> si hay un alma sincera, esa es la mía.

The rejection of preestablished patterns of perception—already recognized in "La página blanca"—is thus linked with naked honesty and sincerity. The symbol that is drawn upon to develop this point is the star—like the one that shines in Pegaso's forehead (p. 630):

> Por eso ser sincero es ser potente:
> de desnuda que está, brilla la estrella;
> el agua dice el alma de la fuente
> en la voz de cristal que fluye d'ella.
>
> Tal fué mi intento, hacer del alma pura
> mía, una estrella, una fuente sonora,
> con el horror de la literatura
> y loco de crepúsculo y de aurora.

The image of unobstructed communication with the essence and energy of creation that emerges from "Yo soy aquel que ayer no más decía" and from the first quatrain of "Pegaso" is elaborated in the remaining ten lines of the sonnet. Acoustically the emphatic tone of the *alejandrinos mixtos* of lines 1, 3, 5, and 7 combines with the trochaic and dactylic alexandrines to reinforce the sense of power and flight. The poet's declaration of confidence is even stronger if lines 9 and 10 are also read as mixed alexandrines with accents on the initial "yo"'s. This self-assertiveness is derived, at least in part, from the poet's special relationship with Apollo, "el Rey del día," who is the source of truth and harmony and who singles him out for illumination and glory.[13] Apollo's daily conquest of the forces of evil and ignorance is the poet's guide as he proceeds forward in control of his native talents and in touch with the absolute.

In contrast to the mythic images of "Pegaso," Darío employs hyperbolic language in "¡Torres de Dios! ¡Poetas!" (p. 641) to reassert the strengths of the artist (ellipsis in original):

> ¡Torres de Dios! ¡Poetas!
> ¡Pararrayos celestes
> que resistís las duras tempestades,
> como crestas escuetas,
> como picos agrestes,
> rompeolas de las eternidades!
>
> La mágica esperanza anuncia un día
> en que sobre la roca de armonía
> expirará la pérfida sirena.
> ¡Esperad, esperemos todavía!
>
> Esperad todavía.
> El bestial elemento se solaza
> en el odio a la sacra poesía
> y se arroja baldón de raza a raza.
> La insurrección de abajo
> tiende a los Excelentes.
> El caníbal codicia su tasajo
> con roja encía y afilados dientes.
>
> Torres, poned al pabellón sonrisa.
> Poned, ante ese mal y ese recelo,
> una soberbia insinuación de brisa
> y una tranquilidad de mar y cielo . . .

By becoming a "tower of God," the poet is able to protect himself against those who take comfort in hating what they cannot comprehend. His towerlike nature is not, however, the poet's means of locking himself away from the world. The tower structure permits him to come into contact with the eternal order of creation. Another passage from "Yo soy aquel que ayer no más decía" sheds light on this point (pp. 628–629):

> La torre de marfil tentó mi anhelo;
> quise encerrarme dentro de mí mismo,
> y tuve hambre de espacio y sed de cielo
> desde las sombras de mi propio abismo.

As evident in these four lines, Darío turns inward but is dissatisfied with what he finds. He is forced to look beyond himself and seek solutions in the harmony of the heavens. Similarly, in "¡Torres de Dios! ¡Poetas!" the initial images underscore the poet's defensive posture, but it is not a posture that operates at the expense of his longing to join ranks with those elements of nature that are in touch with the order of the cosmos. The comparisons with "crestas escuetas," "picos agrestes," and "rompeolas de las eternidades" break the reader's expectation that the towers are the ivory towers of "arty" creation. Quite the contrary: the poet foresees the death of false art, which is represented by the siren, who drives men crazy with her song. She will die on the rock of harmony once the true poet translates the music of existence into art. Until that day the poet must wait patiently while striving to embody the calm of the heavens and seas.

The poet's struggle to rise above the hatred of the ignorant takes on clear religious connotations once again in "Mientras tenéis, oh negros corazones" (p. 643). In this case, the sense of distance from the unenlightened is heightened by the elevation of the poet to divine status.

> Para ti, pensador meditabundo,
> pálido de sentirte tan divino,
> es más hostil la parte agria del mundo.
> Pero tu carne es pan, tu sangre es vino.

Though the poet suffers because of his divine nature, he finds consolation in the concluding apocalyptic vision that links Pegasus with the ascension of Christ.[14]

> Dejad pasar la noche de la cena
> —¡oh Shakespeare pobre, y oh Cervantes manco!—
> y la pasión del vulgo que condena.

> Un gran Apocalipsis horas futuras llena.
> ¡Ya surgirá vuestro Pegaso blanco!

The poet is converted into a Christ-like figure who can lead his readers out of the imperfect present world into a paradisiacal future. The Christ-like attributes of the poet that were alluded to in "La página blanca" are thus emphatically reaffirmed. Similar, though more modest, is the comparison of art with Christ in "Yo soy aquel que ayer no más decía" (p. 630):

> Vida, luz y verdad, tal triple llama
> produce la interior llama infinita;
> el Arte puro como Cristo exclama:
> *Ego sum lux et veritas et vita!*

Darío follows this exuberant statement of faith in art as the path toward salvation with a reference to the other aspect of poetic creation that haunts his view of himself and the world, namely, the possibility of his failure either to recognize the divine harmony of the universe or to control the human frailties that prevent its being captured by art (p. 630):

> Y la vida es misterio; la luz ciega
> y la verdad inaccesible asombra;
> la adusta perfección jamás se entrega,
> y el secreto ideal duerme en la sombra.

With this juxtaposition Darío underscores the fundamental tension that exists within himself and his poetry. This tension—highlighted in chapters 2 and 3—increases in his later work and comes to a head in "Divagaciones" (p. 1136), written in 1916, one of Darío's last poems.

> Mis ojos espantos han visto,
> tal ha sido mi triste suerte;
> cual la de mi Señor Jesucristo,
> mi alma está triste hasta la muerte.

> Hombre malvado y hombre listo
> en mi enemigo se convierte;
> cual la de mi Señor Jesucristo,
> mi alma está triste hasta la muerte.

> Desde que soy, desde que existo,
> mi pobre alma armonías vierte.
> Cual la de mi Señor Jesucristo,
> mi alma está triste hasta la muerte.

Darío does not disavow his divine nature; quite the contrary, he reasserts his sense of brotherhood with Jesus Christ. Unlike his earlier stand, however, he does not enthusiastically accept the challenge of his divinity. He sees it as a burden that weighs on his soul and condemns him to martyrdom. Another aspect of his misfortune is his poetic vision, which permits him to see beyond surface realities and observe the horrors of life. This sensitivity to his surroundings increases his anguish and sense of isolation, for—as in "¡Torres de Dios! ¡Poetas!"—the poet perceives the resentment of those less enlightened. As a result, his impulse to attune himself to the divine harmony of existence and, in turn, to convert that harmony into art becomes the unwarranted cause of his despair and death. With the reference to the crucifixion of Jesus Christ, Darío evokes a touchingly intense cry of injustice against his isolation as he executes his divine mission.

This acute discomfort with his poetic responsibilities—especially in the face of death—appears in at least three earlier poems, "Melancolía," "Pasa y olvida," and "¡Ay, triste del que un día . . . !" In "Melancolía" (p. 675), from *Cantos de vida y esperanza*, the poet's desire to see beyond the external appearances of existence leads him into a region where he feels disoriented and blind. His anguish is therefore double: he has lost all confidence in his ability to discover the hidden order of life and he feels that he has failed to fulfill his destiny as poet. He resorts, as he often does in moments of extreme despair, to invoking Christian illumination. He joins ranks with Jesus Christ as he complains that poetry is the shirt of thorns that he wears on his soul. He implores that Jesus *tell* him his light (ellipsis in original):

> Hermano, tú que tienes la luz, díme la mía.
> Soy como un ciego. Voy sin rumbo y ando a tientas.
> Voy bajo tempestades y tormentas
> ciego de ensueño y loco de armonía.
>
> Ése es mi mal. Soñar. La poesía
> es la camisa férrea de mil puntas crüentas
> que llevo sobre el alma. Las espinas sangrientas
> dejan caer las gotas de mi melancolía.

> Y así voy, ciego y loco, por este mundo amargo;
> a veces me parece que el camino es muy largo,
> y a veces que es muy corto . . .
>
> Y en este titubeo de aliento y agonía,
> cargo lleno de penas lo que apenas soporto.
> ¿No oyes caer las gotas de mi melancolía?

The use of the verb "decir" shows Darío's continued faith in the word as a source of enlightenment, though he, the one who should be providing light for others, has no light by which to proceed. The confusion in the poet's soul as he struggles to find his way out of the darkness and despair is heightened by the storms of self-doubt and distrust. The short phrases and repetition of vocabulary in the first quatrain linguistically underscore the poet's anxiety.

Darío's conclusion is simple: "Ése es mi mal. Soñar." His attempts to assume his role as poet have led him to a martyrdom of pain and suffering. The resulting bitterness makes the road of life seem extraordinarily long. These ideas are reinforced acoustically through rhyme: "mundo amargo" / "muy largo." In the face of death, however, the road often appears excessively short, and Darío underscores this attitude with the shortness of the only seven-syllable line of the poem. This ambivalence toward the length of existence is conveyed by the rhyming of "corto" with the line "cargo lleno de penas lo que apenas soporto," the internal rhyme highlighting the poet's suffering.

The poet emphasizes his unending frustration and sense that there is no exit from this intolerable situation by returning in the final tercet to the initial rhyme of the first two quatrains. He is so locked in by his despair that he sees no way out. He can simply inquire if he has made his point. In asking "¿No oyes caer las gotas de mi melancolía?" he has reached the nadir of self-doubt.

The extent to which this suffering is associated with the confrontation of death can be explored in "Pasa y olvida" (pp. 1103–1104) from *El chorro de la fuente,* a sonnet which begins with an epigraph from "Melancolía": "Ése es mi mal: soñar . . . " As in "Melancolía," the poet seems to have lost his sense of direction and is unable to assist his fellow pilgrim in his search for a better path, namely, toward paradise and salvation. Darío's advice to the traveler applies to himself, for, as he states in the poem, he feels that they share a common destiny (ellipses in original):

> Peregrino que vas buscando en vano
> un camino mejor que tu camino,

¿cómo quieres que yo te dé la mano,
si mi signo es tu signo, Peregrino?

No llegarás jamás a tu destino;
llevas la muerte en ti como el gusano
que te roe lo que tienes de humano . . . ,
¡lo que tienes de humano y de divino!

Sigue tranquilamente, ¡oh caminante!
Todavía te queda muy distante
ese país incógnito que sueñas . . .

. . . Y soñar es un mal. Pasa y olvida,
pues si te empeñas en soñar, te empeñas
en aventar la llama de tu vida.

As in "Alma mía," a religious tone develops around the astrological
and theological reverberations of the words "signo" and, in this case,
"peregrino."[15] Another similarity with the earlier poem is the poet's
assurance of his divine nature. But while he reaffirms his superhu-
man qualities, he also recognizes that it is his human nature, the
twice declared "lo que tienes de humano," that will interfere with
achieving his supreme destiny. In this way, Darío alludes to his human weaknesses that will prevent his capturing in language the natural harmony of the universe; he also restates his doubts about his
ability to earn release from the endless series of incarnations. The
death that he carries within himself is not simply his fear of dying. It
is his frailty of character that forces him to fall to temptation and
lose the possibility of attaining reunion with God.

In this light the enigmatic conclusion becomes clear. Darío
feels that he misses the mark in his poetry because instead of being
able to envision "ese país incógnito que sueñas . . . " he is only able
to perceive the surface realities of the cosmos. The struggle to see
beyond causes pain. His advice is therefore "Pasa y olvida." All attempts to dream may be noble, but they may also be illusory. They
may merely distract him from the search for eternal verities by fan-
ning his passion for life.

Very similar advice is given in "¡Ay, triste del que un día . . . !"
(p. 672) from *Cantos de vida y esperanza*.

¡Ay, triste del que un día en su esfinge interior
pone los ojos e interroga! Está perdido.
¡Ay del que pide eurekas al placer o al dolor!
Dos dioses hay, y son: Ignorancia y Olvido.

> Lo que el árbol desea decir y dice al viento,
> y lo que el animal manifiesta en su instinto,
> cristalizamos en palabra y pensamiento.
> Nada más que maneras expresan lo distinto.

The poet expresses his compassion for all those who fight to find the answers to the most profound questions of life and who, as a result, turn to pleasure and pain. But, as in "Pasa y olvida," Darío finds these alternatives unsatisfactory. He suggests that one should not strive to reach the limits of human intelligence or sensuality; he sees a solution in ignorance and oblivion.

This position does not, nevertheless, negate the power of language—especially in its most natural and spontaneous form—to convey the essence of existence that is expressed by the trees and animals. Darío, therefore, reasserts in the second stanza the Romantic, Symbolist, and occultist faith in the unity of the cosmos and the decipherability of the universe. "¡Ay, triste del que un día . . . !" represents Darío's ambivalence regarding the attainability of his poetic goals.

The poet's vacillation between faith and doubt, between optimism and anguish, is even clearer in "Sum . . . " (pp. 733–734) from *El canto errante* (1907). He begins the poem with an expression of confidence in his divine origin.

> Yo soy en Dios lo que soy
> y mi ser es voluntad
> que, perseverando hoy,
> existe en la eternidad.

Underpinning this statement is the occultist belief that the human soul is a spark of the great Soul of the world, that is, a spark of the eternal and divine spirit. Even more significant, however, is the emphatic tone of the declaration. The poet's divinity and destiny are secure, and this sense of security is reflected in the clear, crisp octasyllable lines. But the poet deviates from this optimistic stand. In a similar fashion, the rhyme scheme varies from stanza to stanza. In some the first and third and second and fourth lines rhyme and in others the first and fourth and second and third rhyme. Nevertheless, in all the stanzas, each point is made with striking directness and simplicity.

As positive as the first stanza is, the second is riddled with despair.

> Cuatro horizontes de abismo
> tiene mi razonamiento,
> y el abismo que más siento
> es el que siento en mí mismo.

Reason interferes with perception, for it illuminates only a very small segment of reality. When reason fails, the poet is overwhelmed by self-doubt and turns instead to fantasy and art.

> Hay un punto alucinante
> en mi villa de ilusión:
> la torre del elefante
> junto al quiosco del pavón.

> Aun lo humilde me subyuga
> si lo dora mi deseo.
> La concha de la tortuga
> me dice el dolor de Orfeo.

Through art Darío finds a vital force, and he takes pride in his ability to generate objects of captivating beauty. The music of the lyre, which was created by Orpheus out of a tortoise shell, puts him in touch with humanity, nature, and God.[16] At the same time, however, Darío projects on Orpheus a troublesome concern, one that is more explicitly verbalized in the next quatrain (ellipses in original):

> Rosas buenas, lirios pulcros,
> loco de tanto ignorar,
> voy a ponerme a gritar
> al borde de los sepulcros:

> ¡Señor, que la fe se muere!
> ¡Señor, mira mi dolor!
> *Miserere! Miserere!* . . .
> Dame la mano, Señor . . .

Darío's faith in his ability to perceive the essence of existence in the perfect roses and lilies is limited; his search for answers becomes desperate in the face of death. He turns, in conclusion, to the Catholic beliefs of his childhood in hope of finding comfort.

As indicated with regard to "Divina Psiquis" at the conclusion of chapter 3, the poet's hesitation between occultist world views and Christian doctrine has broad implications for himself and his art. It reflects his continuing search for the right language and symbols that allow him to perceive and capture the immanent paradise of the universe. It also reflects his concern for his soul. If the poetic apocalypse that he hopes to achieve is not realized, he will have failed to fulfill his supreme destiny as a poet, and—in a form of double jeopardy—this failure leaves him without the source of salvation on which he has been counting. For this reason, the poet's anxiety about his role as magus is often increased by references to death. This interweaving of artistic, universal, and personal considerations makes up the fabric of "Nocturno II" (pp. 680–681) of *Cantos de vida y esperanza*.

Although all three "Nocturnos" share a single poetic climate and sense, united by a serious, almost tragic tone of self-examination, it is in "Nocturno II" that Darío proclaims himself the poet/magus who is in touch with the heartbeat of the universe.[17] The first "Nocturno" (pp. 656–657) announces the fundamental themes of all three. In it Darío confronts with horror "lo inevitable desconocido." He is disillusioned with himself, the world, and the relentless passage of time. The distant clavicord never yielded its sublime sonata to the poet's imagination, and he now fears that he must pay the cost of his search for beauty and pleasure. He suspects that his bill for the "azucena tronchada" has come due. Yet he is consoled by the belief that life is merely a nightmarish, fitful sleep from which he will be awakened to see a truer reality. Darío takes up this image in the second "Nocturno."

If life is a fitful sleep, the nights of insomnia become the moments of vision. It is during the dark, sleepless hours that Darío sees with greatest clarity both the illusion of life and the omnipresence of death. He joins in union with all who, in their sleepless self-reflexion, have developed an acute sensitivity to the world that surrounds them. But it is only in the mysterious silence of the night, when the past escapes from the prison of forgetfulness and resurfaces as the voice of conscience, that Darío's companions in nostalgia and regret will come to understand these lines fully. This stipulation underscores both the intensity of the poet's emotions and his sense of inadequacy as he struggles to express this complex interplay of bittersweet recollections (ellipses in original):

> Los que auscultasteis el corazón de la noche,
> los que por el insomnio tenaz habéis oído
> el cerrar de una puerta, el resonar de un coche
> lejano, un eco vago, un ligero rüido . . .
>
> En los instantes del silencio misterioso,
> cuando surgen de su prisión los olvidados,

en la hora de los muertos, en la hora del reposo,
sabréis leer estos versos de amargor impregnados . . .

Como en un vaso vierto en ellos mis dolores
de lejanos recuerdos y desgracias funestas,
y las tristes nostalgias de mi alma, ebria de flores,
y el duelo de mi corazón, triste de fiestas.

Y el pesar de no ser lo que yo hubiera sido,
la pérdida del reino que estaba para mí,
el pensar que un instante pude no haber nacido,
¡y el sueño que es mi vida desde que yo nací!

Todo esto viene en medio del silencio profundo
en que la noche envuelve la terrena ilusión,
y siento como un eco del corazón del mundo
que penetra y conmueve mi propio corazón.

As in "Lo fatal" and "Eheu!" Darío's greatest concern is that he has failed to be what he should have been and that he has lost—because of pleasurable distractions—the kingdom that should have been his. While the poet's unanimity with the beat of universal life suggests the promise of salvation through the assimilation of divine order, it also reinforces the imperatives of the doctrine of transmigration of souls—reminding the poet of the responsibilities of his vocation.

The anguish, which is somewhat modified in the ambiguous final stanza, is most intense in the fourth and penultimate quatrain. The alliteration of the *p*'s emphasizes the echo of "pesar" in "pensar" and evokes the weight of the poet's loss ("pérdida"). Moreover, the masculine rhyme of the second and fourth lines intensifies the poet's cry of remorse for his misspent youth. Nevertheless, his communion with the harmonious and rhythmic universe, suggested in the final quatrain, offers some consolation. Thus "Nocturno II" provides a summary of the feelings of inadequacy that Darío expresses in his later poems as well as of the poet's hopes and pride that remain constant throughout his career. As in the other poems examined in this chapter, the belief in the poet/magus remains a central ideal by which Darío judges his life and art.

5. Paradise Found: Sexual Love in Esoteric Tradition

Throughout his career, Darío addresses—often in highly personal terms—the issue of alienation. His poetry centers on the modern struggle of people to win a paradise from which they have been exiled and that often seems to be beyond their grasp. Nevertheless, Darío's language describing this struggle implies an unflagging faith in the possibility of salvation. This thrust toward integration is particularly poignant in Darío's poetry with regard to sexual love. By affirming the sexual nature of the godhead and by appealing to the myth of the cosmic androgyne, Darío creates a world in which physical desires are reconciled with and aid in the attainment of universal accord.

This sexual view of the cosmos came to Darío primarily from the esoteric Pythagoreanism that underpins his poetic production. Though esoteric Pythagoreanism holds that the whole universe is God—one, eternal, and divine—it also maintains that the Great Monad acts as a creative Dyad. "From the moment God is manifest, He is double, indivisible Essence, divisible Substance, masculine active, animating and passive feminine principles."[1] The female facet of the godhead is thus identified with the spiritual substance that is the potential essence of matter and from which all souls are created. Moreover, since original man was created in God's image, he was similarly androgynous. His sexuality and the other divisions that exist in nature are considered the result of the fall into evil and multiplicity. Human beings, nevertheless, retain the capacity for recovering this lost integrity. The process of redemption is a return that reverses the result of the fall and culminates in the reunion of male and female.[2]

Based on this conception of the universe, Darío came to view woman as the source of all worldly knowledge and the attraction between man and woman as a path to perfection. A return to the union of male and female becomes a means of perceiving the prelapsarian primordial bliss of unity as well as of intuiting the divine state. Darío's erotic poetry, though drawing upon individual experience, reaches beyond it and exalts the attraction between the two generative principles. Moreover, while Darío the man finds in woman, the flesh of creation, his complement and the key to deciphering the universe, Darío the poet finds in language that is impregnated with poetic energy the embodiment of his divine experience. Poetic creation is thus analogous to cosmic creation: "In the beginning the Spirit conceived, the waters gave birth, and the world which was born from their conjunction was the first material image of the Word. . . ."[3] The poem becomes a living microcosm, which gives substance to the order of the universe. The poet becomes demiurge.

It was a sensitivity to this aspect of Darío's poetry that led Guillermo Sucre to recognize that for Darío the experience of love as an exaltation of the body is actually a vision of the world. He goes on to state: "En efecto, Darío no exalta el cuerpo como algo distinto al alma, sino que el cuerpo encarna la unidad de la mujer y a la vez la unidad del universo."[4] More precisely, it is in union with the female body, which links spirit and flesh, that the poet feels that he can re-discover the oneness of the universe. He also feels that he can aspire to re-create paradise on the page.

In this context, the exaltation of woman and of sexual love functions on three semantic planes simultaneously—the cosmic, the personal, and the poetic—and assumes a fusion of the spiritual and the physical. Darío may have found a pattern for this view in popular occultist writings of the nineteenth century, such as: "O love, thou art the latent heat of the earth; the strength of the wine; the joy of the orchard and the cornfield: thou art the spirit of song and laughter, and of the desire of life."[5] A modified but similar design for sexual love had been prevalent in German and English literature since the beginning of the century and was later developed in France by Hugo, Balzac, and Fourier.[6] In the dual esoteric/Romantic tradition Darío found the foundations for converting sexual love "into a kind of cosmology, the center of which is the female body."[7]

Students of Darío from Guillermo Díaz-Plaja to Graciela Palau de Nemes have commented on Darío's elevation of eroticism into a form of mysticism.[8] Pedro Salinas, who sees Darío's poetry as dominated from beginning to end by "el afán erótico," recognized that physical love became the poet's means of achieving union with the origin of the world.[9] But only Enrique Anderson Imbert and Octavio Paz have perceived the influence of esoteric tradition in the formulation of this view, which departs radically from the Catholic doctrine that permeates Hispanic literature as well as Darío's early poetry.[10]

Darío's Catholic formation is apparent in the love poetry prior to *Prosas profanas*, in which the love described is more romantic than passionate, more sentimental than sexual. It may be a love that purifies, or a love that makes a paradise, or a love that gives meaning to existence.[11] In short, this early love leads the poet toward a good, righteous, and pure life. This Catholic perspective reappears years later, toward the end of his life, when Darío adopts an intermediary position regarding carnal pleasure, neither condemning nor exalting it. In the autobiographic novel *El oro de Mallorca*, he no longer describes sexual love as a road toward salvation but rather as the only bit of paradise that he expects to achieve.

> Pero, Dios mío, si yo no hubiese buscado esos placeres que, aunque fugaces, dan por un momento el olvido de la continua tortura de ser hombre, sobre todo cuando se nace con el terrible mal de pensar, ¿qué sería de mi pobre existencia, en un perpetuo sufrimiento, sin más esperanza que la probable de una inmortalidad a la cual tan solamente la fe y la pura gracia dan derecho? Si un bebedizo diabólico o un manjar apetecible o un cuerpo bello y pecador me anticipa, *al contado*, un poco de paraíso, ¿voy a dejar pasar esa seguridad por algo de que no tengo propiamente una segura idea?[12]

Thus, at every stage of his life, love and salvation appear side by side, and Darío finds himself looking beyond the momentary gratification as much as he is attracted to it.[13] At first, pure love saves the poet from the threat of damnation that is posed by the temptation of sexual indulgences. Later, sexual love becomes a means of attaining union with God. Finally, the spectre of damnation reappears as Darío reassesses his life and discovers in sexual pleasure the only piece of eternity that he feels assured of achieving. This unrelenting struggle to reconcile his sexuality with his view of the universe found an artistically—if not personally—satisfying solution in the esoteric beliefs that form the basis of his mystical concept of love.

The center of this mystical view of love is woman, and the best example of Darío's innovative portrayal of woman is "¡Carne, celeste carne de la mujer!" (pp. 668–669). In it, through the fusion of cosmic and concrete, the woman of flesh and blood is spiritualized as the terrestrial reflection of the divine female and the existence of the spiritual female of the godhead is made more immediate through its description as physical and sexual. Moreover, the harmonious perfection of both cosmic and concrete woman and their promise of ideal unity are captured in the flesh of language that has been inseminated with the poet's "ideal music." Language becomes the poet's mystical partner, and poetry becomes a perfect copy of divine and earthly woman.[14] Darío's praise of woman, therefore, extends to his own poetry. As a result, the entire poem functions on three levels that suggestively intertwine and envelop the reader in a powerfully sensual yet transcendent embrace. The climax of the poem, which ends with an ellipsis, parallels the proverbial romantic swoon in which the lover loses his or her sense of finiteness in an amatory paradise.

> ¡Porque en ti existe
> el placer de vivir, hasta la muerte
> y ante la eternidad de lo probable . . . !

The higher vision that is attained allows the reader, like the author, to glimpse the possibility of feeling at home in the universe and even the possibility of eternal salvation.

The first two lines, if not the entire poem, were suggested by an alexandrine from *Le sacre de la femme* by Hugo: "Chair de la femme! argile idéale! ô merveille!"[15] Darío begins with a similar exclamation expressed in a pair of rhyming alexandrine lines which, because of their length, are set off from and serve as an introduction to the rest of the section.

> ¡Carne, celeste carne de la mujer! Arcilla,
> —dijo Hugo—; ambrosía más bien, ¡oh maravilla!

Darío adds the word "celestial" to Hugo's famous phrase because for him womanly flesh is inextricably linked with heaven. He rejects Hugo's suggestion that flesh is clay, rejecting at the same time the implication that it lacks transcendent significance. Instead, he holds that the flesh of woman is best compared to ambrosia, for, like the food of the gods, it offers both pleasure and immortality. This view anticipates Darío's basic contention, which is expressed in the following short, quick, rhymed lines, whose pace reinforces the directness of his thoughts.

> La vida se soporta,
> tan doliente y tan corta,
> solamente por eso:
> roce, mordisco o beso
> en ese pan divino
> para el cual nuestra sangre es nuestro vino.

For Darío sexual love is a means of salvation, a salvation that is both temporary and eternal. Contact with woman converts the poet's life-blood into an intoxicating liquid which allows him to forget the pain and shortness of life. But, as is clear from Darío's recourse to the principal symbols of the Catholic mass, sexual love also has a tran-scendental dimension. Esoteric tradition holds that Adam was the creation of the Spirit breathed into virgin matter and that Christ was similarly conceived of the Spirit and born of the Virgin Mother. Through sexual intimacy man reenacts divine creation and achieves union with the Womb of Creation, that is, with the body of Christ, or, in Darío's words, with "that divine bread." Similarly, through po-etry—conceived rhythmically and sexually—humans also achieve contact with the flesh of creation.

To further support his view of woman, Darío describes her mul-tiple nature through a series of symbols, all of which, like her, func-tion on three planes.

> En ella está la lira,
> en ella está la rosa,
> en ella está la ciencia armonïosa,
> en ella se respira
> el perfume vital de toda cosa.

The lyre and its music, the rose and its natural perfection, and "the harmonious knowledge" all underscore woman's integral role in the cosmos. She is the key to its harmonious workings. On the cosmic, human, and poetic plane woman holds the secret to music and har-mony, to the ordering pulse of life, and to the world's natural, or-ganic patterns. Woman is also the source of the "vital perfume of all things." As the "soul of all things," she is associated with the wind, breeze, air, and, hence, perfume. She is also the ethereal substance that is essential to all life and from which dimension, form, ap-pearance, and art are derived. On the terrestrial level, she is the fem-inine flesh in which one breathes the sensual scent of love and desire.

The second section of the poem is introduced with the juxtapo-sition of the figures of Eve, who symbolizes the material aspect of life or the mother-of-all-things, and Venus, who is the embodiment of the beauty of the world penetrated by the divine idea.[16]

> Eva y Cipris concentran el misterio
> del corazón del mundo.

The heart of the world is its gravitational center, that point at which everything comes together. The cohesive force of the human and nonhuman universe that propels all toward that center is identified with love, which is the mystery that Darío refers to. Celestial and mundane woman and poetry are the essence of that force that will allow man to become one with the universe and to achieve unity with his surroundings.

The rest of the second section, the unity of which is reinforced by the regular rhyme scheme, deals with the reaction of "el áureo Pegaso" when he sees "Anadiomena" nude. The name "Anadiomena" alludes to the legend of Venus's rising out of the sea at birth. This reference not only links Venus with the Virgin Mary, who is also the Water over which the Spirit moved in the beginning of time, but also emphasizes the facet of physical love that corresponds to the desire to return to the womb. This is particularly clear in a poem like "Revelación" (pp. 712–713), in which the sea is a feminine force that is maternal and loving. More often than not, however, the sea is associated with the single pulsating heart of the world which echoes throughout the universe and within Darío's poetry. This reference to poetry is supported by the appearance of Pegasus, who is generally identified with the poet. Here poet and male generative principle fuse as Pegasus's response to Venus recalls the description of the sun in "Helios" (pp. 643–645) as well as of the celestial reaction to the birth of Venus in "Coloquio de los centauros" (p. 575). It may be concluded from this overlap that the meaning attached to Pegasus is also multiple: golden Pegasus represents man as sexual being, poet as human creator, and the sun as divine generative force. All aspects of his being respond exuberantly to woman.

> Cuando el áureo Pegaso
> en la victoria matinal se lanza
> con el mágico ritmo de su paso
> hacia la vida y hacia la esperanza,
> si alza la crin y las narices hincha
> y sobre las montañas pone el casco sonoro
> y hacia la mar relincha,
> y el espacio se llena
> de un gran temblor de oro,
> es que ha visto desnuda a Anadiomena.

Morning is victory, and golden Pegasus hurls himself forward toward life and toward hope magically synchronized with the rhythm of life, with the pulse of the universe.

The next two four-line sections are the most directly devotional of the poem. One begins with "Glory, oh Powerful One . . . ," the other with "Glory, oh Sublime One. . . ." In the first, Darío identifies the female aspects of the universe with the morning star, which is, of course, Venus.

> Gloria, ¡oh Potente a quien las sombras temen!
> ¡Que las más blancas tórtolas te inmolen,
> pues por ti la floresta está en el polen
> y el pensamiento en el sagrado semen!

Darío's description of woman as the "powerful one whom the shadows fear" is congruent with passages in occultist literature which hold that, as the soul of all things, woman dispelled the long night before creation.[17] Earthly woman, like the morning star, can remove the shadows that obscure man's happiness. Poetry, as well, eliminates the darkness of ignorance by shedding the light of knowledge.

Appealing to more blatantly sexual imagery, Darío asserts that it is because of woman that "the forest is in the pollen and thought is in the holy semen." Darío's awesome respect for the elements of sexual union stems from their capacity to hold within themselves the code to all of creation, the magnificence of the forest, the complexity of human thought. Moreover, the thought that is held within the sacred semen is the idea of man that was implanted by God in the Womb of Creation or in the "útero eterno" that appears in the second of the two quatrains.

> . . . ¡oh Sublime, que eres la existencia
> por quien siempre hay futuros en el útero eterno!
> ¡Tu boca sabe al fruto del árbol de la Ciencia
> y al torcer tus cabellos apagaste el infierno!

The quatrains conclude with another reference to the multiple nature of woman. She is linked with physical pleasure, temptation, and the fall of man and with the extinction of the flames of hell.

The final two sections summarize the concepts expressed throughout the poem (ellipses in original):

> Inútil es el grito de la legión cobarde
> del interés, inútil el progreso
> *yankee,* si te desdeña.
> Si el progreso es de fuego, por ti arde.

¡Toda lucha del hombre va a tu beso,
por ti se combate o se sueña!

　　Pues en ti existe Primavera para el triste,
labor gozosa para el fuerte,
néctar, ánfora, dulzura amable.
¡Porque en ti existe
el placer de vivir, hasta la muerte
y ante la eternidad de lo probable . . . !

Darío reiterates his belief that all human energy is expended for woman. The reason is clear: not only does earthly woman offer man the pleasure of life, but both she and poetry, as reflections of divine woman, offer him the ecstasy of divine truth, that is, the knowledge of the harmonious order of the universe. Woman and poetry are means by which man can participate in the fulfillment of universal harmony.

"¡Carne, celeste carne de la mujer!"—one of Darío's most famous poems—was published in *Cantos de vida y esperanza* at the height of his career in 1905. The innovative cosmology on which it is based had appeared, in embryonic form, several years earlier in the less noticed "El salmo de la pluma" (pp. 901–916). This multisection poem was published on March 14, 1889, in *El Eco Nacional* of León, Nicaragua, upon Darío's return from Chile, where it was probably begun. It is written in the style of the alphabetic psalms. Four stanzas, each containing four alexandrine and two heptasyllable lines, are grouped under twenty of the twenty-two Hebrew letters. (The two sections corresponding to the letters Shin and Tau are missing.) In a prophetic tone, Darío praises the function of the pen and those who use it to construct a superior, mystical world.[18] As could be expected, this mystical world includes woman as the source of poetic inspiration, beauty, harmony, and salvation.

　　The first woman to appear in the poem is a muse, who is magically converted into "la Venus ideal" (p. 908). In the next section, Venus is identified with "la gran Naturaleza," who contains within herself all the elements already seen in Darío's threefold woman. She epitomizes what the poet seeks: a Pythagorean paradise whose fundamental nature is harmony and music (p. 908):

　　　　Emperatriz amable, toda ella es hermosura,
　　su bello cuerpo rítmico, su aliento es la dulzura
　　　　y su alma la ilusión.
　　Para ella las canciones de amor, las dulces odas,

> la rima que es el beso y el himno de las bodas
> en la sexual unión.

This image of woman anticipates the portrayal of a sexual universe that is exploding with love. The poet's vision of a loving universe appears in the section under the fourteenth letter of the Hebrew alphabet, Nun (p. 911).

> Amor, amor inmenso de la creación hermosa;
> amor para la estrella y amor para la rosa,
>   deliquio universal;
> beso, inefable cópula de todo lo existente;
> átomo, forma, vida, calor vivo y potente
>   y espíritu inmortal.
>
>   ¡Oh fiesta! ¡Oh gozo enorme del Universo! El gozo
> de la onda que palpita con cantos de alborozo;
>   el gozo de la flor
> casta que ve los cielos; el gozo de la encina
> que siente en sus ramajes un pájaro que trina
>   una canción de amor.
>
>   Tu gozo, ¡oh madre Tierra!; el gozo en que descubres
> a los sedientos labios tus inexhaustas ubres,
>   tu gloria y brillantez;
> en tus eternos partos, Madre amorosa y tierna,
> sin manchas en tu sacra virginidad eterna
>   y en tu eterna preñez.
>
>   ¡Reina morena! Te ama desde su azul el astro,
> el pensamiento de oro, y el tirso de alabastro
>   de la eterna región;
> y como la de Saba, por tu beldad suprema,
> a Febo, el rey pomposo de espléndida diadema,
>   tienes por Salomón.

From the beginning of this section, the departure from traditional Catholic ideology could hardly be more emphatic. The universe is erupting with a sexual love that is simultaneously spiritual, cosmic, personal, and poetic. The pace of the phrases reaffirms the highly charged nature of creation, which, in its passion, fuses all that exists in a universal swoon of rapture. Large and small, universal and particular, eternal and temporal, all elements come together in a joyous, festive, and sexual union.

The almost frantic series of exclamations praising the ongoing joy of creation that begins in the first stanza is continued into the second. At the same time, the ordered and artistic nature of the universe is recalled by the rhythmic movement of the sea, the attraction between the flowers and the heavens, the love song of the birds, and woman. Divine woman and her terrestrial counterparts are exalted as Darío focuses on her reproductive and rejuvenescent qualities.

In the final two stanzas of the section Darío appeals to one of the oldest images of divine androgyny. The ancients represented the hermaphroditism of their supreme divinity by the sun, which was the male generative energy, and by nature, which was the female procreative principle. This conception of the androgynous god may have come from the belief that universal harmony—seen by early peoples in bountiful harvests—is a manifestation of the productive union of the two generative principles. Darío adapts this image and portrays woman as, above all else, the earthly aspect of the divine female: Mother Earth. She is the eternal source of sustenance to the hungry, the womb of all generation, and the loving guardian of all created. She is unstained and forever virgin, for the matter that divides to create reforms and becomes whole in preparation for new births. Thus she is as eternally virgin as she is eternally pregnant. But she is also the lover, the "Reina morena," who mates with the male procreative principle, the sun, "el astro," "el pensamiento de oro," or "el tirso de alabastro de la eterna región." As lover and model of beauty, divine woman is personalized by her comparison to the queen of Sheba, who is adored by Solomon—the sun's male counterpart.

Echoes of this early experiment with a sexual conception of the cosmos occur years later in "Amo, amas . . . " (p. 679). Like "¡Carne, celeste carne de la mujer!," "Amo, amas . . . " was published in *Cantos de vida y esperanza* and is one of the best examples of Darío's mystical concept of love. It contains many of the features of the earlier poem, which have been intensified in the shorter, eight-line format.

> Amar, amar, amar, amar siempre, con todo
> el ser y con la tierra y con el cielo,
> con lo claro del sol y lo obscuro del lodo:
> amar por toda ciencia y amar por todo anhelo.
>
> Y cuando la montaña de la vida
> nos sea dura y larga y alta y llena de abismos,
> amar la inmensidad que es de amor encendida
> ¡y arder en la fusión de nuestros pechos mismos!

The staccato rhythm is maximized with the emphatic repetition "amar, amar, amar, amar" that highlights the imperative, vital beat of the living, sexual universe. The exaltation of the fusion of all that exists is also heightened as microcosm and macrocosm come together in a loving embrace that fulfills universal harmony. Man, in his attempt to achieve divine knowledge, willfully relinquishes his individuality and sees himself almost exclusively as a reflection of divine forces. He therefore must love with all his being, with heaven and earth, with the brilliance of the sun and the darkness of the mud. And, just as microcosm and macrocosm become one, spirit and flesh, intellect and desire, male and female come together in perfect harmony.

This emphasis on fusion continues in the second stanza as Darío resorts to natural images to discuss the individual. Human life is compared to a mountain during the ascent of which one must come to love the heavens that are ablaze with sexual passion. In this way, Darío underscores his conclusion that universal love is the human solution to the problems that one must confront during life's long, uphill journey. As in summary, the final line recapitulates the many dimensions of mystical love. Through it individuals forget mundane anxieties and are transported outside themselves as they fuse with their beloved and with the cosmos.

Another poem in which the universe is portrayed as sexually aware and active is the fourth poem of the series "Los cisnes," "¡Antes de todo, gloria a ti, Leda!" (pp. 650–651), also from *Cantos de vida y esperanza*. As is evident from the title, the poem grows out of the myth in which Zeus visits Leda in the form of a swan. Although Darío begins by praising Leda, whose beauty was so great as to attract the supreme Olympian god, the poem is actually an exaltation of the harmonious workings of the universe, a harmony that incorporates the acceptance and celebration of sexuality.

In the first section, which consists of six ten-syllable lines, Darío conveys the full extent of the heavenly approval of sexual union through his description of what happened when, as he puts it, Leda's "dulce vientre cubrió de seda el Dios."

> . . . ¡Miel y oro sobre la brisa!
> Sonaban alternativamente
> flauta y cristales, Pan y la fuente.
> ¡Tierra era canto; Cielo, sonrisa!

The first phrase immediately establishes the sense of delight. The sweetness of honey and the deep, rich glow of gold permeated the atmosphere and hung in the air, blanketing the world with a sensation of bliss. At the same time, Darío reaffirms that sexuality is part of the harmonious and living cosmos. The union of Zeus and Leda reactivates the pulse of the sexual universe that resonates in Pan's music, in the spring, as well as in Darío's lilting verses. Moreover, as if with personal delight, the earth responds with song and the heavens with an approving smile.

In the second section, however, it becomes clear that union of Leda and the swan not only represents the union of male and female, which is celestial in its ecstasy as well as in its origin, but also epitomizes the unity of all life. By drawing upon a myth in which a god takes on the form of an animal in order to join with a woman, Darío emphasizes the notion that the entire universe is one living extension of God and that he is present throughout, in all forms. Consequently, it is before this union that a pact was made and the details of universal harmony were worked out. Each of the creatures was given certain divine gifts.

> Ante el celeste, supremo acto,
> dioses y bestias hicieron pacto.
> Se dió a la alondra la luz del día,
> se dió a los buhos sabiduría,
> y melodía al ruiseñor.
> A los leones fué la victoria,
> para las águilas toda la gloria,
> y a las palomas todo el amor.

But it is the swan, the form chosen by Zeus to visit Leda, which becomes the focus of the concluding five quatrains. The regularity and even flow of these five stanzas, each of which contains four decasyllables with a ABAB rhyme scheme, underscore the fundamental characteristic of the swan that attracts Darío's attention. The swans appear as the embodiment of rhythmic and harmonious perfection. Moreover, Darío finds in their natural grace and formal beauty standards of artistic excellence.

> Pero vosotros sois los divinos
> príncipes. Vagos como las naves,
> inmaculados como los linos,
> maravillosos como las aves.
>
> En vuestros picos tenéis las prendas
> que manifiestan corales puros.

Con vuestros pechos abrís las sendas
que arriba indican los Dïoscuros.

Las dignidades de vuestros actos,
eternizadas en lo infinito,
hacen que sean ritmos exactos,
voces de ensueño, luces de mito.

De orgullo olímpico sois el resumen,
¡oh blancas urnas de la armonía!
Ebúrneas joyas que anima un numen
con su celeste melancolía.

¡Melancolía de haber amado,
junto a la fuente de la arboleda,
el luminoso cuello estirado
entre los blancos muslos de Leda!

In the first quatrain, Darío, who describes swans as the princes of the animal kingdom, links them to all creatures by alluding to their multiple nature and their ability to survive on water, on land, and in the air. As becomes progressively more evident, their aristocracy is derived from their talent for living in unity with the universe, reflecting in their movements the order of the stars. For example, on water they follow the paths indicated by the Dioscuri, the constellation (Gemini) that was worshipped as the protector of sailors. But most importantly, they follow the eternal order of the infinite, which allows their behavior to become the basis of art ("ritmos exactos," "voces de ensueño," "luces de mito"). Returning to the point of departure, Darío sees swans as ivory jewels brought to life by Zeus and his melancholic nostalgia for the idyllic moment when he too was a swan, with his "luminoso cuello estirado / entre los blancos muslos de Leda!" The description of the swan's neck as "luminoso" emphasizes the divine nature of the act and reaffirms the unity of existence—the fusion of god, human, and animal. Thus the swan becomes a symbol of universal harmony in all its forms, including artistic creation and sexual love.

This reading of these four poems sheds light on the enigmatic conclusions to two well-studied poems, revealing the philosophic underpinnings of both. The first, "Divagación" (pp. 551–556), was written in 1894 and later collected in the 1896 edition of *Prosas profanas*. The second, "Por el influjo de la primavera" (pp. 653–655), was written in 1905 and published, in the same year, in *Cantos de vida y esperanza*. Though they are separated in time by nine years, they are joined by a common faith in universal love. In both, Darío's search for a paradisiacal interlude leads him beyond human experience to a more encompassing view of existence.

In "Divagación," which Darío himself called "un curso de geografía erótica; la invitación al amor bajo todos los soles," he invites his love to one imaginary setting after another: Greece, France, Italy, Germany, Spain, China, Japan, India, and Israel.[19] The journey covers most of the poetic geography of turn-of-the-century France, highlights the artistic achievements of the specific region, and is actually as much a search for an ideal style as for an ideal love. The woman he invites to accompany him is different and more attractive in each new country.[20] But Darío realizes that what he is seeking has little to do with physical attributes or external variations. He is looking for a love—and poetic style—that subsumes all differences and elevates him above the specific. He therefore leads his companion off the map into the world of the transcendental. This break is both structural and conceptual. Darío ends his travels, in the fourth stanza from the end, with an ellipsis.

> Amor, en fin, que todo diga y cante,
> amor que cante y deje sorprendida
> a la serpiente de ojos de diamante
> que está enroscada al árbol de la vida.
>
> Ámame así, fatal, cosmopolita,
> universal, inmensa, única, sola
> y todas; misteriosa y erudita:
> ámame mar y nube, espuma y ola.
>
> Sé mi reina de Saba, mi tesoro;
> descansa en mis palacios solitarios.
> Duerme. Yo encenderé los incensarios.
> Y junto a mi unicornio cuerno de oro,
> tendrán rosas y miel tus dromedarios.

As clearly stated in the first of these three final stanzas, Darío is seeking, above all else, harmony. He wants a love that can sing with a perfection that would surprise the serpent of evil. As woman, this love would reverse the results of the fall and allow the reunion of male and female in simple yet eternal bliss. As poetry, this love would reveal a prelapsarian vision that would transport poet and reader beyond the here and now. It is this reaching beyond the particular that leads Darío to a cosmic vision in which his love is identified with divine woman—universal, personal, and poetic. She is, therefore, fatal, the controller of his fate; cosmopolitan, common to all the world; universal, pertaining to and occurring throughout the cosmos; and immense. She is simultaneously one and many, archetype and individuals—the Mother Goddess of the Earth, the female consort of God, and the *prima materia* of creation. She is the source of knowledge and the key to paradise. She is the Water over which the Spirit moved in the beginning of time, and, as such, Darío calls to her, "ámame mar y nube, espuma y ola."[21] His injunction reverberates with primordial, religious, and erotic implications.

At first Darío longed to see his love as many different women possessing the distinctive, appealing charms of the females of the many countries on his erotic and poetic itinerary. He realized, however, that there was a common denominator to what he sought, namely, a sexual and artistic union that would put him in touch with the essence of existence. As a result, after the activity and movement of most of the poem, he concludes by asking his love to rest in his secluded palaces and to be his queen of Sheba, the symbol of the eternal woman in occultist literature.[22] The words "descansa" and "solitarios" establish a sense of calm. When Darío suggests that his love sleep as he lights the censers, the quiet takes on a religious quality that is reinforced by the mention of a unicorn—associated with Christ—and dromedaries, which bring to mind biblical scenes of desert life.[23] As in chapter 4, Darío is identified with Christ and is converted into a poetic savior.

Like its predecessor, "Por el influjo de la primavera" consists of a series of erotic images. Spring arrives with the rains, the flowers, visions of the past, heightened sensuality, and music. The impression that emerges from this profusion of images that gushes over the reader in a narrow (eight-syllable), rapid stream of words—like the runoff of spring waters—is that the universe is reawakening to harmonious, artistic, and sexual generation. The concluding six lines underscore this fusion of spirit, body, and soul and point to a higher vision derived from esoteric tradition.

> ¡Y todo por ti, oh alma!
> Y por ti, cuerpo, y por ti,
> idea, que los enlazas.
> ¡Y por Ti, lo que buscamos
> y no encontraremos nunca
> jamás!

Darío's exaltation of sexual passion is not in spite of his soul but because of it. Sexual love restores his integrity, puts him in touch with the order of the cosmos, and permits him to create a vision of life by inseminating the flesh of poetry with his ideas that are, in their essence, music. All is done "por Ti," for a glimpse at idyllic, Pythagorean harmony in which human beings are whole, God is knowable, paradise is accessible, and art is perfectible. In this case, the vision is not attained and Darío despairs, but he does not reject the path that he has chosen—that of sexual love.

Based on the esoteric conception of a sexual godhead, Darío finds in love much more than a personal and immediate solution to his sense of anguish, isolation, and alienation. He discovers in sexual love a means of intuiting the divine state and of perceiving the prelapsarian, primordial bliss of unity. This unity encompasses the reconciliation of fundamental Western dichotomies—human and divine generation, male and female, body and soul. At the same time, this view leads to the exaltation of woman as the source of all knowledge and to the elevation of the attraction between man and woman as a path to perfection. The following chapter shows how Darío's search for integration leads him one step further—to a syncretic world view and the reconciliation of varying religious beliefs and symbols.

6. Toward a Syncretic World View

What emerges from these readings of Darío's poetry is his overriding desire to perceive and capture in language the harmonious unity of all creation. This perspective permeates his concept of the world and his view of art. Darío aspired to emulate in his poetry the perfection of the universe that is hidden from most, and he found in the art of various periods and different cultures the freedom and beauty that he sought. Indeed, this propensity to draw upon disparate techniques from the past and blend them all into a personal style is a well-recognized characteristic of Modernist poetry.[1] But this reconciliation of artistic modes and trends is merely a reflection of a deeper concern. Paz recognizes in the attraction for Modernists of the most distant past and the most remote countries—medieval and Byzantine legends and figures from pre-Columbian America and the Orient—a profound "nostalgia for a true presence."[2] In search of this "true presence" Darío, under the influence of esoteric tradition, extends his syncretic vision to religious beliefs and symbols.

Occultists hold that the basic assumptions of all religions can be reduced to *philosophia perennis*, that is, to a core of wisdom that has been the property of the wise since the beginning of time. They therefore believe in the fundamental unity of all religions and that each religion perpetuates through its emblems and allegories the same fundamental truths. This faith provided Darío with a framework with which he could aspire to discover a transcendental and unified view of the cosmos by reconciling Catholic dogma, which left an irrefutable and indelible mark on his vision of the world, with ancient esoteric belief systems.

From his earliest writings, Darío manifests a predilection for a syncretic world view. In 1881, at the age of fourteen, he links Socrates with Christ and envisions Christ, Vishnu, Buddha, and Brahma as a spiritual unity which is being destroyed by the forces of reason.[3]

Three years later, in a letter "A Juan Montalvo" (pp. 347–359), he attributes divine wisdom to Plato.

> Por boca de Platón habla Dios mismo,
> porque Platón es sabio; y el Eterno
> es foco de la gran sabiduría.

In a more fantastical piece, the short story "Rojo" (1892), Darío once again strikingly brings together the pagan and the Catholic, underscoring an early sensitivity to the unity of religions and religious images. "El [Palanteau] poseía, como todos los soñadores, el espíritu y el ansia del misterio. El pintor de las blancas anadyomenas desnudas se sentía atraído por el Madero de Cristo; el artista pagano, se estremecía al contemplar la divina media-luna que de la frente de Diana rodó hasta los pies de María."[4] In *Los raros*, in which Darío often singles out in others qualities that he finds in or desires for himself, there are many references to the syncretic nature of *fin de siècle* poetry. A great deal of his admiration for the work of both Leconte de Lisle and Jean Moréas is based on their ability to find material for their poetry in all ages and to synthesize the various elements into a refreshing whole. With regard to Leconte de Lisle, he writes, "Tiempos primitivos, Edad Media, todo lo que se halla respecto a nuestra edad contemporánea como en una lejanía de ensueño, atrae la imaginación del vate severo."[5] About Moréas he writes, "En resumen, Moréas posee un alma abierta a la belleza como la primavera al sol. Su Musa se adorna con galas de todos los tiempos, divina cosmopolita e incomparable políglota. La India y sus mitos le atraen, Grecia y su teogonía y su cielo de luz y de mármol, y sobre todo la edad más poética, la edad de los santos, de los misterios, . . . la Edad Media."[6]

The syncretic tendency and techniques which he so admired in other poets and which he himself adopted in his earliest poetry matured under the influence of esoteric tradition until they became a crucial aspect of his work. This progress toward a serious incorporation of a syncretic perspective is apparent in "Año nuevo" (pp. 589–590) and "Diálogo de una mañana de año nuevo" (pp. 990–993) in which the play of images appears, at first, more decorative than philosophic but actually develops out of a firm ideological stance. "Año nuevo" was published in the 1896 edition of *Prosas profanas*; "Diálogo de una mañana de año nuevo" was written one year later and remained uncollected. The two poems are markedly similar in tone, technique, and theme. In both, the New Year underscores the passage of time and symbolizes the start of a new way of life.

In "Año nuevo" the passage of time parallels the passage of Saint Sylvester through the heavens. Though the image of the lavishly dressed pope may have originated as a real-life religious float being carried into the streets on New Year's Eve—the Saint's Feast Day— Darío's description places him among the constellations and virtually transforms him into an astronomical figure, one that dominates the skies and subordinates the celestial bodies identified with classical antiquity. The brilliant jewels worn by Saint Sylvester and the radiant stars become one. Sirius, Arcturus, and Orion are the diamonds of the pope's tiara; his feet are covered by the jewels of the Great Dipper; he wears a cape of stars and, around his neck, the Southern Cross. The intensity of these visual images tends to obscure the full implication of the fusion of the classical and the Christian. This implication becomes clear as the poem draws to a close.

Saint Sylvester journeys east, toward dawn, and toward the "triunfo del rey Enero," who every year delivers twelve arrows to the Archer, Sagittarius. This year's twelve have been spent, and Sagittarius awaits the renewal of time "at the edge of the mysterious abyss of Eternity." The figure that arrives with the conquering light of day and with the hope of salvation brings together, like the previous description, pagan and Christian imagery. He frightens away nocturnal evils and is greeted by ecclesiastical music. He is simultaneously "King January" and Jesus Christ. With divine authority, he blesses the world and embraces the Archer. Thus, as the old year surrenders to the new, so the old gods defer to the new supreme but syncretic deity, Jesus Christ, who is ushered in on January 1—his Feast Day—by Saint Sylvester. Darío's statement is emphatic. The pagan, as symbolized by the Archer "que no se cansa de flechar," though subsumed under Christianity, continues to live.

Unlike "Año nuevo," in which the New Year brings an affirmation of the supremacy of Christianity over the pagan beliefs and symbols out of which it emerged, in "Diálogo de una mañana de año nuevo," the New Year heralds a resurgence of ancient truths, a reacceptance of the harmonious order of the universe, and a reawakening to the sexual nature of existence. These truths resurface not as destructive of the dominant Christian ideology but rather as its complement. The initial reference to Saint Sylvester's New Year's Eve sally and the prose description of the activity in the street the morning after make clear that the setting for "Diálogo de una mañana de año nuevo" is a Catholic community. The sacristan has rung for the first mass, and two devout women are entering the church. Yet there is a pagan quality to the description as well. Atalanta, the young woman of the poem, who is herself a figure from classical mythology, lies awake, unexpectedly naked, preparing to gratify the spirits of the garden with her perfume. This unusual mixture of allusions is particularly poignant in the poet's speech to Atalanta, as he relies upon a persuasive combination of pagan and Catholic symbols to convince her of the propriety of her sexual desires (p. 991):

> Y en ese abismo, ¡oh pura!, y en ese abismo, ¡oh bella!
> ¿has asistido al brillo cirial de alguna estrella,
> a la degollación de corderos rituales?
> ¿Y comulgaste santamente, tiernamente,
> con el trigo que crece junto a la santa fuente?
> ¿Y fué todo tan puro y sagrado y divino?
> ¿Mezclaste la miel casta con las hostias y el vino?
> ¿Y por, y de, y sobre, y ante
> el Amante,
> una nube de fuego delicioso no hizo
> que temblases en un torbellino de hechizo,
> y que se derritiese como una virgen cera
> tu corazón, Paloma de la Primavera?

The poet's references to the sacraments of the Church give sexual desire an aura of saintliness which is supported by the esoteric view that love is the human means of reaching beyond the personal and of coming into contact with the divine order of existence. At the same time, however, the sensuality of the context highlights the poet's departure from orthodox Catholic doctrine. To these claims, Atalanta must respond.

The classical Atalanta was abandoned by her father in infancy and was suckled by a she-bear, the symbol of Artemis, who is identified with Diana. After she had grown up, she lived in pure maidenhood. When her father, who subsequently recognized her as his daughter, wanted her to marry, she required every suitor to contend with her in a foot race, because she was the most swift-footed of mortals. She was at length overcome by a suitor with the assistance of Aphrodite. The Atalanta of the poem is not unlike her classical namesake: she feels that she is the spiritual daughter of the chaste Diana and cannot bring herself to violate the laws that she has so faithfully followed. But now, at the dawn of a new age, she feels stirrings in her soul that she never experienced before. Guided by the poet, she finds reconciliation. Darío concludes the poem with a summary of the syncretic ideas presented by the poet (p. 993; ellipsis in original):

> Saludemos la Hora que nace. El Año Nuevo
> llegó; sobre la alegre cima del campanario
> un pájaro de oro se posó hace un instante.
> Cristo está sobre el brillo del día de diamante;
> mas Pan y Apolo y la potente diosa velan
> por la salud de la vibrante tierra. Vuelan
> de los nidos las aves; y la suave sonrisa
> de las cosas, anuncia que el Mal no existe. ¡Oh hermosa
> Atalanta! . . . ¡Ya es mía
> tu vibrante armonía,
> y la antorcha, y la tórtola, y la copa, y la rosa!

It is appropriate that it is the poet who convinces Atalanta of the reconcilability of her sexual desires with her Catholic upbringing, for it is the poet who most strongly senses the dictates of the "vibrant earth" and the sexual beat of universal life. He also perceives Christ's approval as he looks down from the heavens, which are aglow with spiritual illumination and physical warmth. Pan, Apollo, and Venus appear as his underlings in charge of the felicitous execution of divine order on earth. Their success is reflected in the smile of the living universe and in the poet's enthusiastic conclusion, in which he recalls the power of sexual love to reveal the harmonious bliss of the divine state.

Whereas neither "Año nuevo" nor "Diálogo de una mañana de año nuevo" has attracted very much critical attention, the unexpected syncretic vision of the final stanza of "Responso a Verlaine" (pp. 594–595)—which like "Año nuevo" was written in 1896, within a week of Verlaine's death, and published in *Prosas profanas*—has aroused a great deal of commentary.[7] Most critics have attempted to justify the inclusion of the cross in what is essentially a pagan setting on the basis of thematic and biographic considerations. Even Darío, years later, offered a limited interpretation based on the troubled life of the French poet, with whom he felt an extraordinary spiritual affinity: "Hago ver las dos faces de su alma pánica: la que da a la carne y la que da al espíritu; la que da a las leyes de la humana naturaleza y la que da a Dios y a los misterios católicos, paralelamente."[8] But, as recognized by Alan S. Trueblood, the poem requires a more extensive reading, one which takes into consideration Darío's poetic cosmology, which he formulated under the influence of esoteric tradition.[9]

In his article, Trueblood points out that it is the sixth and penultimate stanza, with its triple darkness, that is the turning point of the poem. The first five stanzas, rather than expressing pain at the loss of the great poet and master, present a sense of acceptance derived from an awareness of the harmonious and musical order of existence—an awareness that Darío feels the two poets shared. The first five stanzas are, therefore, filled with light, serene, and even sensual scenes. The sixth, on the other hand, is dark and brooding.

> De noche, en la montaña, en la negra montaña
> de las Visiones, pase gigante sombra extraña,
>   sombra de un Sátiro espectral;
> que ella al centauro adusto con su grandeza asuste;
> de una extra-humana flauta la melodía ajuste
>   a la harmonía sideral.

The "Sátiro espectral," whose shadow passes over the mountain of Visions, is the only trace left in "Responso" of Verlaine's satanism, but its satanic dimension is quickly tempered by the musical order that prevailed earlier in the poem. "Cuando le vemos ajustar la melodía de una extra-humana flauta a la armonía sideral, es claro que Darío está fundiendo, bajo el signo pitágorico de la música de las esferas, lo pánico con lo apolíneo, fundiendo también en una unidad superior dos vertientes del arte de Verlaine, e intuyendo ya en el pitagorismo un supremo ideal artístico. . . . Es decir, lo sensual, en su forma brutal, queda dominado junto con lo demoníaco."[10] Since it is the imposition of the harmonious order of existence that conquers the demonic, it is also the harmonious order of existence that purifies the world, preparing it for the cross and the ultimate savior, Jesus Christ.

> Y huya el tropel equino por la montaña vasta;
> tu rostro de ultratumba bañe la luna casta
>   de compasiva y blanca luz;
> y el Sátiro contemple, sobre un lejano monte,
> una cruz que se eleve cubriendo el horizonte,
>   ¡y un resplandor sobre la cruz!

The satyr that contemplates the cross does not mourn the death of Pan and the other ancient gods; quite the contrary, his identification with Pan suggests that the ancient gods, like the satyr himself, live on and are attracted to the new faith which Darío presents as syncretic and rooted in the Pythagorean concept of order. Darío therefore suggests that the personal reconciliation sought by Verlaine—and by himself—is attained through esoteric Christianity, which emphasizes its continuity with previous religions as well as the promise of salvation—the glow of the cross—for those who possess a profound understanding of the artistically harmonious universe.

This syncretic world view reappears five years later in "La espiga" (p. 615), the first poem in a series of thirteen entitled "Las ánforas de Epicuro," which Darío added to the 1901 edition of *Prosas profanas*. As indicated in chapter 2, "La espiga" presents a highly refined and sophisticated vision of the world based on the Pythagorean concept of the unity of life. Even more extraordinary—as in the case of "Responso a Verlaine"—is the introduction, in the final stanza, of standard Christian symbols with which Darío achieves a remarkable fusion of Catholic doctrine and Pythagorean pantheism.

If, as Marasso suggests, "La espiga" was produced under the influence of Verlaine's "C'est la fête du blé . . . ," Darío chose to intensify the pantheistic view expressed in the French poem.[11] The elements of nature are described in such a way that, from the outset, it is clear that the poet's concern is not with external appearances but with the hidden realities that they represent. The key word is "signo," for all of nature is seen as a sign of the unity of life in and through God.

> Mira el signo sutil que los dedos del viento
> hacen al agitar el tallo que se inclina
> y se alza en una rítmica virtud de movimiento.
> Con el áureo pincel de la flor de la harina
>
> trazan sobre la tela azul del firmamento
> el misterio inmortal de la tierra divina
> y el alma de las cosas que da su sacramento
> en una interminable frescura matutina.
>
> Pues en la paz del campo la faz de Dios asoma.
> De las floridas urnas místico incienso aroma
> el vasto altar en donde triunfa la azul sonrisa.
>
> Aun verde está y cubierto de flores el madero,
> bajo sus ramas llenas de amor pace el cordero
> y en la espiga de oro y luz duerme la misa.

"La espiga" is a sonnet in alexandrines, a form preferred by the Parnassians for its symmetry (fourteen fourteen-syllable lines).[12] Darío exploits the flexibility given to the fourteen-syllable line by the Modernists by combining trochaic, ternary, and French alexandrines to modulate the rhythm in accordance with the conceptual substance.[13] For example, in the first three lines Darío presents the scene out of which the underlying concepts of the poem develop. A sign is seen in the movement of a plant which is being stirred by the "fingers of the wind." These three lines run on unbrokenly in a steady yet gentle "movement" (the word emphasized by its final position in the third line) that conveys the rhythmic swaying of the wheat in the wind. The use of synecdoche points to the presence and anticipates the appearance of an anthropomorphic force that governs the universe. The sign made is subtle, noticed only by the enlightened poet, who now directs the reader's attention to it. The movement of the plant, in which the sign is seen, is described by "se inclina y se alza," as if the blade were praying or bestowing a blessing. This phrase brings out a secondary meaning of the word "signo"—a sign that is made as a benediction, like that made during the mass—and clearly sets the poem in a religious framework. The religious tone is reinforced by the words "virtud" and "rítmica," which evoke the concept of moral law and, more specifically, the Pythagorean injunction that individuals should set their souls in order by understanding and imitating the orderliness seen in nature, since both human beings and the universe are aspects of the harmonious unfolding of God. This conception of the cosmos forms the basis of the next five lines, which interpret the initial scene poetically and philosophically through a series of metaphors.

The poet envisions the swaying stem as a golden brush with which the fingers of the wind paint upon the blue canvas of the sky. They sketch "el misterio inmortal de la tierra divina / y el alma de las cosas." In other words, it is in all the elements of nature working together in cosmic harmony (one as the painter, one as the paint brush, and one as the canvas) that the eternal mystery of the divine and the soul—the single soul—of all things become evident. And, in the tradition that links the spirit with the wind, it is the morning freshness that is the sign of God's internal and spiritual effect ("el sacramento") offered by the universal soul. The uninterrupted flow of lines 4 through 8 serves to reinforce both the soothing and the unending qualities of the morning breeze, and the tinkle of the *t*'s in "matutina" further enhances the reader's perception of the refreshing morning air. Darío thus creates a scene of paradisiacal harmony and bliss in which time has been suspended. Though the term "sacramento" is used in this non-Catholic context, Darío draws upon its association with the "sacramento del altar." He strengthens the allusion to the Eucharist by describing the indefinite "tallo" of the second line as "el áureo pincel de la flor de la harina." Because the plant/brush is golden, it is linked to the sun, God, and fruitfulness;[14] because it is "la flor de la harina," it is associated with the special flour into which it will be milled to make the host.

The end-stopped ninth line, "Pues en la paz del campo la faz de Dios asoma," stands apart as the turning point of the poem. It summarizes the concepts present in the two quatrains and introduces the concluding section of the sonnet. The "paz del campo" underscores the fact that all the elements of nature are working in harmony. The universal force, whose fingers moved the initial ear of wheat, now shows its "face" and is readily identified as God. In lines 10 and 11 the countryside, where God becomes visible, is metaphorically converted into a temple and its elements into religious objects. Flowers become "floridas urnas" and their scent becomes a "místico incienso" which perfumes "el vasto altar" where God triumphs. Thus the implied religiosity of the quatrains becomes explicit.

The God that triumphs is blue—a color identified with heaven, heavenly love, and truth—because he is the divine mystery that can be seen on the "tela azul del firmamento."[15] He is a "smile" for two fundamental reasons. After examining the harmonious workings of nature, Darío senses that the divine force governing the universe is friendly, benevolent, and beneficent. The smiling, happy God of the countryside is therefore implicitly opposed to the angry, punishing God of the Old Testament or the suffering Catholic Christ. In addition, Darío projects his own happiness upon being able to perceive a divine force. For him it is a wish come true, a wish that he clearly expresses later in "Helios" (p. 644): "Que sientan las naciones / el volar de tu carro."

Throughout the quatrains and the first tercet, Darío presents a world view that is congruent with esoteric Pythagoreanism. In the second tercet, he focuses upon the esoteric belief in the fundamental unity of all religions. With the introduction of standard Christian symbolism, he clarifies his previous allusions to the Eucharist and makes evident his reconciliation of Catholic doctrine with his pantheistic vision. He focuses on a different element in the countryside described: a tree trunk still green and covered with flowers. The final position and consequent linking of the words "madero," "cordero," and "misa" remove all doubt that the "madero" is the cross of redemption. That it is still alive means that it has not yet served its ultimate purpose. The fact that beneath it "pace el cordero" indicates that Christ has not yet been sacrificed. The branches of the tree are "filled with love," because the scene described is of the time before the fall.

To complete this idyllic vision, Darío returns to the "áureo pincel de la flor de la harina," which is now "la espiga de oro y luz." Clearly, the ear of wheat is made of the golden light of the sun, which Darío, under the influence of occultist symbolism, associates with the supreme deity. (This point is central to "Helios," the next poem to be discussed.) By stressing the presence of the divine within the "espiga," he emphasizes the pantheism of the poem and the dispersion of God throughout nature. At the same time, he affirms the Catholic belief that God is in the host. Darío achieves a reconciliation of Catholic and occult doctrine by holding that "en la espiga . . . duerme la misa." In other words, even in this paradisiacal, pre-Christian, prelapsarian setting, God is in the wheat. But, since there is as yet no need for the mass, it will be dormant within the ear of wheat until Christ is sacrificed.

While in "La espiga" Darío achieves an artistic reconciliation of the Catholic belief in transubstantiation with the pantheistic world view of esoteric Pythagoreanism, in "Helios" (pp. 643–645) he blends pre-Christian, Christian, and occultist symbolism to create a unified poetic vision of the supreme deity. This God seems to be, on first impression, Helios, the sun god in Greek mythology. In reality, however, he is a syncretic figure that symbolizes Darío's idealized conception of the ruling force of the universe.

It is fitting that the study of the syncretic aspect of Darío's poetic cosmology should include the sun, for its adoration is well recognized as one of the most ancient and widely diffused forms of religious expression. Since ancient times the sun has been identified with God. The Church Fathers turned to this image, drawing upon scriptural and classical passages. Later on, the sun became a central symbol in Spanish religious poetry of the sixteenth and seventeenth centuries.[16] In the nineteenth century, occultists emphasized this hidden relationship between complex modern theologies and the more primitive solar religions. They point out that aboriginal peoples adored the sun as the efficient cause of all generation and associated it with the principle of good. They also hold that nearly all the salient incidents recorded in the four Gospels have their correlations in the movements, phases, or functions of the heavenly bodies. These occultists preach that the image of the sun god was carried into Christianity by those who chronicled the life and acts of Jesus. Annie Besant presents a summary of the sun god myths, focusing on those features that appear in the New Testament as well.

> The eventful life of the Sun-God [is] spanned within the first six months of the solar year, the other six being employed in general protecting and preserving. He is always born at the winter solstice, after the shortest day in the year, at midnight of the 24th of December, when the sign Virgo is rising above the horizon; born as this sign is rising, he is born always of a

virgin, and she remains a virgin after she has given birth to her
Sun-Child, as the celestial Virgo remains unchanged and unsullied when the Sun comes forth from her in the heavens. . . .
[He is] born when the days are shortest and the nights are long-
est. . . . But . . . the day lengthens toward the spring equinox,
till the time comes for the crossing over, the crucifixion. . . .
After this he rises triumphantly and ascends into heaven, and
ripens the corn and the grape, giving his very life to them to
make their substance and through them to his worshippers.
The God who is born at the dawning of December 25 is ever
crucified at the spring equinox, and ever gives his life as food
to his worshippers—these are among the most salient marks
of the Sun-God.[17]

Even the concept of the Trinity is believed to be derived from
the powers and principles of the sun, from the three distinct phases
of the sun in the course of the day: rising, midday, and setting. God
the Father, the creator of the world, is symbolized by dawn and his
color is blue—a fact that is relevant to the analysis of "Helios"—because the rising sun is veiled in the blue mist. God the Son, the illuminating one sent to bear witness of his Father, is the globe at
midday, the Golden-haired Savior of the World: his color is yellow.
God the Holy Ghost is the sunset phase and his color is red.[18] In addition to these specific associations, the sun is also a source of light,
that is, a source of both physical and intellectual illumination. Thus
it becomes identified with the true light, the supreme benefactor
who, after dying each night, rises again and restores all things to life;
in short, the sun becomes linked with Jesus Christ.[19]

This complex interrelationship of associations forms the background to the poetic cosmology expressed in "Helios" and to the development of the poem's central figure. As a whole, the poem reflects Darío's formulation of an orderly, harmonious universe in
which evil can be conquered through spiritual, intellectual, and artistic illumination. In "Helios" the poet is in touch with the hidden
order of the cosmos, an order that is in its essence ideal music and
artistic perfection. He exuberantly praises the glory of God, who is
present in the workings of the heavens and throughout the universe.
In addition, the poem, like "La espiga," occurs in a paradisiacal interlude that is outside time and that is the perfect setting for the final
syncretic vision.

"Helios" is written in *silva* form, which traditionally consisted
of seven- and eleven-syllable lines with no fixed stanzas or rhyme
scheme. The Modernists increased the flexibility of this form by in-

troducing other rhythms.[20] Darío takes full advantage of this flexibility. He includes fourteen-syllable lines, which slow down the pace of the poem and make the style more serious and declamatory. These longer lines appear in the later sections of the poem, in which the poet reflects upon his experiences. The shorter lines provide a sensation of movement and are used most in the first two sections, where Darío is describing the movement of the sun across the sky. At the same time, Darío's selection of strong rhymes—with many rhyming couplets throughout the poem—enhances the sense of harmony and order.

The lack of fixed stanzas also offers Darío a greater opportunity to accommodate form to content. Each section presents a new phase of the poet's perception of the sun. The first two sections focus on the sun's ascent into the heavens at dawn and through the morning. The third section recalls the night that has been overcome, while the fourth and fifth develop the theological implications of the previous three. Finally, the sixth section, with its introduction of Christian symbolism, concludes the poem with a syncretic reconciliation that underscores the timelessness of the poet's vision.

The poem opens with a reference to celestial music, thereby establishing from the outset the existence of universal harmony (p. 643):

> ¡Oh rüido divino!
> ¡Oh rüido sonoro!
> Lanzó la alondra matinal el trino,
> y sobre ese preludio cristalino,
> los caballos de oro
> de que el Hiperionida
> lleva la rienda asida,
> al trotar forman música armoniosa,
> un argentino trueno,
> y en el azul sereno
> con sus cascos de fuego dejan huellas de rosa.
> Adelante, ¡oh cochero
> celeste!, sobre Osa
> y Pelïon, sobre Titania viva.
> Atrás se queda el trémulo matutino lucero,
> y el universo el verso de su música activa.

Throughout the first two sections, Darío draws upon a series of musical images, which add to the artistic unity of the poem and highlight his perception that universal order coincides with musical and rhythmic patterns. He writes of the "trino," the "preludio," the "música armoniosa," the "instrumento sacro," and Pegasus's "rítmicos saltos." Moreover, since the sounds are described as "divine," they are perceived to belong to a god. At first this god seems to be Helios, son of the Titan Hyperion (hence the name "Hiperionida" in line 6) and the Titaness Thea; later it becomes clear that he is a syncretic figure whose essence is harmony.

The third line determines the time of the poem: day is dawning. "Lanzó la alondra matinal el trino." The word "trino" is, of course, a musical term which corresponds to the others already mentioned. It is also an adjective that, by designating that which has three distinct things, anticipates the appearance of the divine Trinity. The "trino" serves as a prelude to the "música armoniosa," "un argentino trueno," produced as the golden horses trot through the sky. While gold is the metal normally associated with the sun, the use of the adjective "argentine" has a long tradition upon which Darío relies to form a novel synesthetic image. White or silver signifies life, purity, innocence, joy, and light. The thunder is silver because it is not the thunder of dark, menacing storm clouds but rather a pure and innocent thundering of the solar chariot's passage through the sky sonorously announcing the joyous reawakening of the universe.

All this activity takes place in the "azul sereno," in which Helios's horses "dejan huellas de rosas." While this image evokes a brilliant sunrise in which gentle traces of color are left behind as the sun begins its daily ascent, it acquires greater resonance with the understanding that the Greeks accepted the rose as a symbol of the dawn.[21] As the fiery hoofs of the sun's horses step upon the blue firmament, they leave impressions of the sunrise.

The poet spurs the driver on: "Adelante, ¡oh cochero celeste!" At first glance, the adjective "celeste" appears to relate simply to heaven, but the last line of the poem—"¡cochero azul que riges los caballos de oro!"—clarifies its full implications. The blue coachman —God the Father—is in the sky guiding the chariot with his omnipotence. The chariot is to pass over Osa and Pelion, two mountains which the Titans, in their war with the gods, are said to have attempted to heap on Olympus in order to scale heaven. To this myth Darío joins that of the origin of humanity according to the Orphics. In it, the Titans gave toys to the infant god Dionysus and, while his attention was thus distracted, killed him and feasted on his flesh. As punishment Zeus hurled a thunderbolt to burn the Titans. From the soot arose the human race.[22] The fusion of these two myths produces the neologism "Titania." The "Titania viva" is humanity, which Darío sees as arrogantly daring to aspire to the status of gods. This phrase is a sophisticated echo of feelings he expressed earlier in the fourth section of "El porvenir" (p. 371) and in "El poeta a las musas" (pp. 330–333), which ends: "¿cómo cantar en este aciago tiempo / en que hasta los humanos orgullosos / pretenden arrojar a Dios del cielo?"

The final two lines of the first section capture the final moments of dawn as the morning star is left behind. Here, once again, Darío develops the symbolic dimension of the scene he presents. The morning star, the star that rises before the sun, is also known as "Lucifer" or "the false light," for it is overcome by the true light of the sun, which similarly has a scriptural parallel. Like the sun, Christ's illumination overpowers misleading distractions. Significantly, the morning star is "trémulo," the Spanish equivalent of the musical term "tremolo." With this word Darío connects the visual —the image of the flickering star—with the aural—the echoes of celestial music. This allusion is picked up in the last line, as Darío reaffirms the musical order of divine (and poetic) creation: "el universo el verso de su música activa."

The second section of the poem describes the first moments of bright sunlight and begins by emphasizing the force that controls the universe and directs the sun's magic carriage (p. 644):

> Pasa, ¡oh dominador, oh conductor del carro
> de la mágica ciencia! Pasa, pasa, ¡oh bizarro
> manejador de la fatal cuadriga
> que al pisar sobre el viento
> despierta el instrumento
> sacro! Tiemblan las cumbres
> de los montes más altos
> que en sus rítmicos saltos
> tocó Pegaso. Giran muchedumbres
> de águilas bajo el vuelo
> de tu poder fecundo,
> y si hay algo que iguale la alegría del cielo,
> es el gozo que enciende las entrañas del mundo.

Movement, life, and harmony come together in Darío's adaptation of the image of the universal monochord, which, in the poem, is strummed by the hoofs of Helios's horses after having lain silent all night. Not only does Darío, in this way, link the Pythagorean and the mythological, but he also underscores the rhythmic essence of all existence. These vibrations of the resonating "instrumento sacro" correspond, in turn, to the cadenced pulse of the poet's art—represented as the responsive peaks of the highest mountains touched by Pegasus.[23] This cosmic beat develops into a praise of procreation— universal, personal, and poetic—in the next five lines, the nucleus of which is the eagle.

The eagle was the appointed bird of Jupiter and signified the swiftly moving forces of the Demiurgus.[24] As such, it was identified with the sun and with the idea of male reproductive activity.[25] Since the eagle reinforces the sexual associations of the sun, the universe appears doubly aroused and fertile, and this living, feeling, sexual universe responds with human delight. The joy of the heavens is reflected in the pleasure of the earth, which is inseminated with the heat of passion and generation.

Darío turns from his praise of the sun as procreator to its exaltation as conquering hero, who triumphs over the sinister forces of the night (p. 644):

> ¡Helios!, tu triunfo es ése,
> pese a las sombras, pese
> a la noche, y al miedo, y a la lívida Envidia.
> Tú pasas, y la sombra, y el daño y la desidia,
> y la negra pereza, hermana de la muerte,
> y el alacrán del odio que su ponzoña vierte,
> y Sátan todo, emperador de las tinieblas,
> se hunden, caen. Y haces el alba rosa, y pueblas
> de amor y de virtud las humanas conciencias,
> riegas todas las artes, brindas todas las ciencias;
> los castillos de duelo de la maldad derrumbas,
> abres todos los nidos, cierras todas las tumbas,
> y sobre los vapores del tenebroso Abismo,
> pintas la Aurora, el Oriflama de Dios mismo.

Sections 2 and 3 are linked by the retrospective "ése," which serves as a hinge referring back to "el gozo que enciende las entrañas del mundo" and forward to the following thirteen lines. Helios's triumph is creation—divine, human, intellectual, artistic, and moral— despite the evil that inhabits the night. This ability to defeat the forces of darkness has long been joined with myths of descent into the netherworld. The idea of the sun's invincibility is reinforced by its comparison with the moon, which must suffer fragmentation before it can reach its monthly stage of three-day disappearance. The sun, on the other hand, does not need to die in order to descend into hell; it can reach the ocean or lake of the Lower Waters and cross it without being dissolved.[26] Hence, the sun's ability to conquer evil is associated with the idea of resurrection. Darío takes full advantage of the easy application of this image to this syncretic context. He develops the figure of Helios with a masterful play of light and dark, ascent and descent, creation and destruction.

Lines 2 through 7 of section 3 are filled with references to evil, darkness, and death. The scorpion, for example, was called by ancients the backbiter, and it is the symbol *par excellence* of deceit, perversion, and wickedness. It is also the sign of the Zodiac which corresponds to the span of human life under the threat of death.[27] In line 8, Darío specifies the fate of these black forces: "se hunden, caen." This fall of evil and the ascension of good is reinforced in the chiasmus of lines 11 and 12 of this section. Not only does Helios throw down and destroy the entombing castles of grief and wickedness, but he also makes possible the upward flight of souls—traditionally represented by winged creatures—by opening all nests. This image is further enhanced by that of closing all tombs, for by conquering death Helios frees souls from their earthly limitations, allowing them to soar to the highest of heights.

If the first half of this section is dominated by the dark ("sombras," "noche," "negra pereza," "tinieblas"), the second combines the symbolism of the sun as the efficient cause of all generation and as the source of physical, intellectual, and spiritual illumination to produce vibrant images of fertility in all areas of human endeavor. Helios, like Apollo, presides over law and order as well as the arts. He therefore generates love, virtue, conscience, art, and science. This conquest of the dark side of existence is represented by Helios's emergence at dawn, which is metaphorically converted into God's battle standard. This metaphor is carried into the next section. If dawn is God's battle standard, Helios is his standard-bearer (p. 644):

> ¡Helios! Portaestandarte
> de Dios, padre del Arte,
> la paz es imposible, mas el amor eterno.
> Danos siempre el anhelo de la vida,
> y una chispa sagrada de tu antorcha encendida,
> con que esquivar podamos la entrada del Infierno.

In section 4 Darío begins to ponder the divine characteristics he has attributed to Helios and to clarify the separation between Helios, the youthful hero and son, and God the Father, who is in heaven. Darío's thoughts reflect his mature compromise with the enigmas of existence: art is blessed, spiritual peace is impossible, but love is eternal.[28] It is Darío's faith in art, in love, and in their harmonious nature that sustains him. This desire to live is what he needs and requests, along with a spark of sacred illumination with which to avoid the entrance of hell.

More frightening than damnation, however, is the fear that life has no transcendental significance at all. This fear is the focus of the first eight lines of the fifth section (pp. 644–645):

> Que sientan las naciones
> el volar de tu carro; que hallen los corazones
> humanos, en el brillo de tu carro, esperanza;
> que del alma-Quijote y el cuerpo-Sancho Panza
> vuele una psique cierta a la verdad del sueño;
> que hallen las ansias grandes de este vivir pequeño
> una realización invisible y suprema;
> ¡Helios! ¡Que no nos mate tu llama que nos quema!
> Gloria hacia ti del corazón de las manzanas,
> de los cálices blancos de los lirios,
> y del amor que manas
> hecho de dulces fuegos y divinos martirios,
> y del volcán inmenso,
> y del hueso minúsculo,
> y del ritmo que pienso,
> y del ritmo que vibra en el corpúsculo,
> y del Oriente intenso
> y de la melodía del crepúsculo.

Darío implores Helios to give all peoples hope by letting them feel the music of the spheres, thereby informing them of the existence of a divine being. This longing for cosmic assurances is common to both aspects of human nature, that is, both to the "alma-Quijote," which lives on an ideal spiritual plane, and to the "cuerpo-Sancho Panza," which indulges in the material world. The single dream of both is realized by Psyche, the force of reconciliation in Darío's poetry.[29] Darío's hope is simple: "que hallen las ansias grandes de este vivir pequeño / una realización invisible y suprema." This poetic phrase highlights the center of the issue: human anxiety is inversely proportional to the sense of transcendental worth. Yet the desire for divine illumination bears with it the possibility of exposing a destructive truth; for this reason, Darío adds: "¡Helios! ¡Que no nos mate tu llama que nos quema!"

Midway through section 5, the poet's attitude suddenly changes. He stops making requests and begins to praise. He seems determined, on one hand, to find beauty and harmony in what he can see and, on the other, to stop concerning himself with the inapprehensible. He establishes pairs, some antithetical and some complementary, which form the basis of his new faith. The "corazón de las manzanas," which brings to mind the fall and original sin, is coupled with the "cálices blancos de los lirios," which are associated with purity and goodness and, more specifically, with the Virgin Mary, who is the receptive, feminine aspect of human spiritual transformation.[30] In addition, the "cáliz" is more than just the calyx of the lily; it is also a chalice, that is, the cup used for the Holy Communion. Thus, in this pair Darío captures all of human history from Adam and Eve to the present day, from original sin to redemption through the mass.[31] These concepts are reinforced by the fact that faith in Helios comes from the love that issues from him and that is made of "dulces fuegos y divinos martirios." This statement, with its allusion to the martyrdom of Christ and the saints, echoes the Christian idea that human love of God is a reflection of his love of humanity. It also recalls the divine pulse which, emanating from God, echoes throughout the universe. The reverberations of the divine presence are sensed in the following three pairs: in the large, tumultuous, and destructive ("del volcán inmenso") and the small, quiet, and regenerative ("del hueso minúsculo"); in the universal heartbeat felt by the poet and incorporated in his art ("del ritmo que pienso") and the vital pulsation evident in nature ("del ritmo que vibra en el corpúsculo"); in the brilliant sunrise ("del Oriente intenso") and the peaceful, harmonious sunset ("y de la melodía del crepúsculo").

In the sixth and final section, Darío confirms the syncretic vision that he develops subtly throughout the first five (p. 645):

> ¡Oh rüido divino!
> Pasa sobre la cruz del palacio que duerme,
> y sobre el alma inerme
> de quien no sabe nada. No turbes el destino.
> ¡Oh rüido sonoro!
> El hombre, la nación, el continente, el mundo,
> aguardan la virtud de tu carro fecundo,
> ¡cochero azul que riges los caballos de oro!

Since the cross is immediately associated with Christianity, it does not appear in this basically non-Christian milieu unintentionally. The "cruz del palacio" is the cross of a church that is not yet a church because it antedates Christianity; for this reason, it is a "palacio que duerme"—just as the mass sleeps in the "espiga." The soul is "inerme" because it cannot defend itself against perdition. The individual to whom it belongs "no sabe nada," that is, he knows nothing about salvation because the Church does not yet exist. At the same time, Darío echoes the pre-Christian longings for the Messianic Age, for the coming of the savior, with "El hombre, la nación, el continente, el mundo, / aguardan la virtud de tu carro fecundo." Though the context is pre-Christian, these lines also convey the longings of Darío's own age for the Second Coming—a desire expressed more directly in "Canto de esperanza" (p. 642). By thus fusing past, present, and future, Darío not only achieves a reconciliation of Catholic and occultist doctrine and symbolism, but he also creates a poetic vision in which the harmonious order of the universe is the fundamental nature of the divinity. The human inability to perceive God and attain a paradisiacal integration with the surroundings is due to the inability to perceive the order of the cosmos. Since this order is in its essence ideal music and artistic perfection, it falls upon the poet to discover the "cochero azul que rige los caballos de oro"—who is a syncretic, triune God and the "true presence" that Paz places at the center of the Modernist search.[32]

7. Modernism and Its Legacy

Spanish American Modernism, in contrast to the explanation implied by some earlier theories, did not take shape in relative isolation as a reaction against and negation of the preceding literature.[1] The fundamental nature of the movement was molded by the Romantic metaphysics of integration and the unrelenting Romantic quest for innocence that came to Spanish American writers primarily by way of France. The emphasis by critics on the well-crafted, elaborate quality of Modernist verse, almost to the exclusion of other artistic features, has further diverted attention from the true origins of the movement and from its serious philosophic substructure. Moreover, this unbalanced reading has inadvertently brought into question the enduring influence of the Modernists.[2] Because of a (re)current distrust of "artificiality" in art and its association with affectation, insincerity, superficiality, and a lack of concern for the basic issues of life, the critical focus on Modernism's highly contrived forms has made the movement appear obsolete. This position is inaccurate and blocks the perception of the vestiges of Modernist art that continue to function in contemporary Hispanic literature.

Without purporting to present a detailed survey of the literary movements that follow Modernism, this concluding chapter highlights the significant links between Modernist poetry and more recent Hispanic literature which have now become recognizable in the light of this study and its examination of Modernism's sophisticated philosophic underpinnings. This chapter focuses on the debt that contemporary writers owe to the earlier poets, thereby underscoring the continuing influence of Darío and the other Modernists. It should, nevertheless, be understood that the relationships between Modernism and later movements that are outlined here are merely the salient points of a terrain that still remains to be explored.

As has been indicated throughout this study, the major characteristics of Modernist art have their basis in a cosmology formulated under the influence of the esoteric beliefs popular among European writers of the nineteenth century. The formal manifestations of Modernist art do not define the movement; rather they are reflections of a profound struggle to come to grips with the meaning of existence and the perplexities of poetic responsibility. Though Darío and other Modernists sought answers in a variety of religions, sects, and ideologies, adopting a flexible, syncretic world view, they found, like the Romantics and Symbolists before them, a unifying notion and philosophic keystone in the concepts of unity and harmony. They hoped to redeem their contemporaries, whom they saw as fragmented—out of touch with themselves, others, and with nature— by fostering a reconciliation with an orderly, benevolent universe. In Darío's case, the aspiration to harmony underpins his entire poetic production and is particularly relevant to the poems that center on the five occultist tenets examined here.

Early in his career, Darío took harmony as an artistic standard, which he then enlarged into an ideal associated with divine perfection, the Good, and the Beautiful. He found support for these beliefs in esoteric Pythagoreanism, to which he was introduced by the writers of the period. In it he also found support for a premise central to Romantic and Symbolist poetics, namely, that all the elements of nature are signs that indicate the unity of the universe in and through God. It is the poet/magus who can read and interpret these signs, conveying their message of unity and harmony to the rest of humanity.

Faith in this unity forms the basis of the doctrine of reincarnation, to which Darío turned in order to express his judgment about his ability to achieve spirituality and to fulfill his poetic responsibility of translating into human language the signs of the universe. The doctrine of transmigration of souls provided him with the ideal metaphoric structure through which to discuss his self-doubts, for within this framework all the elements of creation are torn between their aspiration toward a harmonious union with God and the temptations of the flesh. But Darío's sense of moral weakness and his inability to resist these temptations provoked great internal discord. He therefore extended his search for harmony—and for resolution of his personal turmoil. In the occultist belief that the Great Monad acts as a creative Dyad, Darío found a pattern for human behavior based on sexual union. Human love is thus a microcosmic parallel to the macrocosmic order and provides a means by which one can achieve direct and immediate consciousness of divine truth and God by joining with him in fulfillment of universal harmony.

Finally, the fundamental syncretic nature of the dominant occultist sects provided Darío with a means of reconciling or "harmonizing" discordant doctrine. And, since the esoteric belief in the unity of all religions extended to their symbolism, it taught him to draw upon and blend the ideas and imagery of all ages and to use concepts as "hubs" around which to create unified artistic compositions by attaching "spokes" from disparate ages. Underlying this approach to beliefs and symbols is a significant development. The specific symbols and their original religious context have become less important than their new role in their new poetic structure that attempts to capture the essence of the harmonious universe. Darío thus implicitly denies the absolute authority of any one belief system. Consequently, Darío's recourse to either occultism or Catholicism does not necessarily represent a vacillation of personal beliefs. The appeal to one symbolic code rather than another reaffirms the artist's freedom to attempt to match the words with "la iniciación melódica" (p. 622). At the same time, however, he silently acknowledges the tentative nature of poetic discourse with which he hopes to capture truth through the magic of language.

This view of language and of the world is not unique to Darío. Recent studies have begun to recognize the primary importance of these characteristics of Darío's poetry to other writers of the period. As Grass and Risley acknowledge in their introduction to *Waiting for Pegasus: Studies of the Presence of Symbolism and Decadence in Hispanic Letters*, the artistic phenomenon to which Modernism belongs is both international and long-lived—continuing at least until the rise of the avant-garde.[3] Moreover, increased attention has been focused on the influence of the esoteric tradition that was adopted by Romantic and Symbolist writers of the nineteenth century. One of the first to observe the unorthodox vein running through Modernism was Ricardo Gullón, who noted the presence of Pythagorean thought in the poetry of Herrera y Reissig, the appearance of the doctrine of transmigration of souls in the writings of Lugones, and the interest demonstrated by Valle-Inclán in hermeticism and numerology.[4] Jensen's study of *Las fuerzas extrañas* by Lugones and the works on Valle-Inclán by Maier, Sperrati-Piñero, and Risco—to mention just a few—support Gullón's earlier findings.[5] Similar conclusions have been reached with regard to Amado Nervo and José Martí.[6]

As Schulman points out in "Modernismo, revolución y pitagorismo en Martí," an undercurrent of Pythagorean thought runs throughout Martí's political writings and poetry. In an earlier article, "Génesis del azul modernista," Schulman clearly shows how Martí anticipates many of the aesthetic issues later taken up and developed by Darío.[7] This dual political/artistic nature of Martí's Pythagoreanism appears in "Canto religioso" from *Versos libres* (1882). In this poem Martí describes a pantheistic fusion of God, nature, and humanity that reaches its spiritual climax within the poet. The religious vocabulary underscores the sacred nature of the poet's task to spread the word of universal beauty and human perfectibility.

> Y sigo a mi labor, como creyente
> a quien unge en la sien el sacerdote
> de rostro liso y vestiduras blancas.
> Practico: en el divino altar comulgo
> de la naturaleza: es mi hostia el alma humana.[8]

Later, in "¡Vivir en sí, qué espanto!" from *Flores del destierro* (1882–1891), Martí finds in this faith in the unity of life the strength to overcome the despair of isolation. He takes consolation in the simple soul of creation that rhythmically flows throughout all the elements of nature.

> Del aire viene al árbol alto el jugo:
> de la vasta, jovial naturaleza
> al cuerpo viene el ágil movimiento
> y al alma la anhelada fortaleza.
> ¡Cambio es la vida! Vierten los humanos
> de sí el fecundo amor: y luego vierte
> la vida universal entre sus manos
> modo y poder de dominar la Muerte. . . .[9]

As in Darío's poetry, the rhythm of the universe becomes a primary factor in the poet's world view. In Verso 17 of *Versos sencillos* (1891), it is their rhythmic nature that unites woman with poetry and that allows both to represent the essence of creation.

> ¡Arpa soy, salterio soy
> dónde vibra el Universo:
> vengo del sol, y al sol voy:
> soy el amor: soy el verso![10]

In Nervo's case, the recourse to unorthodox beliefs is motivated by a search for alternatives to the positivistic rationalism against which he struggled all his life. He rejects the compartmentalized vision of life achieved through established patterns of perception in favor of a poetic knowledge of the harmonious unity of existence. "El éxtasis poético," writes Nervo, "semejante a todos los éxtasis, no

es más que el acceso a una dimensión nueva y la consiguiente de-
leitosa y admirable sensación de que se han quebrantado *los límites*
que encierran nuestras percepciones del universo como rejas invisi-
bles."[11] Nervo's attempts to break the shackles of rationalism would
eventually lead him—like Antonio Machado—to Bergsonian intuitionism, but, as is clear from the early poem "Implacable" (1895), he
first explores other nontraditional belief systems. After his rejection
of the doctrine of transmigration of souls (in section 2), he comments ironically on the intricacies of his search.

III

(Nota bene: El poeta continúa
su proceso de todos los sistemas,
de todas las obscuras teogonías,
de todas las marañas esotéricas;
de todos los programas positivos
que derrumban altares y desdeñan
la hipótesis de Dios, de todo el triste
delirar de las razas, anestesia
con que aduermen las razas su amargura
de cruzar como sombras por la tierra,
y el romance concluye de la suerte
que verá en breve término quien lea.)[12]

A tentative response to his despair is expressed later in the same
poem and is simultaneously syncretic and relativistic—maintaining
a skeptical perspective throughout.[13]

A poetic solution—not unlike the solutions offered by Darío
during the same period—is suggested by Nervo in the group of
poems written in 1901 entitled *La hermana agua*.[14] In the prose introduction, "A quien va a leer," Nervo explains how he has found
answers in the sonorous simplicity of flowing water.

Un hilo de agua que cae de una llave imperfecta, un hilo de
agua, manso y diáfano, que gorjea toda la noche y todas las
noches cerca de mi alcoba; que canta a mi soledad y en ella me
acompaña; un hilo de agua: ¡qué cosa tan sencilla! Y, sin em-
bargo, esas gotas incesantes y sonoras me han enseñado más
que los libros.

El alma del Agua me ha hablado en la sombra—el alma
santa del Agua—, y yo la he oído con recogimiento y con amor.
Lo que me ha dicho está escrito en páginas que pueden com-

pendiarse así: *ser dócil, ser cristalina: ésta es la ley de los profetas;* y tales páginas han formado un poema.

In "El agua multiforme," of the same group, the poet suggests that he be like the water, that is, that he respond in perfect harmony to his surroundings and that he "Pythagorize" his being. The reference to a universe of pristine simplicity, the identification of an aquatic soul, and the cheerful surrender to divine purpose reflect the poet's faith in the possibility of following the command "sé como el agua." He expresses an optimistic view of his ability to rediscover and follow in his life and verse the harmonious order of creation.

The search for the hidden order of creation and the longing for belonging and integration remain the foundation of Modernist poetics from beginning to end. In 1907 one of the youngest Modernists, Herrera y Reissig, wrote "Panteo," a poem that expresses, through the figure of Job, his anguished desire to find in the universe a responsive force that converts his insensitive surroundings into a sympathetic companion. In "Panteo" Herrera rejects scientific knowledge in favor of feelings and intuitions and thus, simultaneously, reaffirms the Modernist emphasis on the symbolic, noncognitive comprehension of existence (ellipses in original):

> Sobre el césped mullido que prodiga su alfombra,
> Job, el Mago de acento bronco y de ciencia grave,
> vincula a las eternas maravillas su clave,
> interroga a los astros y en voz alta los nombra . . .
>
> Él discurre sus signos . . . Él exulta y se asombra
> al sentir en la frente como el beso de un ave,
> pues los astros le inspiran con su aliento süave
> y en perplejas quietudes se hipnotiza de sombra.
>
> Todo lo insufla. Todo lo desvanece: el hondo
> silencio azul, el bosque, la Inmensidad sin fondo . . .
> Transustanciado él siente como que no es el mismo,
>
> y se abraza a la tierra con arrobo profundo . . .
> Cuando un grito, de pronto, estremece el abismo:
> ¡y es que Job ha escuchado el latido del mundo![15]

In other poems, Herrera's references are less traditional. The appearance of the Kabbala, Islam, Brahmanism, Zoroaster, Nirvana, and so forth, underscores the dual nature of Modernist syncretism. Not only does it suggest an alternative to the positivistic emphasis on quantifiable truths; it reasserts the poet's freedom to attempt to go beyond the limits of established symbolic codes.

This recognition of the need to explore the "occult" aspects of language and reality continues into the "Postmodernist" period. For example, González Martínez's classic Postmodernist sonnet, "Tuércele el cuello al cisne . . . " (1911), reflects these dominant concerns (ellipsis in original):

> Tuércele el cuello al cisne de engañoso plumaje
> que da su nota blanca al azul de la fuente;
> él pasea su gracia nomás, pero no siente
> el alma de las cosas ni la voz del paisaje.
>
> Huye de toda forma y de todo lenguaje
> que no vayan acordes con el ritmo latente
> de la vida profunda . . . y adora intensamente
> la vida, y que la vida comprenda tu homenaje.
>
> Mira al sapiente búho cómo tiende las alas
> desde el Olimpo, deja el regazo de Palas
> y pasa en aquel árbol el vuelo taciturno . . .
>
> El no tiene la gracia del cisne, mas su inquieta
> pupila, que se clava en la sombra, interpreta
> el misterioso libro del silencio nocturno.[16]

González Martínez is not criticizing Darío's Modernist swan, whose natural grace is the embodiment of the rhythm of the universe. Rather he is reacting against the superficial imitations of Modernist verse which substituted "deceitful plumage" for contact with "the soul of things" and "the voice of the landscape." The Postmodernist rejection of those forms that became hollow echoes of Modernist versification and, therefore, obstacles encumbering the vision of harmony can only be fully understood as a continuation of the Modernist desire to create a living language that captures the rhythm of existence. González Martínez's careful selection of a new emblem highlights this continuity with Modernism. As the Mexican poet acknowledges, the owl does not have the grace of the swan, but its vision can penetrate the dark. The obvious attention to formal beauty is thus replaced by an emphasis on clarity of perception. The underlying faith reflected in this change is that if the order of the universe is perceived, beauty will follow or, in other words, that the universe is perfectly consonant with poetic values.

These views which have their roots in the dual Romantic/esoteric tradition that came to Spanish America from Europe and which have been underscored as the fundamentals of Modernist poetics appear most elaborately and coherently developed in Spanish literature in the writings of Valle-Inclán, particularly in *La lámpara maravillosa*, which was published five years after "Tuércele el cuello al cisne," in 1916. In this aesthetic treatise, Valle-Inclán expresses views on language and the cosmos that set him apart from his Spanish companions. He is less preoccupied with particularistic issues and nationalistic solutions than with the universal concerns and nontraditional answers already established as crucial to Modernism. In *La lámpara maravillosa* he outlines his hopes for integration and harmony and for the achievement of a pristine vision of the universe. His ideas and language reflect the influence of Pythagoreanism, Neoplatonism, Kabbalism, and Eastern religions.

The basis of Valle-Inclán's aesthetics, what he calls "quietismo estético," is the recognition that beauty is a means to salvation through which the poet achieves a timeless fusion with the great soul of the world by reaching beyond words.

> . . . aprendí que los caminos de la belleza son místicos caminos por donde nos alejamos de nuestros fines agoístas [*sic*] para transmigrar en el Alma del Mundo. Esta emoción no puede ser cifrada en palabras. Cuando nos asomamos más allá de los sentidos, experimentamos la angustia de ser mudos. Las palabras son engendradas por nuestra vida de todas las horas, donde las imágenes cambian como las estrellas en las largas rutas del mar, y nos parece que un estado del alma, exento de mudanza, finaría en el acto de ser. Y, sin embargo, ésta es la ilusión fundamental del éxtasis, momento único en que las horas no fluyen y el antes y el después se juntan como las manos para rezar. Beatitud y quietud, donde el goce y el dolor se hermanan, porque todas las cosas al definir su belleza se despojan de la idea del Tiempo.[17]

The poet/seer is aware of the harmony of existence present in microcosmic perfection in all the elements of creation, even in the apparently insignificant grain of wheat. He also has the unusual ability to share this knowledge with the rest of humanity. Valle-Inclán states: "El conocimiento de un grano de trigo, con todas sus evocaciones, nos daría el conocimiento pleno del Universo. . . . Allí donde los demás hombres sólo hallan diferenciaciones, los poetas descubren enlaces luminosos de una armonía oculta. El poeta reduce el número de las alusiones sin transcendencia a una divina alusión cargada de significados. Abeja cargada de miel!"[18] Valle-Inclán's faith in the poet is thus twofold: not only can he read the gestures of the invisible world, but he can also break the restrictive bonds of language by relying on the evocative music of poetry. He therefore synthesizes the revolutionary aspect of Modernist poetics by proposing, "Hagamos de toda nuestra vida a modo de una estrofa, donde el ritmo interior despierta las sensaciones indefinibles aniquilando el significado ideológico de las palabras."[19] For him, as for Darío before him, music is the ideal model for capturing "el número" and "la pautas de las verdades demostradas."[20] At the heart of Valle-Inclán's treatise is the belief that the poet must aspire to create a new language through which an original vision of the world can be achieved. The initiate does not accept previous images of the world, but finds new modes of expression, thereby producing an edenic view of existence in which the unity of creation is expressed in the sexual fusion of form and essence.[21]

Though Valle-Inclán is well established as the most "Modernist" member of the Generation of '98, the common ground shared by writers on both sides of the Atlantic is too extensive to be obscured by generalizations about the different nature of the two groups.[22] A close reading of the poetry of Antonio Machado, for example, reveals links with Modernist verse which confirm the pervasive impact of Modernist solutions. Correa, in a recent article, shows the lasting influence of Darío's Pythagoreanism upon Machado's poetics and demonstrates that music functions as a central metaphor in the Spaniard's poetry.[23] Like Darío before him, Machado holds that the poet must be receptive to the rhythm of life and to the profound truths of the universe thereby communicated. Both poets sought in the music of poetry answers not found in the dry positivism of the nineteenth century. As Cano Ballesta points out, Machado assigns to lyric poetry the mission of capturing existence and time in its perpetual flow; the poet does so under the influence of Bergsonian intuitionism, which proposed an alternative to the mechanistic and static materialism of the day.[24]

Machado found in Bergson's teachings a philosophy based on intuition, that is, on the "immediate consciousness" or direct awareness of reality. The object of such intuition is movement, becoming, and duration, or, in other words, that aspect of existence that is destroyed or distorted by reductive analysis. The human experience of one's own duration is an intuition of the creative activity of the cosmic vital impulse. This Bergsonian concept of *élan vital* is central to Machado's poetic vision and recalls the ancient belief in the soul of the world, which resurfaces throughout Modernist poetry as the cosmic pulse to which poets must attune their art. As a result, though Machado claims to have set a different path for himself from that of Darío, he echoes Darío's concern that the poet write in responsive accord with the profound order of the universe. Machado admits:

> Yo también admiraba al autor de *Prosas profanas*, el maestro incomparable de la forma y de la sensación, que más tarde nos reveló la hondura de su alma en *Cantos de vida y esperanza*. Pero yo pretendí—y reparad en que no me jacto de éxitos, sino de propósitos—seguir camino bien distinto. Pensaba yo que el elemento poético no era la palabra por su valor fónico, ni el color, ni la línea, ni un complejo de sensaciones, sino una honda palpitación del espíritu; lo que pone el alma, si es que algo pone, o lo que dice, si es que algo dice, con voz propia, en respuesta animada al contacto del mundo.[25]

The Modernist search for a new language with which to achieve communion with nature is evident once again a few years later in the poetry of the Generation of '27. Recourse to surrealistic imagery and structural innovation reflects a recognition of the inadequacy of existing patterns of expression. Furthermore, the optimism of the earlier works of the Generation of '27 may be traced to a Romantic faith in a decipherable, orderly universe, whose secrets can be unlocked in and through poetry. By picking up this aspect of Modernism but not adopting overtly occultist thought, the Generation of '27 reaffirms the conservative, traditional nature of Spanish poetry. This conservatism emerged, at least in part, as a response to the radical nature of *vanguardista* or *ultraísta* poetry that reached its greatest popularity in Spain between 1918 and 1921.[26] The struggle to arrive at integration with the universe is strikingly evident, for example, in the poetry of Vicente Aleixandre prior to *Historia del corazón*—in *Ámbito, Pasión de la tierra, Espadas como labios, La destrucción o el amor, Mundo a solas, Sombra del paraíso,* and *Nacimiento último.*

Modernism, therefore, comes to an end not with Postmodernism or the Generation of '27 but with the Vanguardia, in which the search for harmony and unity is converted into an investigation of its loss. This assertion of a sense of loss took the form of protests against previous literary traditions, self-conscious emphasis on the playful, superficial aspects of art, and deliberate attempts to ridicule bourgeois sensibilities as vacuous and stultifying. Thus, when the Modernist legacy of Pythagorean numerology appears in *vanguardista* poetry—such as *Trilce* by César Vallejo—the allusions evoke not a harmonious, ordered, and orderly universe, but rather a world in chaos, abandoned by God.[27] And later, as the anger and indignation of the early Vanguardia subsided, authors continued to find in occultist systems of belief alternative modes of conceiving the role of the individual, language, and the order (or disorder) of the universe. This recourse to occultism is important in the writing of Cortázar, Carpentier, and Borges, to name just a few of the most prominent authors. This recourse also underscores the centrality to Modernism of an aspect of contemporary literature that is often overlooked in the earlier movement, namely, a sense of rupture.

The Modernist attempt to break the dominance of logic and conceptual coherence anticipates the distrust of language that is key to twentieth-century art. As Modernism progressed, the poetic sign became increasingly more hermetic, illogical, anomalous, and removed from natural discourse, and the Modernist poets began to exceed the limits of everyday perception in the hope of reestablishing semantic efficiency.[28] Carlos Fuentes in the concluding section of his *La nueva novela hispanoamericana* emphasizes this aspect of the Spanish American reaction against positivism as crucial to the development of the new novel. The positivistic tradition "concede a la palabra una función amable colindante con la bufonería: el escritor puede divertir, incluso advertir . . . pero no puede, llanamente y sin prefijos, verter. Pero sólo la palabra vertida puede descolorar eso que pasa por 'realidad' para mostrarnos lo real: lo que la 'realidad' consagrada oculta: la totalidad escondida o mutilada por la lógica convencional (por decir: de conveniencia)."[29] But this common point of departure leads in two different directions. Yurkievich, in his perceptive analysis of the dual nature of the absurd, outlines the two paths taken by Spanish American authors. The "positive absurd" liberates poets from empirical causality and allows them by means of unshackled imagination to invent unknown worlds (Huidobro's "Creationism") or to return, through myth, to their origin and primordial source. The "negative absurd" alienates reason and reveals the insignificance of existence and the insurmountable otherness of things (*Trilce, Residence on Earth, Altazor*).[30] For the Modernist— especially Darío—what is imagined to remain imprisoned behind the bondage of habitual categories coincides with ancient images of peace and tranquillity. For the contemporary writer the underlying reality most often does not correspond to any single set of preestablished views; on the contrary, the fundamental truth about life and literature is often conceived of as the inversion of traditional images. The resulting emergence of the unexpected is particularly striking in novels and short stories by Julio Cortázar.[31]

In chapter 99 of *Hopscotch*, Cortázar summarizes his point of view in the discussion among Horacio, Étienne, Gregorovius, Perico, and Babs regarding the inadequacy of language and the need to break through its limitations. Horacio comments upon Morelli's theories:

> The only thing clear in everything that the old man [Morelli] has written is that we still utilize language in its current key, with its current finalities, we shall die without ever knowing the real name of the day. It's almost stupid to repeat that life is sold to us, as Malcolm Lowry said, that it's given to us pre-fabricated. Morelli is also a little stupid when he insists on that, but Étienne has hit the nail on the head: the old man shows himself by the way he does it and he shows us the way out. What good is a writer if he can't destroy literature?

Horacio continues his attack on literature in response to Babs' query about the implications of this approach. Horacio rejects as insufficient the previous view of language that formed the foundation of Romantic, Symbolist, and Modernist poetics. "Until about twenty years ago there was the great answer: Poetry, silly, Poetry. They would gag you with the great word. Poetical vision of the world, conquest of a poetical reality. But then after the last war, you must have noticed that it was all over."[32]

The rejection of language, therefore, is not simply rejection of the dry intellectualization of positivism and its limited perspective; the attack is against all fixed views of reality. Later in the same discussion, Horacio makes clear that his criticism is wide-ranging. "The idea is that reality, whether you accept the version of the Holy See, or of René Char, or of Oppenheimer, is always a conventional reality, incomplete and divided."[33] In agreement with this assessment, Étienne comments: ". . . that true reality, I repeat, is not something that is going to happen, a goal, the last step, the end of an evolution. No, it's something that's already here, in us. You can feel it, all you need is the courage to stick your hand into the darkness."[34] The problem that Étienne's comment highlights and that Cortázar examines throughout *Hopscotch* is that people often do not have the courage to stick a hand into the darkness. Cortázar exposes the possibility not only that modern individuals are incapable of penetrating reality but that they intentionally avoid contact with reality by escaping into habit and routine—the most obvious of which is linguistic.[35]

The modern individual's reluctance to stick a hand into the

darkness is based on fear that the reality that exists behind appearances and established patterns may be so alien as to seem horrible and terrifying.[36] The possibility suggested by the end of the narrative that Horacio's only way of reaching heaven is by falling on his head into the hopscotch reinforces this fearsome vision of "the other side." Also, the possibility suggested by Étienne and agreed to by Horacio that "Right in the middle of the center itself there's probably a perfect emptiness" offers little consolation.[37] Even Horacio, who sees himself as a searcher, recognizes his own ambivalence when it comes to immersing himself in the metaphysical rivers of existence.[38] This hesitancy to go "beyond" is especially evident to him when he compares himself to La Maga: ". . . but once again I imposed the false order that hides chaos, pretending that I was dedicated to a profound existence while all the time it was one that barely dipped its toe into the terrible waters. There are metaphysical rivers, she swims in them like that swallow swimming in the air, spinning madly around a belfry, letting herself drop so that she can rise up all the better with the swoop. I describe and define and desire those rivers, but she swims in them."[39]

In *Hopscotch*, as in Modernist verse, the problem of language is thus linked with the positing of an occult reality. And, as in Modernist verse, *Hopscotch* brings together many forms of the human quest for the beyond: Zen Buddhism, Kabbalism, Chinese philosophy, Zoroastrianism, Orphism, Theosophy, jazz, art, and so forth. In his recent article, Gareth Davies focuses on the influence of the Theosophic basis of abstract art as formulated by Mondrian.[40] In this recourse to occultism in order to discuss the issues of language and reality, Cortázar demonstrates a hidden affinity with Modernism. At no point is this link clearer than in chapter 36, with two references to González Martínez's sonnet "Tuércele el cuello al cisne." While the violent, iconoclastic command that entitles the poem highlights Cortázar's assertion of rupture and transgression, the rest of the poem functions in the novel as a self-reflective and silent commentary on Horacio's search.[41]

As indicated earlier in this chapter, the swan whose neck is to be wrung is of "engañoso plumaje." The bird's offense is deceit or, more specifically, the willingness to use the superficial, attractive niceties of life to hide the deeper and perhaps darker realities of existence. Its neck is to be wrung not simply because it represents established patterns of behavior and expression but because "no siente el alma de las cosas ni la voz del paisaje." Though it masquerades as the Modernist swan, it is not. It is a false, facile copy that fails to embody the order of the universe. Similarly, Horacio—at least the

Horacio of "From the Other Side"—claims to want to come into touch with life, but, more often than not, he fails to emerge from behind established behavioral and linguistic patterns.[42] His attempts to break these molds are often violent affronts to middle-class sensibilities—such as his behavior with the *clocharde* of chapter 36, the chapter in which the sonnet is cited. These attempts are Horacio's wringing of the swan's neck, but the poem's relevance to *Hopscotch* does not stop with the title.

The advice of the second quatrain is particularly poignant for Horacio at the point in the novel when he evokes the sonnet, for Horacio has blocked—willfully or unwittingly—with ideas, books, and assumed roles any direct perception of life. Despite his erudition, he is not the poet/seer that La Maga is, and she tells him so in chapter 3. "'You believe in the principle [that thought must precede action],' said La Maga. 'How complicated. You're like a witness. . . . You think that you're in this room, but you're not. You're looking at the room, you're not in the room.'"[43] Even later, in Argentina, Traveler criticizes Horacio for his way of searching. He tells Horacio, "You're looking for that thing called harmony, but you're looking for it precisely in the place where you just said it didn't exist. . . ."[44] In contrast, it is La Maga who follows the sonnet's command "to adore life intensely" and who, as proposed in the second quatrain, senses that life understands her idiosyncratic praise. She is the one who, in Horacio's words, reaches the great timeless plateaus that the others were all seeking through dialectics.[45]

But the sonnet does not simply underscore Horacio's failings. The point suggested by the final six lines appears to be that, like the owl, Horacio aspires to leave Minerva's lap and "interpret the mysterious book of the nocturnal silence." The owl's greatest strength is not its intellect but its vision. Having left the easy comfort of Pala's protection, Horacio penetrates the dark side of humanity and the mysteries of existence. The final tercet highlights his rejection of traditional paths toward perception. He opts instead to follow the example set by La Maga, whose time is the night.[46] His moments of greatest perception occur during his nocturnal descents into the netherworld of the *clochards* or into the hellish morgue of the insane asylum.[47]

The descent into the basement of the insane asylum represents an entry into the infrastructure of sanity which confines and orders the fluid and unrestrained movement of the darker side of existence. It also represents a descent into that side of life that is simultaneously magic and terror—precisely that side of life personified by Johnny Carter in "El perseguidor." In *Hopscotch*, Cortázar first emphasizes the magic. "In some way they had got into another thing, into that something where one could be dressed in gray and be dressed in pink, where one could have died of drowning in a river . . . and appear in a Buenos Aires night to reproduce on the hopscotch the very image of what they had just attained, the last square, the center of the mandala, the dizzy Ygdrasil through which one came out onto an open beach, an extension without limit, the world beneath the eyelids that the eyes turned inward recognized and obeyed."[48] Yet once the underside of reality is glimpsed, routine crumbles and established molds are shattered. Chapter 56 documents the uneasy tension between magic and terror and highlights —as does Robert Michel's fate in "Las babas del diablo"—the essential impotence of human beings in the face of these unleashed forces. Cortázar appears to suggest that the dissolution of habitual structures exposes a world in which people, as known in Western culture, cannot survive. Only in cases of false success and incomplete penetration of reality—as with Bruno in "El perseguidor"—is one able to continue.

A different perspective on the same issues is provided by Alejo Carpentier in his 1962 novel, *Explosion in a Cathedral*. Like *Hopscotch*, *Explosion in a Cathedral* contains many references to occultism, but with its initial epigraph from *The Zohar*, Carpentier appears to emphasize Kabbalism as the principal esoteric system to which the novel alludes. Basing his analysis of *Explosion in a Cathedral* on the centrality of the Kabbalistic conception of the cosmos, Roberto González Echevarría, in his groundbreaking study of Carpentier's novels, concludes that Carpentier abandons the conceit of writing as the result of the communion between nature and the self and turns instead to a view of the writer as a transmitter of the emanations from a plenum of nothingness. "If Carpentier's fiction in the forties sought its foundation in a theological, transcendental source from which it received order, his new writing will have a much more dialectical conception of the source. . . . In *Explosion in a Cathedral*, for the first time, there is a clear separation between worldly and divine realms. The presence of the Kabbala points precisely at the secondary status of writing and of the world."[49] It does so because it holds that the cosmos emanates from its creator but that the source of that emanation is a void. There develops, as a result, in Carpentier's later novels—beginning with *Explosion in a Cathedral* —a move toward a writing that focuses on the fissure between thought and language and that underlines the hollow materiality of signs.[50]

This aspect of the novel comes to the fore in those sections in which the contemplation of nature does not produce a glimpse of its source but rather elicits a commentary on its derivative signs. In chapter 22, for example, Esteban's enthusiastic response to the "Tree" only allows him to discover in it the basis of later symbols. "The great symbols of the Tau, the Cross of Saint Andrew, the Brazen Serpent, the Anchor and the Ladder, were implicit in every tree, the Created anticipated the Constructed, providing patterns for the future Builder of Arks."[51] Only future echoes of the Tree are perceived. In other words, nature does not refer back to the occult reality from which it emanates but rather projects forward to human constructs.[52] The proliferation of signs emphasizes the development of multiplicity and not, as in the syncretism of Modernism, a rooting in a hidden unity. Thus, while appealing to occultism, Carpentier concludes—in opposition to the earlier optimism of the Romantics, Symbolists, and Modernists—that modern individuals are unable to "read" the symbols of nature. This view of the natural world is juxtaposed with that of the fate of revolutionary symbols. Immediately after his experience with the Tree, Esteban comments, "New-born children were now being called Cincinnatus, Leonidas, or Lycurgus, and were being taught to recite a Revolutionary Catechism which no longer corresponded with reality—just as at the recently formed Jacobin Club they continued to talk about the Incorruptible as if he were still alive."[53] As in nature, the language of the revolution does not refer back to its origins but rather projects forward into a future in which it may or may not coincide with its original intent.[54]

Like Carpentier, Jorge Luis Borges is influenced by the Kabbalistic conception of the role of language in the creation of the universe.[55] And, as in Carpentier's *Explosion in a Cathedral*, the obfuscation of origins and the consequent emphasis on the hollow materiality of signs are central to Borges's short stories. In a coincidence of phrases that highlights the similarity of their perspectives, Carpentier and Borges allude to the human frailties that undermine the continuity of symbolic action. At the beginning of chapter 4 of *Explosion in a Cathedral*, in subchapter 29, Esteban observes a Frenchman's manifestation of religiosity. "He slowly crossed himself, with a movement that was so unusual in these times that Esteban found it the height of originality."[56] In the epigraph to "The Immortal," the first story of *El Aleph*, Borges quotes Francis Bacon, "Salomon saith, *There is no new thing upon the earth.* So that as Plato had an imagination, *that all knowledge was but remembrance; so Salomon giveth his sentence, that all novelty is but oblivion.*"[57] Though the passage from *Explosion in a Cathedral* does not immediately reveal the breadth of the second quote, both authors are alluding to the hollow repercussions of signs. Because of their inability to remember or perceive symbolic links with creation, human beings are cut off from original signification and are forced to make empty gestures that either blindly parallel or parody all that precedes them. These alternatives are summarized by Borges in the fourth section of "The Immortal":

> Death (or its allusion) makes men precious and pathetic. They are moving because of their phantom condition; every act they execute may be their last; there is not a face that is not on the verge of dissolving like a face in a dream. Everything among the mortals has the value of the irretrievable and the perilous. Among the Immortals, on the other hand, every act (and every thought) is the echo of others that preceded it in the past, with no visible beginning, or the faithful presage of others that in the future will repeat it to a vertiginous degree. There is nothing that is not as if lost in a maze of indefatigable mirrors.[58]

Signs, whether in nature or in language, hide the profound reality of existence and human beings—the species—are left to construct symbolic labyrinths which never lead back to the source of meaning.

Jaime Alazraki, in a perceptive comment alluding to Borges's recourse to religious doctrine, underscores the author's lack of faith in human intelligence to go beyond one's own creations:

> Al bajarlas del pedestal divino y convertirlas [las doctrinas religiosas] en literatura fantástica, Borges sublima su escepticismo esencial en arte. En este punto descansa gran parte de su originalidad: al hacer literatura con las doctrinas de la teología y las especulaciones de la filosofía, ha mostrado que su valor reside no en ser la revelación de la voluntad divina o el diseño del esquema universal—tareas que, para Borges, exceden el poder de la inteligencia humana—, sino en ser invenciones o creaciones de la inquieta imaginación de los hombres.[59]

As indicated in this statement, throughout Borges's stories individuals are locked within their humanity unable or unwilling to step "beyond." In "El Aleph" the first interference is linguistic. The narrator cannot hope to capture with language, which is successive and, therefore, partial, what he saw, which was simultaneous and infinite.[60] But in the long run, the narrator rejects his divine vision, preferring instead his human forgetfulness.[61] At the end of the story, he expresses doubts about what he convincingly described earlier. By questioning the existence of the Aleph, which he specifically points out represents the En Soph or unlimited and pure divinity, and by comparing his recollection of the Aleph to the eroded vision of Beatriz, the narrator (Borges) ironically underscores both the generative power of language—its power to create a credible world—and its power of falsification. Linguistic creations—like the development of the story itself—inevitably replace previous conceptions, removing one further from the source.

Moreover, attempts to penetrate into the "beyond," as in "El Aleph" or in Cortázar's *Hopscotch*, offer a fearsome vision. In "The God's Script," the ascension to divinity would lead to the annihilation of the protagonist. In this regard Sosnowski indicates, "Borges parece sugerir que la coexistencia de lo divino y lo humano es imposible, que el hombre deberá optar por una solución, que aun el infierno humano es preferible a un poder que no le pertenece."[62]

This view of what remains hidden behind routine and habitual patterns is antithetical to that held by Darío and other Modernists, who maintained that poetry—specifically the musical nature of poetry—could reveal the order and beauty of the universe that had been shrouded by cognitive constructs. The dual Romantic/esoteric tradition offered a basis for believing in the decipherability of the universe, in other words, that the universe consists of symbols that ultimately lead back to the source. These symbols must simply be discovered and "translated" into human language. The consequent Romantic, Symbolist, and Modernist aspirations to liberate signs from rigid cognition by freely choosing the "right" word or symbol from any of a number of symbolic systems exposed the inherent independence of signs. It thus became possible to conceive of signs as totally removed from original signification. This transition from the struggle to free language from its positivistic limitations to the acceptance of its labyrinthian nature is captured by Borges in his essay "The Mirror of Enigmas."[63] After beginning with the Kabbalistic belief that the sacred scriptures have a symbolic value and with León Bloy's interest in the implications of this assumption, Borges leads the reader away from the supposed interpretability of the universe. He proceeds from a quotation by de Quincy that echoes Modernist tenets. " 'Even the articulate or brutal sounds of the globe must be all so many languages and ciphers that somewhere have their corresponding keys—have their own grammar and syntax; and thus the least things in the universe must be secret mirrors to the greatest.' "[64] Borges concludes with the profound unknowability of existence.

While Darío's faith may appear naive in comparison with Borges's skepticism, his poetic struggle was not. It brought Hispanic poetry into the mainstream of modern literature and opened the way for all that came after.

Notes

1. Modernism and the Romantic/Esoteric Tradition

1. The term "Modernism" is used in this study to refer to the Hispanic literary movement *el modernismo*, which began in Spanish America toward the end of the nineteenth century and should not be confused with the European and Anglo-American movements of the same name. In their article "The Name and Nature of Modernism," Malcolm Bradbury and James McFarlane conclude that the European and Anglo-American movements are characterized by anti-representationalism in painting, atonalism in music, *vers libre* in poetry, and stream-of-consciousness narrative in the novel (in *Modernism*, ed. Malcolm Bradbury and James McFarlane, pp. 19–55). The non-Hispanic Modernisms are therefore closer to Hispanic *vanguardismo*, though all Modernisms share certain features, most notably, an intense awareness of their own modernity. For an insightful study of the development of the concept of modernity and its relationship to the various Modernist movements, see Matei Calinescu, *Faces of Modernity: Avant-Garde, Decadence, Kitsch*.

2. Octavio Paz, "The Siren and the Seashell," in *The Siren and the Seashell and Other Essays on Poets and Poetry*, trans. Lysander Kemp and Margaret Sayers Peden, pp. 52–53. This essay was originally published in Spanish as "El caracol y la sirena," in *Cuadrivio*, pp. 11–65.

3. Ricardo Gullón, "Pitagorismo y modernismo," *Mundo Nuevo*, No. 7 (1967), 22–32; Enrique Anderson Imbert, "Sincretismo religioso," in *La originalidad de Rubén Darío*, pp. 197–213.

4. Miguel de Unamuno's prologue to the poetry of José Asunción Silva, 1918, as quoted in Ned J. Davison, *The Concept of Modernism in Hispanic Criticism*, p. 1.

5. Pedro Salinas, "El problema del modernismo en España, o un conflicto entre dos espíritus," *Literatura española siglo XX*, pp. 13–25; Juan Ramón Jiménez, *El modernismo: Notas de un curso*, ed., Ricardo Gullón and Eugenio Fernández Méndez.

6. Donald L. Shaw, "*Modernismo*: A Contribution to the Debate," *Bulletin of Hispanic Studies*, 46 (1967), 196.

7. Shaw, "*Modernismo*," p. 201.

8. Donald L. Shaw, "Toward the Understanding of Spanish Romanticism," *Modern Language Review,* 58 (1963), 192.

9. Angel del Río, "Present Trends in the Conception and Criticism of Spanish Romanticism," *Romantic Review,* 39 (1948), 239.

10. For later implications of Spanish conservatism, see John W. Kronik, "The Introduction of Symbolism in Spain: A Call to Arms," in *Waiting for Pegasus: Studies in the Presence of Symbolism and Decadence in Hispanic Letters,* ed. Roland Grass and William R. Risley, pp. 31–38.

11. E. A. Peers, *Historia del movimiento romántico español.*

12. See Angel Rama, *Rubén Darío y el modernismo,* p. 26.

13. Gullón, "Pitagorismo y modernismo," p. 54.

14. Rubén Darío, "El pueblo del Polo," *Letras, Obras completas,* I, 545.

15. Octavio Paz, *Children of the Mire: Modern Poetry from Romanticism to the Avant-Garde,* trans. Rachel Phillips, p. vi.

   In simplest terms, the notion of analogy holds that correspondences exist between the material world and spiritual realities. Language is the key that unlocks these hidden relationships. The primary importance of analogy to Romanticism has long been recognized. For example, Morse Peckham reconciles the opinions of Wellek and Lovejoy regarding the fundamental characteristics of Romanticism by demonstrating their origin in dynamic organicism ("Toward a Theory of Romanticism," *PMLA,* 66 [1951], 5–23).

16. For the following discussion of the recourse to esoteric and biblical conceptions of the world by Romantic authors I am particularly indebted to Meyer Howard Abrams's discussion in "The Circuitous Journey: Pilgrims and Prodigals," in his *Natural Supernaturalism: Tradition and Revolution in Romantic Literature,* pp. 141–195. Like Abrams, Gwendolyn Bays, in *The Orphic Vision: Seer Poets from Novalis to Rimbaud,* and Denis Saurat, in *Literature and Occult Tradition: Studies in Philosophical Poetry,* contend that Romantic and Symbolist writings are permeated with Kabbalistic and Hermetic thought. Bays adds Gnosticism, Manicheanism, Pythagoreanism, Mesmerism, and Spiritualism to the occult philosophies that influenced English, German, and French literary creation during the nineteenth century. Saurat underscores the presence of fragments of Madame Blavatsky's summary of occultism in the writings of the period. He sees her importance in the fact that *The Secret Doctrine* distills from a modern perspective all the data found in occult works since the Renaissance as well as a great deal of Indian doctrine, though the fusion of Oriental and occult doctrine is not unique to Madame Blavatsky. Bays notes that "the descent into the self so characteristic of the whole Romantic movement received at least some of its impetus from the large body of Eastern works translated in the late eighteenth century." The translation of Oriental manuscripts "stimulated interest in, and reevaluation of, a more familiar body of Orientalism, the occult doctrines of the Middle East which had existed in Europe since the Middle Ages—Gnosticism, Kabbalism, and Neoplatonism. . . .

These systems were not so unfamiliar to the Western mind and were therefore easier to grasp" (pp. 31, 32–33). John Senior, in *The Way Down and Out: The Occult in Symbolist Literature*, suggests that, among modern occultists, Abbé Alphonse-Louis Constant, better known as Eliphas Lévi, has the single greatest influence on Symbolism. In his various works, Lévi attempts a synthesis of the various kinds of occult thought in an effort to show that the Kabbala is behind all of them. Two other works popular among the Symbolist poets were also based on the Kabbala. They are Stanilas de Guaita's *Au seuil de mystère* and Papus's *Traité élémentaire de science occulte*. See also Theodore W. Jensen's recent article, "*Modernista* Pythagorean Literature: The Symbolist Inspiration," in *Waiting for Pegasus*, pp. 169–179.

17. Abrams, *Natural Supernaturalism*, pp. 170–171.

18. Ibid., p. 169.

19. Wayne Shumaker, *The Occult Sciences in the Renaissance*; François Secret, *Le Zohar chez les kabbalistes chrétiens de la renaissance*; Frances A. Yates, *Giordano Bruno and the Hermetic Tradition*.

20. Meyer Howard Abrams, *The Mirror and the Lamp: Romantic Theory and the Critical Tradition*, pp. 216–218; Abrams, *Natural Supernaturalism*, p. 170.

21. Abrams, *Natural Supernaturalism*, pp. 171–172.

22. Abrams, at the conclusion of *The Mirror and the Lamp*, underscores how Romantic criticism had led to the falling together of poetry and religion, even though the first generation of Romantic critics had kept poetry separate from religion (p. 335).

23. Though it is generally acknowledged that Baudelaire formulated this view of poetry under the influence of the esoteric tradition, especially the writings of Swedenborg, its connection with the expressive theory of the earlier Romantics should not be disregarded. As Abrams notes, "Some romantic extremists, inspired by the philosophy of Fichte, made the work of art out to be, in a fashion even more absolute than the world of perception, an expression of unadulterated spirit." In 1813, Mme. de Staël, in *De l'Allemagne*, a sentimentalized version of the doctrines that she had learned from August Schlegel, writes that to conceive "the true grandeur of lyric poetry, one must wander in thought into the ethereal regions . . . and regard the whole universe as a symbol of the emotions of the soul . . . ; were it not for the difficulties of language he would, like the sybil and the prophets, improvise the sacred hymns of genius" (Abrams, *The Mirror and the Lamp*, pp. 90–91).

24. It should be noted that very early in his career Darío encountered similar ideas about the role of the poet and language in the poetry of Gustavo Adolfo Bécquer. It was not, however, until after his contact with the more sophisticated English and French writers that Darío began to formulate what later would be recognized as the foundations of the Modernist movement.

25. This designation is so common that it is impossible to cite all the critics who have used it; those whose studies are based on the association of

Darío's work with Pythagoreanism are most notably: Gullón in his "Pitagorismo y modernismo," Erika Lorenz in her *Rubén Darío: "Bajo el divino imperio de la música,"* trans. Fidel Coloma González, and Raymond Skyrme in his *Rubén Darío and the Pythagorean Tradition.*

26. The mixing of these four philosophies actually has some basis in history. Pythagoreanism had a strong impact not only on Neo-Pythagoreanism but also on Platonism. Neo-Pythagoreanism, which in turn drew widely on Platonic, Aristotelian, and Stoic beliefs as well as on hermetic literature and the Chaldaic Oracles, prepares the ground for Neoplatonism. As Frederick Copleston, S.J., notes, "In the system of Plotinus, then, the Orphic-Platonic-Pythagorean strain of 'other-worldliness,' intellectual ascent, salvation through assimilation to and knowledge of God, reach their most complete and systematic expression" (Part 2 of *Greece and Rome,* Vol. 1 of *A History of Philosophy,* pp. 190–215).

27. Arturo Marasso, *Rubén Darío y su creación poética,* pp. 12–13. Schuré, as both a poet and an occultist, moved freely in the world of letters and thus enjoyed a unique opportunity for influencing the Symbolists as well.

28. As Annie Besant (with whose writings Darío was familiar) explained, "religions are branches from a common trunk—Divine Wisdom" (*Esoteric Christianity,* p. 6).

29. Schuré, in articles published in *Revue des Deux Mondes* and in *Nouvelle Revue,* wrote: "Today neither the Church, imprisoned in dogma, nor science, locked up inside matter, any longer knows how to make men whole. Science need not change its tradition, but it must understand its origins, its spirit and its significance" (*The Great Initiates: A Study of the Secret History of Religions,* trans. Gloria Rasberry, introd. Paul M. Allen, p. 19).

Attempts to make occultism widely acceptable by demonstrating the overlap between science and religion were extremely common at the end of the nineteenth and beginning of the twentieth century. Many articles in popular journals reflect the desire to legitimize faith in occult phenomena. For example, a series of articles published in *España Moderna* under the heading "Ciencias ocultas" or "Ocultismo" includes accounts of rigorous experiments that take place in the homes of incredulous observers as well as anthropological descriptions of non-European peoples and their unorthodox beliefs. In "Ocultismo" by Fernando Araujo (*España Moderna,* Año 14, Tomo 157 [1902], 206–207) a story published by Professor A. Zuccarelli about a vision he had of his uncle is cited at length. In the article the professor gives a scientific explanation for the transmission of the image, comparing the vibrating waves of clairvoyance with X-rays and wireless telegraphy. In another of his articles on occultism entitled "El más allá" (*España Moderna,* Año 14, Tomo 159 [1902], 190–192) Araujo discusses mediums. He writes, "Cierto o no, ese y los demás descubrimientos de las habilidades de los *medios* de profesión no disminuyen el valor de los muy serios experimentos que no pueden hacer dudar ya de la existencia del más allá á todo espíritu exento de prejuicios." In "El milagro moderno" (*España Moderna*, Año 14, Tomo 160 [1902], 179–182) Araujo comments on the "pequeñas religiones de París." He states that the movements headed by Péladan, Guaita, and Blavatsky are now being investigated by scientific groups that are truly disinterested and critical. His faith in the scientific approach is evident in his belief that these groups will discover ("desocultarán") the occult secrets and that our knowledge of ourselves will gain a great deal. In "La ciencia del soplo: Fakires y yoguis" (*España Moderna*, Año 15, Tomo 176 [1903], 179–186) Araujo reports on an article by Julio Bois published in *La Revue* in which Bois explains in great detail the customs and philosophies of these two groups of Indians. In all, there are at least thirty-nine articles published in *España Moderna* (most of them by Fernando Araujo and many of them based on articles from *La Revue*) from 1901 to 1910.

30. Anderson Imbert, *La originalidad de R. D.*, pp. 203–204.
31. Charles D. Watland, *Poet-Errant: A Biography of Rubén Darío*, p. 44.
32. Rubén Darío, *Autobiografía, Obras completas*, I, 36.
33. Anderson Imbert, *La originalidad de R. D.*, p. 52.
34. Schuré, *The Great Initiates*, p. 314. All further references to this work appear in the text. N.B.: References to Pythagoras, the Pythagoreans, and Pythagoreanism relate, unless otherwise specified, to their meaning within the esoteric tradition.
35. Francis Macdonald Cornford, *Before and After Socrates*, pp. 66–68.
36. A central hypothesis of Raymond Skyrme's study *Rubén Darío and the Pythagorean Tradition* is that under the influence of Pythagoreanism Darío came to equate the ordering principle of the cosmos with music.
37. See Abrams, *The Mirror and the Lamp*, pp. 126–132.
38. Besant, *Esoteric Christianity*, pp. 154–155.
39. Anna Kingsford and Edward Maitland, *The Perfect Way*, p. 333.
40. For the development of the use of the term "love" for this universal "centripetal force" and a discussion of its role in Romantic literature, see Abrams, *Natural Supernaturalism*, pp. 292–299.
41. See Abrams, *Natural Supernaturalism*, chapters 4 and 5, pp. 197–324.
42. Ernest Robert Curtius, *European Literature and the Latin Middle Ages*, trans. Willard R. Trask, pp. 557–558.
43. Paz, *Children of the Mire*, p. 76.
44. Abrams, *Natural Supernaturalism*, p. 447.
45. Abrams points out that the prototype of Rimbaud's poet is to be found in a stubbornly recurrent Christian heresy which asserts not merely the permissibility of sin but also the holiness of sin (*Natural Supernaturalism*, pp. 416–417).
46. Paz, *Children of the Mire*, p. 56.
47. Rubén Darío, "Dilucidaciones," *El canto errante, Poesías completas*, ed. Alfonso Méndez Plancarte, augmented by Antonio Oliver Belmás, pp. 699–711. All further references to Darío's *Poesías completas* appear in the text.
48. Paz, *The Siren and the Seashell*, p. 29.

49. Severo Sarduy, Tomás Segovia, and Emir Rodríguez Monegal, "Nuestro Rubén Darío," *Mundo Nuevo*, No. 7 (1967), 36.
50. See Abrams, "Romantic Analogues of Art and Mind," *The Mirror and the Lamp*, pp. 47–69.
51. This variation of "La fuente" is found in both *Prosas profanas, Obras completas*, and *Poesía*, V, 848, ed. Ernesto Mejía Sánchez. In the version in *Poesías completas* line 6 begins with "basta" instead of "busca."
52. Paz, *The Siren and the Seashell*, p. 37.
53. This point of view is presented by Stephanie Merrim in "Darío and Breton: Two Enigmas," *Latin American Literary Review*, 4, No. 9 (1976), 48–62, and by Paz in *The Siren and the Seashell*, p. 39.
54. Alan W. Watts, *Myth and Ritual in Christianity*, p. 47.
55. See Abrams, "The Poem as Heterocosm," *The Mirror and the Lamp*, pp. 272–285.
56. Paz, *Children of the Mire*, p. 77.
57. Rubén Darío, *Obras desconocidas: Escritas en Chile y no recopiladas en ninguno de sus libros*, ed. Raúl Silva Castro, pp. 168–169, 170; my italics.
58. Merrim, "Darío and Breton," p. 56.
59. An interesting Marxist interpretation of the Modernist's struggle to find a place in society is provided by Françoise Pérus in *Literatura y sociedad en América latina: El modernismo.*
60. Alberto Zum Felde, *Crítica de la literatura uruguaya*, p. 201, as quoted in Davison, *The Concept of Modernism*, p. 27; Paz, *Children of the Mire*, pp. 88–89.
61. Zum Felde, *Crítica de la literatura uruguaya*, p. 43, as quoted in Davison, *The Concept of Modernism*, p. 30.

2. Esoteric Pythagoreanism in Darío's Vision of the Universe

1. Pedro Salinas, *La poesía de Rubén Darío*, pp. 283–286.
2. Miguel Enguídanos, "Inner Tensions in the Work of Rubén Darío," *Rubén Darío Centennial Studies*, trans. Cecile Wiseman, ed. Miguel González-Gerth and George D. Schade, pp. 14–15.
3. At the height of his career, Darío recalled from his childhood that he often withdrew from merriment and went all by himself to look at things in the sky and sea because of his sad and pensive nature. He adds: "Debo decir que desde niño se me infundió una gran religiosidad que llegaba a veces hasta la superstición" (Rubén Darío, *Autobiografía, Obras completas*, I, 28–29).
4. Rubén Darío, *Poesías completas*, ed. Alfonso Méndez Plancarte, augmented by Antonio Oliver Belmás, pp. 248–251. Quotations in the text are from this edition.
5. While in El Salvador from 1882 to 1883, Darío came to know Hugo's poetry well under the tutelage of Francisco Gavidia and undoubtedly was exposed to Hugo's pantheistic and gnostic beliefs—many of which stemmed from his readings of occultist literature (Enrique Anderson Im-

bert, *La originalidad de Rubén Darío*, pp. 21, 24–25). By 1888, when he wrote "Catulle Mendès: Parnasianos y decadentes," Darío already had a sound understanding of Symbolist aesthetics.

6. Edouard Schuré, *The Great Initiates: A Study of the Secret History of Religions*, trans. Gloria Rasberry, intro. Paul M. Allen, pp. 331–339.

7. Arturo Marasso, "Nuevos aspectos de Rubén Darío: La canción de los osos: Filosofía y hermetismo," *La Nación*, Buenos Aires, 22 julio 1951, 53. Although Marasso acknowledges the presence of occultist themes in the poem, he fails to explore the fundamental role that esoteric tradition had in the poem's formulation and execution. See also Arturo Marasso, *Rubén Darío y su creación poética*, pp. 73–108, and the more recent "El universo el verso de su música activa" by Guillermo Sucre in *La máscara, la transparencia: Ensayos sobre poesía hispanoamericana*, pp. 35–38. Other studies of "Coloquio" have focused almost exclusively on the question of literary sources and models. María Teresa Maiorana, for example, discusses the poem in comparison with "Le centaure" by Maurice de Guérin, "La mort du centaure" by Luis de Ronchard, and "La Grèce et la Sicile" by J. M. de Hérédia ("'El coloquio de los centauros' de Rubén Darío," *Boletín de la Academia Argentina de Letras*, 23 [1958], 185–263). Réné Durand sees Darío's centaurs as the product of a long tradition as well as of immediate literary and cultural trends ("El motivo del centauro y la universalidad de Rubén Darío," *La Torre*, 15 [1967], 71–97). Marie-Josèphe Faurie examines the French sources of "Coloquio" in *Le modernisme hispano-américain et ses sources françaises*, pp. 29–48. Arturo Echevarría takes as his point of departure the poem's mythological sources. He then proceeds to develop insightful observations regarding its structure and central themes ("Estructura y sentido poético del 'Coloquio de los centauros,'" *La Torre*, 17 [1969], 95–130).

8. Rubén Darío, *Historia de mis libros, Obras completas*, I, 209.

9. For example, Salinas, in his summary statement, indicates a similar split in the nature of Darío's eroticism: "Pero este eroticismo rubeniano, ése tan complejo, por razón de su naturaleza trágica y agónica, de su condición insatisfactoria, funciona con respecto a las potencias del ser humano, por modo centrífugo, impulsándolas del otro lado de la raya de su círculo lindante, disparándolas ansiosamente hacia otro espacio. Por eso se le puede dar como última y definitiva calificación la de *lo erótico transcendente*" (*La poesía de R. D.*, pp. 208–209). In his discussion of the figure of the centaur, however, his emphasis is slightly different. He indicates a split between "lo erótico del animal" and "lo humano." ". . . lo erótico del animal—fuerza ciega del instinto, poder bruto—se combina con lo humano, significando la dualidad que yace en el amor, lo posesivo puro, animal, y algo que es superior, que está por encima, lo puesto por el hombre" (*La poesía de R. D.*, p. 93).

10. Maiorana, "'El coloquio de los centauros' de R. D.," p. 192.

11. Darío, *Historia*, p. 209.

12. Alan S. Trueblood, "Rubén Darío: The Sea and the Jungle," *Comparative Literature Studies*, 4 (1967), 427.

13. Trueblood, "R. D.: The Sea and the Jungle," pp. 431–432.

14. Tomás Navarro Tomás, *Métrica española: Reseña histórica y descriptiva*, pp. 420–421.

15. Raymond Skyrme in *Rubén Darío and the Pythagorean Tradition* compares this passage with Baudelaire's "Correspondances" and Hugo's attempts to "lire / Dans cet hiéroglyphe énorme: l'univers" (pp. 20–21, 30–31).

16. Skyrme, *R. D. and the Pythagorean Tradition*, p. 27. Similar ideas are developed in chapter 5, "Paradise Found: Sexual Love in Esoteric Tradition."

17. As Marasso indicates, not only did Darío take characters from *The Metamorphoses*, but, what is more, he incorporated many of their stories into the poem, *Rubén Darío*, pp. 79, 96.

18. Darío's affirmation that Venus was born of the blood of Uranus, who was Chiron's grandfather, is not altogether accurate. As Marasso notes, this misconception came from Hérédia's sonnet, "La naissance d'Aphrodite," *Rubén Darío*, p. 84.

19. Marasso identifies many likely sources for the images used by Quirón in the passage describing the birth of Venus: "Darío en el elogio de Venus, está cerca de Hesíodo y del himno a Venus del *Khirón* de Leconte de Lisle, sin olvidar a Lucrecio: *Hominum divumque voluptas, Alma Venus*. Laurant Tailhade escribió con este encabezamiento un *Hymne a Aphrodite*. . . . En los alejandrinos descriptivos de Venus y de su cortejo marino, el poeta no olvida el siglo XVIII, la apoteosis de la diosa en los cuadros de Albani y de Boucher que reproduce Ménard en su *Mitología*; el poeta adapta algunas expresiones del texto de Ménard y de la explicación de la pintura: 'hocicos de hipocampos', 'tritónicas melènas.'" Marasso also recalls the unforgettable painting by Botticelli (*Rubén Darío*, p. 84).

20. Schuré, *The Great Initiates*, pp. 315–316.

21. Cf. "Yo soy aquel que ayer no más decía," in which Darío wrote (p. 629):
    Mas, por gracia de Dios, en mi conciencia
    el Bien supo elegir la mejor parte;
    y si hubo áspera hiel en mi existencia,
    melificó toda acritud el Arte.

22. Ovid, *The Metamorphoses*, trans. Horace Gregory, p. 331.

23. J. E. Cirlot, *A Dictionary of Symbols*, trans. Jack Sage, p. 173.

24. Edith Hamilton, *Mythology*, p. 271.

25. Marasso suggests Lucian as a primary influence, but the consequent conclusion that Quirón opted to die in order to escape the monotony of life is not in keeping with the rest of the poem (*Rubén Darío*, p. 75).

26. Schuré, *The Great Initiates*, pp. 339, 340.

27. Cf. "Helios" (pp. 643–645) and analysis in chapter 6.

28. Trueblood, "R. D.: The Sea and the Jungle," p. 430.

29. G. S. Kirk and J. E. Raven, *The Presocratic Philosophers*, p. 228.

30. Ibid., p. 228.

31. Ricardo Gullón points out that Modernists held this belief to be central to both Pythagoreanism and their own poetic creation ("Pitagorismo y modernismo," *Mundo Nuevo*, No. 7, [1967], 23).

32. Francisco Rico in *El pequeño mundo del hombre* sees this point as the core of the poem's meaning and calls "Ama tu ritmo . . . " "una declaración de la microcosmía humana, en los términos familiares de la estirpe pitagórica" (p. 287).

33. Although Marasso suggests that the "irradiación geométrica" is the rays given off by or the illumination from the divine idea, the universal monad (*Rubén Darío*, p. 162), it seems more likely that, with the use of the adjective "nocturna," Darío was referring to the night sky. However, the two views are easily reconciled. One need only recall that the universe is created in God's image and that the harmony seen there is patterned on the harmony inherent in God.

34. Cf. Darío's use of this image in two of his earlier "Rimas" (pp. 501, 507).

35. *Rubén Darío: "Bajo el divino imperio de la música,"* trans. Fidel Coloma González, pp. 31–32.

36. Sucre, *La máscara, la transparencia*, p. 42.

37. Cf. "Revelación" (lines 7–9): "Y sentí que sorbía en sal y viento / como una comunión de comuniones / que en mí hería sentido y pensamiento" (p. 712).

38. The tortuga is not merely, as suggested by Erika Lorenz, the symbol of the lyre, the body of which was originally a tortoise's shell.

39. Skyrme presents a detailed study of "La tortuga de oro . . . " as a key example of the fusion of the principles of mystery and music in Darío's conception of "la concorde unidad del universo" (*R. D. and the Pythagorean Tradition*, pp. 33–43).

40. Octavio Paz explains, "The divine work is the cyclic revolution that places what was down, up, and obliges everything to be transformed into its opposite: it immolates the Minotaur and petrifies Medusa" (*The Siren and the Seashell and Other Essays on Poets and Poetry*, trans. Lysander Kemp and Margaret Sayers Peden, p. 53).

41. In "La espiga," as we saw above, the ear of wheat is seen as a golden brush with which the fingers of the wind paint upon the blue canvas of the sky.

42. Marasso, *Rubén Darío*, p. 245.

43. Trueblood, "R. D.: The Sea and the Jungle," p. 443.

3. "Under the Sign of a Supreme Destiny": Reincarnation and Poetic Responsibility

1. Rubén Darío, *Historia de mis libros, Obras completas*, I, 223.

2. Enrique Anderson Imbert, *La originalidad de Rubén Darío*, p. 130.

3. Anna Kingsford and Edward Maitland, *The Perfect Way*, p. 24. Although the fundamental concepts regarding the transmigration of souls hardly vary within the broad range of occultist literature, the following discus-

sion of reincarnation is taken from Schuré's statement on the evolution of the soul, a statement that had a strong influence on Darío (Edouard Schuré, *The Great Initiates: A Study of the Secret History of Religions*, trans. Gloria Rasberry, intro. Paul M. Allen, pp. 320–345).

4. The most noteworthy example of Darío's reference to Buddha appears in "A la razón," in which "Cristo, Vichnú, Budha y Brahama" are overthrown by reason (Rubén Darío, *Poesías completas*, ed. Alfonso Méndez Plancarte, augmented by Antonio Oliver Belmás, p. 28).

5. Gullón also sees in this association "el desinterés de los poetas por la coherencia lógica; estaban interesados—y eso les bastaba—en la coherencia del sentimiento" ("Pitagorismo y modernismo," *Mundo Nuevo*, No. 7 [1967], 25).

6. Joseph L. Henderson, in "Ancient Myths and Modern Man," underscores this point. "It is this finality of the Christian concept of the resurrection (the Christian idea of the Last Judgment has a similar 'closed' theme) that distinguishes Christianity from the other god-king myths. It happened once, and the ritual merely commemorates it. But this sense of finality is probably one reason why early Christians, still influenced by pre-Christian traditions, felt that Christianity needed to be supplemented by some elements of an older fertility ritual. They needed the recurring promise of rebirth; and that is what is symbolized by the egg and the rabbit of Easter" (in *Man and His Symbols*, ed. Carl G. Jung et al., p. 108).

7. Anderson Imbert, in his analysis of "Yo persigo una forma," makes this point with references to "La fuente" ("Joven . . . la fuente está en ti mismo") and "Yo soy aquel que ayer no más decía" ("el agua dice el alma de la fuente / en la voz de cristal que fluye d'ella"), *La originalidad de R. D.*, p. 101.

8. See J. E. Cirlot's discussion of the forest symbolism in *A Dictionary of Symbols*, trans. Jack Sage, p. 107.

9. These associations with the figures of Pan and Apollo in the poetry of Rubén Darío are studied by Alejandro Hurtado Chamorro, *La mitología griega en Rubén Darío*, pp. 125, 132–133, 140, by Dolores Ackel Fiore in *Rubén Darío in Search of Inspiration (Greco-Roman Mythology in His Stories and Poetry)*, pp. 121–122, and by Erika Lorenz, *Rubén Darío: "Bajo el divino imperio de la música,"* trans. Fidel Coloma González, pp. 37, 39–40.

10. Anderson Imbert, *La originalidad de R. D.*, XIII, 141–147.

11. Ibid., p. 147.

12. Carlos D. Hamilton points out that Mallorca "tuvo tal fuerza de purificación para el alma del poeta enfermo y triste sin ya más primavera que cantar . . . , que llegó a hacer estallar en él una crisis religiosa y moral, en una accidentada y atormentada 'conversión'" ("Rubén Darío en la Isla de Oro," *Cuadernos Hispanoamericanos*, Nos. 212–213 [1967], 567; ellipsis in original).

13. *La poesía de Rubén Darío*, p. 172.

14. "The Siren and the Seashell," in *The Siren and the Seashell and Other*

Essays on Poets and Poetry, trans. Lysander Kemp and Margaret Sayers Peden, p. 55.

15. Cirlot, *A Dictionary of Symbols,* p. 143.

4. The Poet as Magus: Deciphering the Universe

1. Meyer Howard Abrams, *The Mirror and the Lamp: Romantic Theory and the Critical Tradition,* p. 335.
2. Marcel Raymond, *From Baudelaire to Surrealism,* p. 2.
3. Maurice Z. Shroder, *Icarus: The Image of the Artist in French Romanticism,* p. 67.
4. For a discussion of Hugo's profound involvement with the occult, see John Senior, *The Way Down and Out: The Occult in Symbolist Literature.*
5. Shroder, *Icarus,* pp. 67–68.
6. Annie Besant, *Esoteric Christianity,* pp. 154–155.
7. Anna Kingsford and Edward Maitland, *The Perfect Way,* pp. 333–334.
8. See "El poeta" (1880, pp. 8–9), "Ingratitud" (1882, pp. 13–14), "El poeta" (1882, p. 14), "El poeta" (pp. 240–244), "Introducción" to *Epístolas y poemas* (1885, pp. 323–329), "El arte" (pp. 442–452), *Poesías completas,* ed. Alfonso Méndez Plancarte, augmented by Antonio Oliver Belmás. All further references to Darío's *Poesías completas* appear in the text. See also "El rey burgués" and "El sátiro sordo," *Cuentos completos,* ed. Ernesto Mejía Sánchez, pp. 57, 113.
9. Besant, *Esoteric Christianity,* p. 154.
10. Cf. analysis of "Ama tu ritmo . . . " in chapter 2.
11. J. E. Cirlot, *A Dictionary of Symbols,* trans. Jack Sage, p. 240; Dolores Ackel Fiore, *Rubén Darío in Search of Inspiration,* p. 105.
12. As Abrams points out, the importance of "sincerity" to poetry was a natural corollary of the expressive poetics of the Romantics. Carlyle, for example, held that sincerity was the chief measure of his hero, whether in the avatar of prophet, priest, or poet (*The Mirror and the Lamp,* pp. 317, 319). Anderson Imbert sees in Darío's emphasis on sincerity an echo of Verlaine's "Art Poétique," in which the French poet proclaims, "Et tout le rest est littérature" (*La originalidad de Rubén Darío,* p. 122).
13. See analysis of "Ama tu ritmo . . . " in chapter 2.
14. For the role of the apocalypse in Western culture see Abrams, *The Mirror and the Lamp,* pp. 37–38.
15. See analysis of "Alma mía" in chapter 3.
16. See analysis of "En las constelaciones" and "La tortuga de oro" in chapter 2.
17. Julio Ycaza Tigerino, *Los nocturnos de Rubén Darío y otros ensayos,* p. 20.

5. Paradise Found: Sexual Love in Esoteric Tradition

1. Edouard Schuré, *The Great Initiates: A Study of the Secret History of Religions,* trans. Gloria Rasberry, intro. Paul M. Allen, p. 315.
2. For the Neoplatonic basis for Romantic recourse to this image, see

Meyer Howard Abrams, *Natural Supernaturalism: Tradition and Revolution in Romantic Literature*, pp. 152–154.

3. Alan W. Watts, *Myth and Ritual in Christianity*, p. 47. See discussion of the identification of woman and poetry in chapter 1.

4. Guillermo Sucre, *La máscara, la transparencia: Ensayos sobre poesía hispanoamericana*, p. 43.

5. Anna Kingsford, *Clothed with the Sun*, p. 257.

6. Abrams, *Natural Supernaturalism*, IV and V, 197–324.

7. Sucre, *La máscara, la transparencia*, p. 43.

8. Guillermo Díaz-Plaja, *Modernismo frente a noventa y ocho*, p. 148; Graciela Palau de Nemes, "Tres momentos del neomisticismo poético del 'siglo modernista': Darío, Jiménez y Paz," in *Estudios sobre Rubén Darío*, ed. Ernesto Mejía Sanchez, pp. 536–552.

   Mysticism is generally held to be the doctrine or belief that through contemplation and love a person can achieve a direct and immediate consciousness of God or of divine truth without the use of reason or any of the ordinary senses. It is in this sense, which bears no necessary connection to Catholic dogma, that the term is used.

9. Pedro Salinas, *La poesía de Rubén Darío*, pp. 66, 205. Along similar lines, Skyrme suggests that "Whatever physical stimulus the man may have found in woman, the poet certainly saw in the female body the incarnation of the enigma of the universe, and in the act of love a sacrament of communion with its motive spirit, music and mystery in one. . . ." (*Rubén Darío and the Pythagorean Tradition*, p. 27).

10. Enrique Anderson Imbert, *La originalidad de Rubén Darío*, pp. 89–90; Octavio Paz, *The Siren and the Seashell and Other Essays on Poets and Poetry*, trans. Lysander Kemp and Margaret Sayers Peden, pp. 50–51.

11. Rubén Darío, *Abrojos, Poesías completas*, ed. Alfonso Méndez Plancarte, augmented by Antonio Oliver Belmás, pp. 463–464; also "A Emelina," p. 157, and "Rimas," pp. 509–511. All further references to Darío's *Poesías completas* appear in the text.

12. Rubén Darío, *El oro de Mallorca*, quoted from the article by Max Henríquez Ureña, "En torno a las prosas de Rubén Darío," *La Torre*, 15 (1967), 175.

13. Pedro Salinas has called this phenomenon "lo erótico insuficiente." Salinas holds that the presence of death in the act of creation, the fleeting gratification, and the aftertaste of guilt color Darío's entire poetic production. This dissatisfaction led Darío, according to Salinas, through a psychologically complicated process, to find a means of transcending the erotic without dismissing it (Salinas, *La poesía de R. D.*, pp. 205–211).

14. This identification of woman and art had already appeared in Bécquer's poetry, most notably in the famous "Poesía . . . eres tú" of Rima XXI. As a result, this image began to develop in Darío's poetic imagination rather early. It is, for example, central to "Sonatina" (pp. 556–557) (see Anderson Imbert *La originalidad de R. D.*, pp. 85–86) and to "El cisne" (pp. 587–588).

15. Arturo Marasso, *Rubén Darío y su creación poética*, p. 252.
16. Dolores Ackel Fiore, *Rubén Darío in Search of Inspiration (Greco-Roman Mythology in his Stories and Poetry)*, p. 142.
17. Anna Kingsford and Edward Maitland, in *The Perfect Way*, offer an example of the use of this occult metaphor (p. 350):
    I am the Dawn, Daughter of Heaven and of the Deep: the sea-mist covers my beauty with a veil of tremulous light.
    I am Aphrodite, the sister of Phoibas, opener of Heaven's gates, the beginning of Wisdom, the herald of the Perfect Day.
    Long had darkness covered the deep: the Soul of all things slumbered: the valleys were filled with shadows: only the mountains and the stars held commune together. . . .
    Then from the Deep I arose, dispeller of Night: the firmament of heaven kindled with joy beholding me.
18. Anderson Imbert, *La originalidad de R. D.*, pp. 45–46.
19. Rubén Darío, *Historia de mis libros*, *Obras completas*, I, 207–208.
20. Salinas discusses the multiplication of the single beloved, *La poesía de R. D.*, pp. 130–135.
21. Darío describes Venus rising out of the sea at birth in "Coloquio de los centauros"; in "¡Carne, celeste carne de la mujer!"; and in an unpublished poem which ends:
    Yo no sé en que dulce horizonte
    nunca he podido separar
    a Cristo en su cruz en el monte
    y a mi Venus sobre el mar.
    See Fiore, *R. D. in Search of Inspiration*, p. 145.
22. Anderson Imbert, *La originalidad de R. D.*, p. 92.
23. J. E. Cirlot, *A Dictionary of Symbols*, trans. Jack Sage, p. 338.

6. Toward a Syncretic World View

1. Ned J. Davison, *The Concept of Modernism in Hispanic Criticism*, p. 22.
2. Octavio Paz, "The Siren and the Seashell," in *The Siren and the Seashell and Other Essays on Poets and Poetry*, trans. Lysander Kemp and Margaret Sayers Peden, pp. 23–25.
3. Rubén Darío, "Máximo Jérez" and "A la razón," *Poesías completas*, ed. Alfonso Méndez Plancarte, augmented by Antonio Oliver Belmás, pp. 22–26, 27–28. All further references to Darío's *Poesías completas* appear in the text.
4. Rubén Darío, *Cuentos completos*, ed. Ernesto Mejía Sánchez, p. 163.
5. Rubén Darío, "Leconte de Lisle," *Los raros*, *Obras completas*, II, 277.
6. Rubén Darío, "Jean Moréas," *Los raros*, pp. 361–362.
7. A summary of this criticism can be found in A. J. Carlos, "La cruz en el 'Responso a Verlaine,'" *Hispania*, 48 (1965), 226–229.
8. Rubén Darío, *Historia de mis libros*, *Obras completas*, I, 211.
9. See Alan S. Trueblood, "El 'Responso' a Verlaine y la elegía pastoril tra-

dicional," *Actas del Tercer Congreso Internacional de Hispanistas*, pp. 861–870.

10. Trueblood, "El 'Responso,'" p. 869.
11. Arturo Marasso, *Rubén Darío y su creación poética*, p. 154.
12. Enrique Anderson Imbert, *La originalidad de Rubén Darío*, p. 98.
13. Tomás Navarro Tomás, *Métrica española: Reseña histórica y descriptiva*, pp. 419–423.
14. Clara Erskine Clement, *A Handbook of Christian Symbols and Stories of the Saints*, p. 9.
15. Clement, *A Handbook*, p. 9.
16. See M. Louise Solstad, "Sun Motifs in Sixteenth-Century Spanish Religious Poetry," *Bulletin of Hispanic Studies*, 40 (1978), 211–230.
17. Annie Besant, *Esoteric Christianity*, pp. 109–110.
18. Manly P. Hall, *An Encyclopedic Outline of Masonic, Hermetic, Qabbalistic and Rosicrucian Symbolical Philosophy*, p. xlix. J. E. Cirlot comments: "With his 'youthful' and filial characteristics, the Sun is associated with the hero, as opposed to the father, who connotes the heavens, although the two (sun and sky) are sometimes equated" (*A Dictionary of Symbols*, trans. Jack Sage, p. 302).
19. Hall, *An Encyclopedic Outline*, p. l; Cirlot, *A Dictionary of Symbols*, p. 303.
20. Navarro Tomás, *Métrica española*, p. 449.
21. Hall, *An Encyclopedic Outline*, p. cxxxix.
22. W. K. C. Guthrie, *The Greeks and Their Gods*, pp. 319–320.
23. See reading of "Pegaso" in chapter 4.
24. Hall, *An Encyclopedic Outline*, p. lxxxix.
25. Cirlot, *A Dictionary of Symbols*, p. 87.
26. Ibid., p. 303.
27. Ibid., p. 268.
28. Though "mas" appears in Darío's *Poesías completas* with an accent, the internal logic of the poem dictates its elimination. Ernesto Mejía Sánchez removed the accent in the Biblioteca Ayacucho edition of Darío's *Poesía* (p. 259).
29. See comments on "Reino interior" (pp. 603–605) and "Divina Psiquis" (pp. 665–666) in chapter 3.
30. Alan W. Watts, *Myth and Ritual in Christianity*, pp. 46–47. Cf. "El poeta pregunta por Stella" (p. 580).
31. Cf. stanza 37 of "Poema del otoño" (p. 775).
32. See Paz, "The Siren and the Seashell," pp. 23–25.

7. Modernism and Its Legacy

1. The most famous exponent of the reaction theory is Federico de Onís, *Antología de la poesía española e hispanoamericana, 1882–1932*, p. xiii.
2. See Edgardo Buitrago, "Consideraciones polémicas acerca de la vigencia y actualidad de Rubén Darío," in *Estudios sobre Rubén Darío*, ed. Ernesto Mejía Sánchez, pp. 596–625.

3. Roland Grass and William R. Risley (eds.), *Waiting for Pegasus: Studies of the Presence of Symbolism and Decadence in Hispanic Letters,* pp. 11–12.

4. Ricardo Gullón, "Pitagorismo y modernismo," *Mundo Nuevo,* No. 7 (1967), 24–25.

5. Theodore W. Jensen, "El pitagorismo en *Las fuerzas extrañas* de Lugones," in *Otros mundos otros fuegos: Fantasía y realismo mágico en Iberoamérica,* Memoria del XVI Congreso Internacional de Literatura Iberoamericana, ed. Donald A. Yates, pp. 299–307; Carol S. Maier, "Valle-Inclán y *La lámpara maravillosa*: Una poética iluminada," Diss. Rutgers 1975; Emma Susana Sperrati-Piñero, *El ocultismo en Valle-Inclán;* Antonio Risco, *El demiurgo y su mundo: Hacia un nuevo enfoque de la obra de Valle-Inclán.*

6. Theodore W. Jensen, "*Modernista* Pythagorean Literature: The Symbolist Inspiration," in *Waiting for Pegasus: Studies of the Presence of Symbolism and Decadence in Hispanic Letters,* ed. Grass and Risley, p. 172; Ivan Schulman, "Modernismo, revolución y pitagorismo en Martí," *Casa de las Américas,* No. 73 (1972), 45–55.

7. "Génesis del azul modernista," in *Estudios críticos sobre el modernismo,* ed. Homero Castillo, pp. 168–189.

8. José Martí, *Poesías completas,* prólogo y notas de Luis Alberto Ruiz, p. 82.

9. Martí, *Poesías completas,* p. 182.

10. Ibid., p. 139.

11. Amado Nervo, *Obras completas,* ed. Francisco González Guerrero and Alfonso Méndez Plancarte, II, 651.

12. Amado Nervo, *Poemas,* p. 92.

13. Ibid., pp. 95–96.

14. Ibid., pp. 139–151.

15. Julio Herrera y Reissig, *Poesías completas,* pp. 158–159.

16. Enrique González Martínez, *Poesías completas,* p. 135.

17. Ramón del Valle-Inclán, *Obras completas,* II, 563.

18. Ibid., p. 567.

19. Ibid., p. 568.

20. Ibid., p. 570.

21. Ibid., pp. 578, 581, 591, 617. Valle-Inclán, like Darío, incorporates into his poetics a sexual view of the universe derived from occultism. He refers to the "concepto teológico del logos espermático" (*Obras completas,* pp. 571, 572).

22. An early study by Guillermo Díaz-Plaja (*Modernismo frente a noventa y ocho*) set the pattern for contrasting generalizations about the two groups.

23. Gustavo Correa, "Una 'lira inmensa': El ritmo de la muerte y de la resurrección en la poesía de Antonio Machado," in *Estudios sobre Antonio Machado,* ed. José Angeles, pp. 121–162.

24. Juan Cano Ballesta, "Antonio Machado y la crisis del hombre moderno," in *Estudios sobre Antonio Machado,* ed. José Angeles, pp. 73–96.

25. Antonio Machado, "Prólogo a *Soledades*" in *Páginas escogidas*, ed. Calleja, as quoted in *Antología de su prosa*, ed. Aurora de Albornoz, II, 106.
26. Andrew P. Debicki highlights this contrast in his *Estudios sobre poesía española contemporánea: La generación de 1924–1925*, p. 43. Debicki adds: "Surgen [los poetas que estoy estudiando] más bien arraigados en la tradición hispánica, y en vez de alzarse contra esto o aquello están inspirados por un deseo positivo de crear un arte trascendente. Frente a los 'ultraístas' parecen un movimiento de afirmación de lo positivo, de profundización, de interiorización."
27. See Eduardo Neale-Silva, "Pitagorismo: Esencia e imagen," in *César Vallejo en su fase trílcica*, pp. 507–529.
28. Saúl Yurkievich develops this point in the second chapter of his book *Celebración del modernismo*, pp. 11–23. In this work Yurkievich adopts a forward-looking perspective and "celebrates" Modernism as Spanish America's entrance into the modern era. In particular, he focuses on features that are fundamental to the Vanguardia and that first appear in Modernist poetry.
29. Fuentes, *La nueva novela hispanoamericana*, p. 85.
30. Yurkievich, *Celebración del modernismo*, p. 17.
31. See Sara Castro-Klarén's discussion of Cortázar's view of reality in "Ontological Fabulation: Toward Cortázar's Theory of Literature," in *The Final Island: The Fiction of Julio Cortázar*, ed. Jaime Alazraki and Ivar Ivask, pp. 140–150.
32. Julio Cortázar, *Hopscotch*, trans. Gregory Rabassa, p. 451.
33. Ibid., p. 454.
34. Ibid., p. 455.
35. The second epigraph to the novel, from César Bruto's *What I Would Like to Be If I Wasn't What I Am*, refers to this escape into habit and human surrender to weakness. The last sentence of the section quoted underscores the role of individual responsibility. "I jes hope what I been writin down hear do somebody some good so he can take a good look at how he livin and he dont be sorry when it too late and everythin is gone down the drain cause it his own fault" (Cortázar, *Hopscotch*, n.p.).
36. "Behind" or "beyond" is the metaphor used by Cortázar, who, even in the Spanish version, indicates a preference for the English "yonder" (Cortázar, *Hopscotch*, p. 443).
37. Cortázar, *Hopscotch*, p. 177.
38. "It was about that time I realized that searching was my symbol, the emblem of those who go out at night with nothing in mind, the motives of a destroyer of compasses" (Cortázar, *Hopscotch*, p. 16).
39. Cortázar, *Hopscotch*, pp. 105–106.
40. Gareth A. Davies, "Mondrian, Abstract Art, and Theosophy in Julio Cortázar's *Rayuela*," *Proceedings of the Leeds Philosophical and Literary Society*, 16, Part 6, 127–147.
41. See Margery A. Safir's reference to the poem in support of her theory of transgressive behavior in "An Erotics of Liberation: Notes on Transgres-

sive Behavior in *Hopscotch* and *Libro de Manuel*," in *Final Island*, pp. 84–96.

42. For example, he recalls in chapter 1 that the day he met La Maga, "Everything had been going badly that afternoon because the habits I had brought from Argentina would not permit me to cross from one sidewalk to the other to look at silly items in the dimly lit shop windows on streets I don't remember any more" (Cortázar, *Hopscotch*, p. 14).

43. Cortázar, *Hopscotch*, p. 29.

44. Ibid., p. 291.

45. Ibid., p. 34.

46. Madame Léone captures La Maga's essence with the following description: "'She is suffering somewhere. She has always suffered. She is very gay, she adores yellow, her bird is the blackbird, her time is night, her bridge is the Pont des Arts'" (Cortázar, *Hopscotch*, p. 15).

47. See Safir, "An Erotics of Liberation," p. 85.

48. Cortázar, *Hopscotch*, pp. 333–334.

49. Roberto González Echevarría, *Alejo Carpentier: The Pilgrim at Home*, pp. 241–242.

50. González Echevarría, *Alejo Carpentier*, p. 256.

51. Alejo Carpentier, *Explosion in a Cathedral*, trans. John Sturrock, p. 162.

52. This pattern occurs throughout the novel. Sofía sees ". . . prodigious sunsets building allegorical tableaux in a sky where each cloud could be read as a sculptural group—the battles of Titans, a Laocoön, a quadriga, or the fall of angels" (p. 80). Later Esteban, upon contemplating a conch shell, comments, "Out of a sea at the mercy of lunar cycles—fickle, furious or generous, curling and dilating, forever ignorant of modules, theorems and equations—there appeared these surprising shells, symbolising in number and proportion exactly what the Mother lacked, concrete examples of linear development, of the laws of convolution, of a wonderfully precise conical architecture, of mass in equilibrium, of tangible arabesques which hinted at all the baroquisms to come" (p. 180). He also discovers caves "from whose roofs giant cacti hung head downwards, their red and yellow flowers extended in festoons like curious theatrical chandeliers, serving as a sanctuary for some strange and enigmatic geometrical shape, isolated and mounted on a plinth—a cylinder, a pyramid, or a polyhedron—like a mysterious object of veneration, a Stone of Mecca, a Pythagorean symbol, the materialisation of an abstract cult" (p. 194).

53. Carpentier, *Explosion in a Cathedral*, p. 164.

54. See González Echevarría's discussion of Esteban's contemplation of the spiral shape of the conch shell at the end of subchapter 24, *Alejo Carpentier*, pp. 246–247.

55. See Jaime Alazraki, *La prosa narrativa de Jorge Luis Borges*; Jaime Alazraki, "Kabbalistic Traits in Borges' Narration," *Studies in Short Fiction*, 8 (1971), 78–92; Jaime Alazraki, "Borges and the Kabbalah," *TriQuarterly*, No. 25 (1972), 240–267; Jaime Alazraki, "'El golem' de J. L. Borges," in *Homenaje a Casalduero*, pp. 9–19; Oscar Hahn, "El motivo

del Golem en 'Las ruinas circulares' de J. L. Borges," *Revista chilena de literatura*, 4 (1971), 103–108; Saúl Sosnowski, *Borges y la Cábala: La búsqueda del verbo*; Saúl Sosnowski, "'The God's Script'—A Kabbalistic Quest," *Modern Fiction Studies*, 19 (1973), 381–394.

56. Carpentier, *Explosion in a Cathedral*, p. 215.
57. Jorge Luis Borges, *Labyrinths: Selected Short Stories and Other Writings*, ed. Donald A. Yates and James E. Irby, p. 105.
58. Borges, *Labyrinths*, pp. 115–116.
59. Alazraki, *La prosa narrativa*, p. 28.
60. Jorge Luis Borges, "El Aleph," *El Aleph*, p. 164.
61. Borges, "El Aleph," p. 167.
62. Sosnowski, *Borges y la Cábala*, p. 68, fn. 92.
63. Borges, *Labyrinths*, pp. 209–212.
64. Borges, *Labyrinths*, p. 209.

Works Cited

Abrams, Meyer Howard. *The Mirror and the Lamp: Romantic Theory and the Critical Tradition*. London: Oxford University Press, 1971.
———. *Natural Supernaturalism: Tradition and Revolution in Romantic Literature*. New York: W. W. Norton and Co., Inc., 1973.
Alazraki, Jaime. "Borges and the Kabbalah." *TriQuarterly*, No. 25 (1972), 240–267.
———. "'El golem' de J. L. Borges." In *Homenaje a Casalduero*. Madrid: Gredos, 1972, pp. 9–19.
———. "Kabbalistic Traits in Borges' Narration." *Studies in Short Fiction*, 8 (1971), 78–92.
———. *La prosa narrativa de Jorge Luis Borges*. Madrid: Gredos, 1968.
Anderson Imbert, Enrique. *La originalidad de Rubén Darío*. Buenos Aires: Centro Editor de América Latina, 1967.
Araujo, Fernando. "La ciencia del soplo: "Fakires y yoguis." *España Moderna*, Año 15, Tomo 176 (1903), 179–186.
———. "El más allá." *España Moderna*, Año 14, Tomo 159 (1902), 190–192.
———. "El milagro moderno." *España Moderna*, Año 14, Tomo 160 (1902), 179–182.
———. "Ocultismo." *España Moderna*, Año 14, Tomo 157 (1902), 206–207.
Bays, Gwendolyn. *The Orphic Vision: Seer Poets from Novalis to Rimbaud*. Lincoln: University of Nebraska Press, 1964.
Besant, Annie. *Esoteric Christianity*. Adyar, Madras: Theosophical Publishing House, 1957.
Borges, Jorge Luis. *El Aleph*. Buenos Aires: Emecé Editores, 1957.
———. *Labyrinths: Selected Short Stories and Other Writings*. Ed. Donald A. Yates and James E. Irby. New York: New Directions, 1964.
Bradbury, Malcolm and James McFarlane. "The Name and Nature of Modernism." In *Modernism*. Ed. Malcolm Bradbury and James McFarlane. New York: Penguin, 1976, pp. 19–55.
Buitrago, Edgardo. "Consideraciones polémicas acerca de la vigencia y actualidad de Rubén Darío." In *Estudios sobre Rubén Darío*. Ed. Ernesto Mejía Sánchez. Mexico: Fondo de Cultura Económica, 1968.
Calinescu, Matei. *Faces of Modernity: Avant-Garde, Decadence, Kitsch*. Bloomington: Indiana University Press, 1977.

Cano Ballesta, Juan. "Antonio Machado y la crisis del hombre moderno." In *Estudios sobre Antonio Machado.* Ed. José Angeles. Barcelona: Editorial Ariel, 1977, pp. 73–96.

Carlos, A. J. "La cruz en el 'Responso a Verlaine.'" *Hispania,* 48 (1965), 226–229.

Carpentier, Alejo. *Explosion in a Cathedral.* Trans. John Sturrock. New York: Harper and Row, 1979.

Castro-Klarén, Sara. "Ontological Fabulation: Toward Cortázar's Theory of Literature." In *The Final Island: The Fiction of Julio Cortázar.* Ed. Jaime Alazraki and Ivar Ivask. Norman: University of Oklahoma Press, 1976.

Cirlot, J. E. *A Dictionary of Symbols.* Trans. Jack Sage. New York: Philosophical Library, 1962.

Clement, Clara Erskine. *A Handbook of Christian Symbols and Stories of the Saints.* Boston: Ticknor, 1889.

Copleston, Frederick. Part 2 of *Greece and Rome.* Vol. 1 of *A History of Philosophy.* 1946; rpt. Garden City, N.Y.: Image-Doubleday and Co., Inc., 1962.

Cornford, Francis Macdonald. *Before and After Socrates.* Cambridge, Eng.: Cambridge University Press, 1964.

Correa, Gustavo. "Una 'lira inmensa': El ritmo de la muerte y de la resurrección en la poesía de Antonio Machado." In *Estudios sobre Antonio Machado.* Ed. José Angeles. Barcelona: Editorial Ariel, 1977, pp. 121–162.

Cortázar, Julio. *Hopscotch.* Trans. Gregory Rabassa. New York: Avon Books, 1975.

Curtius, Ernest Robert. *European Literature and the Latin Middle Ages.* Trans. Willard R. Trask. Princeton, N.J.: Princeton University Press, 1953.

Darío, Rubén. *Cuentos completos.* Ed. Ernesto Mejía Sánchez. Mexico: Fondo de Cultura Económica, 1950.

———. *Obras completas.* 5 vols. Madrid: Afrodisio Aguado, S.A., 1950.

———. *Obras desconocidas: Escritas en Chile y no recopiladas en ninguno de sus libros.* Ed. Raúl Silva Castro. Santiago: Prensas de la Universidad de Chile, 1934.

———. *Poesía.* Ed. Ernesto Mejía Sánchez. Caracas: Biblioteca Ayacucho, 1977.

———. *Poesías completas.* Ed. Alfonso Méndez Plancarte. Augmented by Antonio Oliver Belmás. 11th ed. Madrid: Aguilar, 1968.

Davies, Gareth A. "Mondrian, Abstract Art, and Theosophy in Julio Cortázar's *Rayuela.*" *Proceedings of the Leeds Philosophical and Literary Society,* 16, Part 6. Leeds: Leeds Philosophical Society, 1976, pp. 127–147.

Davison, Ned J. *The Concept of Modernism in Hispanic Criticism.* Boulder, Colorado: Pruett Press, 1966.

Debicki, Andrew P. *Estudios sobre poesía española contemporánea: La generación de 1924–1925.* Madrid: Editorial Gredos, 1968.

del Río, Angel. "Present Trends in the Conception and Criticism of Spanish Romanticism." *Romantic Review,* 39 (1948), 229–248.

Díaz-Plaja, Guillermo. *Modernismo frente a noventa y ocho*. Madrid: Espasa-Calpe, 1951.

Durand, Réné. "El motivo del centauro y la universalidad de Rubén Darío." *La Torre*, 15 (1967), 71–97.

Echevarría, Arturo. "Estructura y sentido poético del 'Coloquio de los centauros,'" *La Torre*, 17 (1969), 95–130.

Enguídanos, Miguel. "Inner Tensions in the Work of Rubén Darío." Trans. Cecile Wiseman. In *Rubén Darío Centennial Studies*. Ed. Miguel González-Gerth and George D. Schade. Austin: University of Texas, Department of Spanish and Portuguese, Institute of Latin American Studies, 1970, pp. 13–29.

Faurie, Marie-Josèphe. *Le modernisme hispano-americain et ses sources françaises*. Paris: Centre de recherches de l'Institut d'études hispaniques, 1966.

Fiore, Dolores Ackel. *Rubén Darío in Search of Inspiration (Greco-Roman Mythology in His Stories and Poetry)*. New York: Las Américas Publishing Co., 1963.

Fuentes, Carlos, *La nueva novela hispanoamericana*. Mexico: Joaquín Mortiz, 1974.

González Echevarría, Roberto. *Alejo Carpentier: The Pilgrim at Home*. Ithaca, N.Y.: Cornell University Press, 1977.

González Martínez, Enrique. *Poesías completas*. Mexico: Asociación de Libreros y Editores Mexicanos, 1944.

Grass, Roland and William R. Risley (eds.). *Waiting for Pegasus: Studies of the Presence of Symbolism and Decadence in Hispanic Letters*. Macomb: Western Illinois University, 1979.

Gullón, Ricardo. "Pitagorismo y modernismo." *Mundo Nuevo*, No. 7 (1967), 22–32.

Guthrie, W. K. C. *The Greeks and Their Gods*. Boston: Beacon Press, 1954.

Hahn, Oscar. "El motivo del Golem en 'Las ruinas circulares' de J. L. Borges." *Revista chilena de literatura*, 4 (1971), 103–108.

Hall, Manly P. *An Encyclopedic Outline of Masonic, Hermetic, Qabbalistic and Rosicrucian Symbolical Philosophy*. Los Angeles: Philosophical Research Society, Inc., 1969.

Hamilton, Carlos D. "Rubén Darío en la Isla de Oro." *Cuadernos Hispanoamericanos*, Nos. 212–213 (1967), 556–573.

Hamilton, Edith. *Mythology*. New York: New American Library, 1953.

Henderson, Joseph L. "Ancient Myths and Modern Man." In *Man and His Symbols*. Ed. Carl G. Jung et al. Garden City, N.Y.: Doubleday, 1964, pp. 104–157.

Henríquez Ureña, Max. "En torno a las prosas de Rubén Darío." *La Torre*, 15 (1967), 155–177.

Herrera y Reissig, Julio. *Poesías completas*. Buenos Aires: Editorial Losada, 1969.

Hurtado Chamorro, Alejandro. *La mitología griega en Rubén Darío*. Avila: Editorial La Muralla, 1967.

Jensen, Theodore W. "*Modernista* Pythagorean Literature: The Symbolist Inspiration." In *Waiting for Pegasus: Studies of the Presence of Symbolism and Decadence in Hispanic Letters.* Ed. Roland Grass and William R. Risley. Macomb: Western Illinois University, 1979, pp. 169–179.

———. "El pitagorismo en *Las fuerzas extrañas* de Lugones." In *Otros mundos otros fuegos: Fantasía y realismo mágico en Iberoamérica.* Memoria del XVI Congreso Internacional de Literatura Iberoamericana. Ed. Donald A. Yates. Pittsburgh: A Publication of the Latin American Studies Center of Michigan State University, 1975, pp. 299–307.

Jiménez, Juan Ramón. *El modernismo: Notas de un curso.* Ed. Ricardo Gullón and Eugenio Fernández Méndez. Mexico: Aguilar, 1962.

Kingsford, Anna. *Clothed with the Sun.* New York: F. J. Lovell and Company, 1889.

Kingsford, Anna and Edward Maitland. *The Perfect Way.* 3rd ed. London: Field and Tuer, 1890.

Kirk, G. S. and J. E. Raven. *The Presocratic Philosophers.* Cambridge, Eng.: University Press, 1964.

Kronik, John W. "The Introduction of Symbolism in Spain: A Call to Arms." In *Waiting for Pegasus: Studies of the Presence of Symbolism and Decadence in Hispanic Letters.* Ed. Roland Grass and William R. Risley. Macomb: Western Illinois University, 1979, pp. 31–38.

Lorenz, Erika. *Rubén Darío: "Bajo el divino imperio de la música."* Trans. Fidel Coloma González. Managua: Ediciones "Lengua," 1960.

Machado, Antonio. *Antología de su prosa.* Ed. Aurora de Albornoz. Madrid: Editorial para el Diálogo, S.A., 1970. Vol. 2.

Maier, Carol S. "Valle-Inclán y *La lámpara maravillosa*: Una poética iluminada." Diss. Rutgers 1975.

Maiorana, María Teresa. "'El coloquio de los centauros' de Rubén Darío." *Boletín de la Academia Argentina de Letras,* 23 (1958), 185–263.

Marasso, Arturo. "Nuevos aspectos de Rubén Darío: La canción de los osos: Filosofía y hermetismo." *La Nación,* Buenos Aires, 22 julio 1951, 53.

———. *Rubén Darío y su creación poética.* Buenos Aires: Biblioteca Nueva, 1946.

Martí, José. *Poesías completas.* Prólogo y notas de Luis Alberto Ruiz. Buenos Aires: Ediciones Antonio Zamora, 1970.

Merrim, Stephanie. "Darío and Breton: Two Enigmas." *Latin American Literary Review,* 4, no. 9 (1976), 48–62.

Navarro Tomás, Tomás. *Métrica española: Reseña histórica y descriptiva.* 3rd ed. Madrid: Ediciones Guadarrama, 1972.

Neale-Silva, Eduardo. *César Vallejo en su fase trílcica.* Madison: University of Wisconsin Press, 1975.

Nervo, Amado. *Obras completas.* Ed. Francisco González Guerrero and Alfonso Méndez Plancarte. Madrid: Aguilar, 1952. Vol. 2.

———. *Poemas.* Buenos Aires: Espasa-Calpe, 1945.

Onís, Federico de. *Antología de la poesía española e hispanoamericana,*

1882–1932. Madrid: Imp. de la Librería y Casa Editorial Hernando, S.A., 1934.

Ovid. *The Metamorphoses.* Trans. Horace Gregory. New York: New American Library, 1960.

Palau de Nemes, Graciela. "Tres momentos del neomisticismo poético del 'siglo modernista': Darío, Jiménez y Paz." In *Estudios sobre Rubén Darío.* Ed. Ernesto Mejía Sánchez. Mexico: Fondo de Cultura Económica, 1968.

Paz, Octavio. "El caracol y la sirena." In *Cuadrivio.* Mexico: Joaquín Mortiz, 1965, pp. 11–65.

————. *Children of the Mire: Modern Poetry from Romanticism to the Avant-Garde.* Trans. Rachel Phillips. Cambridge, Mass.: Harvard University Press, 1974.

————. *Los hijos del limo: Del romanticismo a la vanguardia.* Barcelona: Editorial Seix Barral, 1974.

————. "The Siren and the Seashell." In *The Siren and the Seashell and Other Essays on Poets and Poetry.* Trans. Lysander Kemp and Margaret Sayers Peden. Austin: University of Texas Press, 1976, pp. 17–56.

Peckham, Morse. "Toward a Theory of Romanticism." *PMLA*, 66 (1951), 5–23.

Peers, E. A. *Historia del movimiento romántico español.* 2nd ed. 2 vols. Madrid: Editorial Gredos, 1967.

Pérus, Françoise. *Literatura y sociedad en América latina: El modernismo.* La Habana, Casa de las Américas, 1976.

Rama, Angel. *Rubén Darío y el modernismo.* Caracas: Ediciones de la Biblioteca de la Universidad Central de Venezuela, 1970.

Raymond, Marcel. *From Baudelaire to Surrealism.* London: Methuen and Co. Ltd., 1970.

Rico, Francisco. *El pequeño mundo del hombre.* Madrid: Editorial Castalia, 1970.

Risco, Antonio. *El demiurgo y su mundo: Hacia un nuevo enfoque de la obra de Valle-Inclán.* Madrid: Gredos, 1977.

Safir, Margery A. "An Erotics of Liberation: Notes on Transgressive Behavior in *Hopscotch* and *Libro de Manuel.*" in *Final Island: The Fiction of Julio Cortázar.* Ed. Jaime Alazraki and Ivar Ivask. Norman: University of Oklahoma Press, 1976.

Salinas, Pedro. *La poesía de Rubén Darío.* Buenos Aires: Editorial Losada, 1948.

————. "El problema del modernismo en España, o un conflicto entre dos espíritus." In *Literatura española siglo XX.* Madrid: Alianza Editorial, 1970, pp. 13–25.

Sarduy, Severo, Tomás Segovia, and Emir Rodríguez Monegal. "Nuestro Rubén Darío." *Mundo Nuevo*, No. 7 (1967), 33–46.

Saurat, Denis. *Literature and Occult Tradition: Studies in Philosophical Poetry.* 1930; rpt. Port Washington, N.Y.: Kennikat Press, Inc., 1966.

Schulman, Ivan. "Génesis del azul modernista." In *Estudios críticos sobre el modernismo.* Ed. Homero Castillo. Madrid: Editorial Gredos, 1974, pp. 168–189.

———. "Modernismo, revolución y pitagorismo en Martí." *Casa de las Américas,* No. 73 (1972), 45–55.

Schuré, Edouard. *The Great Initiates: A Study of the Secret History of Religions.* Trans. Gloria Rasberry. Intro. Paul M. Allen. West Nyack, N.Y.: St. George Books, 1961.

Secret, François. *Le Zohar chez les kabbalistes chrétiens de la renaissance.* Paris: Durlacher, 1958.

Senior, John. *The Way Down and Out: The Occult in Symbolist Literature.* Ithaca, N.Y.: Cornell University Press, 1959.

Shaw, Donald L. "*Modernismo:* A Contribution to the Debate." *Bulletin of Hispanic Studies,* 46 (1967), 195–202.

———. "Toward the Understanding of Spanish Romanticism." *Modern Language Review,* 58 (1963), 190–195.

Shroder, Maurice Z. *Icarus: The Image of the Artist in French Romanticism.* Cambridge, Mass.: Harvard University Press, 1961.

Shumaker, Wayne. *The Occult Sciences in the Renaissance.* Berkeley: University of California Press, 1972.

Skyrme, Raymond. *Rubén Darío and the Pythagorean Tradition.* Gainesville: University Presses of Florida, 1975.

Solstad, M. Louise. "Sun Motifs in Sixteenth-Century Spanish Religious Poetry." *Bulletin of Hispanic Studies,* 40 (1978), 211–230.

Sosnowski, Saúl. *Borges y la Cábala: La búsqueda del verbo.* Buenos Aires: Hispamérica, 1976.

———. "'The God's Script'—A Kabbalistic Quest." *Modern Fiction Studies,* 19 (1973), 381–394.

Sperrati-Piñero, Emma Susana. *El ocultismo en Valle-Inclán.* London: Tamesis Books, 1974.

Sucre, Guillermo. *La máscara, la transparencia: Ensayos sobre poesía hispanoamericana.* Caracas: Monte Avila, 1975.

Trueblood, Alan S. "El 'Responso' a Verlaine y la elegía pastoril tradicional." In *Actas del Tercer Congreso Internacional de Hispanistas.* Mexico: El Colegio de México, 1970, pp. 861–870.

———. "Rubén Darío: The Sea and the Jungle." *Comparative Literature Studies,* 4 (1967), 425–456.

Valle-Inclán, Ramón del. *Obras completas.* 3rd ed. Madrid: Editorial Plenitud, 1954. Vol. 2.

Watland, Charles D. *Poet-Errant: A Biography of Rubén Darío.* New York: Philosophical Library, 1965.

Watts, Alan W. *Myth and Ritual in Christianity.* Boston: Beacon Press, 1968.

Yates, Frances A. *Giordano Bruno and the Hermetic Tradition.* Chicago: University of Chicago Press, 1964.

Ycaza Tigerino, Julio. *Los nocturnos de Rubén Darío y otros ensayos.* Madrid: Ediciones Cultura Hispánica, 1964.

Yurkievich, Saúl. *Celebración del modernismo*. Barcelona: Tusquets Editor, 1976.

Zum Felde, Alberto. *Crítica de la literatura uruguaya*. Montevideo: Máximo García, 1921.

Index